Perspectives in Critical Thinking

Studies in the Postmodern Theory of Education

Joe L. Kincheloe and Shirley R. Steinberg
General Editors

Vol. 110

PETER LANG
New York • Washington, D.C./Baltimore • Boston • Bern
Frankfurt am Main • Berlin • Brussels • Vienna • Canterbury

Perspectives in Critical Thinking

Essays by Teachers in Theory and Practice

EDITED BY

Danny Weil and Holly Kathleen Anderson

PETER LANG
New York • Washington, D.C./Baltimore • Boston • Bern
Frankfurt am Main • Berlin • Brussels • Vienna • Canterbury

Library of Congress Cataloging-in-Publication Data

Perspectives in critical thinking: essays by teachers
in theory and practice/ edited by Danny Weil and Holly Kathleen Anderson.
p. cm. — (Counterpoints; vol. 110)
Includes bibliographical references.
1. Critical thinking—Study and teaching. 2. Critical pedagogy.
I. Weil, Danny K. II. Anderson, Holly Kathleen.
LB1590.3.P476 370.15'2 99-045896
ISBN 0-8204-4429-4
ISSN 1058-1634

Die Deutsche Bibliothek-CIP-Einheitsaufnahme

Perspectives in critical thinking: essays by teachers
in theory and practice/ ed. by: Danny Weil and Holly Kathleen Anderson.
–New York; Washington, D.C./Baltimore; Boston; Bern; Frankfurt am Main;
Berlin; Brussels; Vienna; Canterbury: Lang.
(Counterpoints; Vol. 110)
ISBN 0-8204-4429-4

Cover design by Nona Reuter

The paper in this book meets the guidelines for permanence and durability
of the Committee on Production Guidelines for Book Longevity
of the Council of Library Resources.

© 2000 Peter Lang Publishing, Inc., New York

All rights reserved.
Reprint or reproduction, even partially, in all forms such as microfilm, xerography,
microfiche, microcard, and offset strictly prohibited.

Contents

Acknowledgments	vii
Notes on Contributors and Editors	ix
Introduction *Danny Weil and Holly Kathleen Anderson*	xiii
Learning to Reason Dialectically: Teaching Primary Students to Reason Within Different Points Of View *Danny Weil*	1
Making Critical Thinking Critical *Joe L. Kincheloe*	23
Eight Critical Points for Mathematics *Peter M. Appelbaum*	41
Storytelling in the Classroom: Crossing Vexed Chasms *Greg Sarris*	57
The Role of Service-Learning in Critical Thinking *Nancy P. Kraft*	75
Inviting Youth into Civic Action *Jenice L. View*	95
Becoming A Critical Teacher *Raymond A. Horn, Jr.*	139
Using a Journal to Develop Reflective and Critical Thinking Skills in Classroom Settings *Valerie J. Janesick*	173
Just Doing It: Towards a Critical Thinking of Visual Culture *Kevin Tavin*	187
Critical Thinking in Science—How Do We Recognize It? Do We Foster It? *David B. Pushkin*	211

Acknowledgments

We would like to thank all the contributors to this book and applaud the efforts they have made on behalf of children throughout their distinguished careers. We would also like to thank all teachers for their commitment to teaching and learning and especially those teachers struggling to make courageous and meaningful reform in education.

We wish to thank Shirley Steinberg and Joe Kincheloe for making this book possible and recognize their tremendous intellectual scholarship and efforts.

Notes on Contributors and Editors

Holly Kathleen Anderson is a primary school teacher in Santa Maria, California. For more than twelve years she has taught Kindergarten through sixth grade in Los Angeles and in the Central Valley of California. Holly is a Spanish speaker who has worked with migrant children and Chapter I schools. She has edited two books on education, numerous fiction books, and has written several screen plays. She has a Masters in Education and an Administrative Services Credential.

Peter M. Appelbaum teaches mathematics and science education at the William Patterson University of New Jersey. The author of *Popular Culture, Educational Discourse, and Mathematics* (SUNY Press), his research interests are in social and cultural approaches to curriculum.

Raymond A. Horn, Jr. is a social studies teacher who teaches high school.

Valerie J. Janesick is Professor of Educational Leadership and Policy at Florida International University in Miami and Fort Lauderdale, Florida. She teaches classes in Qualitative Research Methods, Curriculum Theory, Curriculum Planning and Evaluation and Action Research and Development. Her research interests include qualitative research methods, ethics in research and comparative curriculum issues. As a former choreographer, dancer art's educator, and researcher on teaching she has tried to incorporate the Arts and Humanities into how we view research. Her text, *Stretching Exercises for Qualitative Researchers*, Sage 1998, and her chapter in *Strategies of Qualitative Inquiry*, Sage 1998, both use dance as a metaphor for clarifying and expanding our notions of qualitative inquiry. Her next project is a text on Ethics and the Qualitative researcher and classes in Irish step dancing.

Joe L. Kincheloe teaches cultural Studies and Education at Penn State University. He is the author of many books including *Getting Beyond the Facts: Teaching Social Studies in the Late Twentieth Century* (Lang:1989); *Curriculum as Social Psychoanalysis: Essays on the Significance of Place* (with William F. Pinar, SUNY: 1991), *Teachers as Researchers: Qualitative Paths to Empowerment* (Falmer, 1991), *The Stigma of Genius: Einstein and Education* (with Shirley R. Steinberg and Deborah J. Tippens, Hollowbrook: 1992), *Toward a Critical Politics of Teacher Thinking: Mapping the Postmodern* (Bergin and Garvey: 1993), *Toil and Trouble: Good Work, Smart workers and the Integration of Academic and Vocational Education* (Lang: 1995), and he is the coeditor, along with Shirley Steinberg, of *Kinder-Culture: The Corporate Construction of Childhood* (Westview: 1997).

Nancy P. Kraft is a Senior Research Associate with RMC Research Corporation in Denver, Colorado. She is the co-author of *Linking IASA* (Improving America's Schools Act) *Programs and Service Learning: A Planning Implementation and Evaluation Guide* that shows schools how to use federal funding to support authentic instruction grounded in the service-learning philosophy. She has directed demonstration site-work in schools across the nation that are incorporating service-learning in Title I (Aid for Disadvantaged Youth), Title IV (Safe and Drug Free Schools and Communities) and Title IX (Indian Education) programs. Her research includes how to enable students, teachers and parents to have voice and ownership in the educational process. Nancy received her doctorate in Education Policy studies from the University of Wisconsin.

David B. Pushkin holds a doctorate in Curriculum and Instruction from Penn State, a Master of Arts in Biochemistry and a Bachelor of Science in chemistry. He is currently an assistant Professor of Science Education at William Paterson University in New Jersey. He has had many teaching and research positions in colleges and university in the area of science and as also taught chemistry and physics in High School. David has authored numerous articles in education relevant publications, including the *Journal of Chemical Education, Chemical and Engineering News, Journal of Research in Science Teaching, The Physics Teacher,* and *Association of Women in Science Magazine.* He has also offered many presentations at academic institutions.

Greg Sarris is a Professor of English at the University of California at Los Angeles. He is the author of the acclaimed HBO tele-drama entitled

Grand Avenue. A novelist, he is the author of numerous books including *Grand Avenue* (Penguin: 1995), *Keeping Slug Woman Alive: A Holistic Approach to American Indian Texts* (University of California Press:1993), *Mabel McKay: Weaving the Dream (Portraits of American Genius, 1)* (University of California Press: 1994), *Watermelon Nights: A Novel* (Hyperion: 1998), and *The Sound of Rattles and Clappers: A Collection of New California Indian Writing* (Arizona Press: 1994).

Kevin Tavin is a Ph.D. candidate in the Department of Art Education at the Pennsylvania University. He is currently working on his dissertation that focuses on the relationship between visual culture, critical pedagogy, cultural studies and art education. He has published articles in the *M.A.E.A. Gazette* and other journals

Jenice L. View is a resident of her native Washington D.C., mother of two school aged children, avid cyclist and occasional artist and writer. Her professional identity included work as: a curriculum development specialist for community-based and social justice organizations; a teacher/trainer using popular education techniques with adults and children; and an evaluator of efforts to include the voices of service recipients, children, low-income communities, workers and other populations typically omitted from policy-making processes. She had a doctorate in Education from the Union Institute Graduate School, an MPA/URP from Princeton University's Woodrow Wilson School, and a BA from Syracuse University. Dr. View currently is co-principal of View Associated in Washington, D.C.

Danny Weil is Director of The Critical Thinking Institute. He is an attorney at law who quit practicing public interest law to become a primary school teacher. He has taught kindergarten, first, and second grades for six years both in Los Angeles and in the Central Valley of California. He has also taught within the California Youth Authority Prison System. Danny is a multi-subject bilingual credentialed teacher who received the teacher of the Year Award from the California Association of Bilingual Educators in California in 1991. He has been published in numerous national and international magazines and journals throughout the United States and Mexico and his books include The Critical Thinking Handbook Grades K-3 (Sonoma State: 1991) and Towards a Critical Multicultural Literacy (Lang: 1998).

Introduction

Danny Weil and Holly Kathleen Anderson

Providing our nation's children with educational opportunities that demand and develop their critical capacities in the interests of *not translating reality* but *transforming it,* should be the chore of each and every one of us as educators no matter what our particular disciplines, grade levels, or pedagogical positions. In the following pages you will read stories from educators who have devoted their efforts to working towards helping students and teachers do just that. They are not unlike the thousands of educators who work daily with students and teachers helping them give birth to critical, self-authored thinking. The experiences you will read about in these articles range from thinking critically with students about science, math, and social studies to helping them critically reflect on their own lives, aspirations and dreams. There are articles that focus on junior high school experiences in Washington DC as well as articles that speak to teaching point of view to young, primary students; articles that deal with service learning and others that speak to storytelling as a powerful form of learning and thinking.

In their diversity of focus, these educators share a common purpose and theme: they all strive to help their students think more critically, to govern and author their own lives and to develop good citizenship practices and interests that are tied to equality and public good. These educators all share a commitment to work and struggle to transform education and educational practices into something that is relevant to the lives of both students and teachers. By offering their stories, they provide theoretical insights as well as practical suggestions as to how we as a community of educators might highlight and build upon the best practices in our fields to achieve our desired educational reforms and visions.

We have purposely asked our contributors to write in a language of accessibility that is both popular and public so that we might abandon the realm of idealism and a particular fetishism of language that has often infected humanistic intellectual theory and practice in the last fifteen years. The contributors to this book have engaged in a language directly concerned with people and their conditions; a language less embellished for the sake of academic ego and power and more interested and vested in the struggles of people for liberation—a language that conveys meaning through populist thought and action.

We are proud to have been able to edit the work of such remarkable educators and we share their vision and commitment to helping students think critically and build and sustain a better world. Again, we would like to thank all contributors to this book for their visions and struggles and we hope that their stories will help you, the reader, promote, sustain and build a new educational theory and practice for liberation.

Learning to Reason Dialectically: Teaching Primary Students to Reason Within Different Points of View

Danny Weil

> Ours is the age that is proud of machines that think and suspicious of men who try.
> —H. Mumford Jones

When as a result of a political debate, a person decides to vote for one particular candidate or issue; when as a result of hearing evidence, a jury renders reasoned judgment about the guilt or innocence of a defendant; when as a result of reading an editorial in the newspaper, one comes to the conclusion that the point of view is incorrect or correct; when as a result of dealing with a family argument, one finds that one argument is superior to another; or when, as a result of reading and thinking about the best approach to, say, parenting and raising children, one concludes that one approach is better than another—one is reasoning within and about different points of view. In fact, whenever we discuss our ideas and beliefs with other people—whether it is the best way to do a job, the best way to resolve a conflict, the best way to raise a family, or the best way to form a relationship—we are reasoning dialectically, within and about different and various points of view.

We all have points of view; we couldn't live without them. The question is, what constitutes our point of view on this or that issue? How did we come to believe what we believe? How do we exchange ideas collaboratively within an environment of inquiry and civility? What other points of view exist on any given issue, and what do they claim or assume? How does our point of view relate to these other points of view and what do we believe in light of what others believe? Are we accurately and precisely capturing and depicting another's point of view as it is being expressed, or are we simply sophistically responding to and interpreting the point of view through our own set of assumptions and conclusions without the ability to accurately formulate the point of view in question, reason from its premises, or embrace its conclusions?

Whenever we think we operate from some point of view or *frame of reference* that helps us conceptualize what we are thinking about. A point of view is simply a system of thought as it relates to a given issue. It involves a line of reasoning that can be understood and analyzed for purposes of assessment. This does not mean that it must be accepted as true, that it is justified or that we have to believe it; nor does it mean that every point of view is equally defensible or equally rational. However, it does mean that the proponent of the point of view is attempting to represent his or her thinking within specific parameters. Our job as thinkers, then, is to recognize and assess the relative merits or shortcomings of a point of view in the interest of greater understanding of ideas, ourselves and others. Understanding that the large questions and issues we face are comprised of a myriad of points of view is the first step to rationally and fairmindedly assessing and then evaluating various points of view—and, it is essential for engaging in fruitful dialogue in the interest of maturation, problem solving and good judgment.

Unfortunately, for many, the process of fairly and accurately characterizing a point of view not keeping with one's own seems a difficult if not impossible task. Learning to listen empathically; learning to question our own belief systems relative to another point of view; and learning to substitute self-questioning for self-righteousness is difficult and for many if not all of us, an often downright threatening process.

Not only are many people uncomfortable when confronting points of view not keeping with their own, I would argue that the natural inclination or norm is to reject that which does not fit into the neatly designed premises and constructs we have fabricated for ourselves. The unfortunate result of such narrow-minded thinking is close-minded debate, unsophisticated argumentation, failed or faulty communication and inevitable bad problem solving and decision making. Some people argue or debate other points of view, not necessarily in the interest of self-awareness and good judgment, but simply to be right or to defeat the point of view, and thus, argumentation or debate often becomes a self-serving, self-justifying process as opposed to a collaborative learning process or a cooperative search for higher understanding.

Part of the problem, in my judgment, rests with our grotesquely individualistic culture and our consequent attachments to ego-centric belief systems, prejudices, biases, and misconceptions. Without opportunities to develop fairminded reasoning about and within diverse points of view, we often fall victim to our own irrational habits of thought—reducing the world to our individual point of view. For the egocentric mind, the world is as it sees it and the tendency is to reject that which does not fit within *the* paradigm or our model of how things should be. I think we often do this unconsciously without ever having the benefit of truly understanding points of view which we have rejected or even knowing why we've rejected them.

Another problem rests in the way we have learned to conceive of issues requiring reasoning and our understanding of the entire notion of reasoned judgment and how it compares and contrasts with simply rendering opinion on a given issue or situation. Because critical thinking involves moving beyond answers that offer a mere preference, its important that we understand reasoned judgment itself and that we are able to differentiate it from mere opinion rendering.

Distinguishing Judgment From Opinion

> I am not ashamed to confess I am ignorant of what I do not know.
> —Cicero

The *Random House Dictionary of the English Language* defines *judgment* as "The ability to judge, make a decision, or form an opinion objectively, authoritatively and wisely. esp. in matters affecting action; good sense; discretion" (Random House, 1973). The same dictionary defines *opinion* as "A belief or judgment that rests on grounds insufficient to produce certainty" (ibid.). This means that an opinion, unlike a judgment, falls short of absolute conviction or certainty. A judgment, on the other hand, connotes an objective, thought-out and critical survey of a situation, problem or decision based on a mental examination that takes into consideration evidence and reasons. So, one can have an opinion without having to really think it through or marshal evidence for their position; in essence, their opinion is an impression or appraisal that concludes that certain facts, ideas or thoughts are *probably* true or likely to prove so. When considering a judgment, however, we remove general impressions and appraisals in favor of reasoning from evidence to conclusions. For example, when a jury is asked to deliberate over the guilt or innocence of a defendant in a criminal matter, they are not asked for their opinions but for a well reasoned and thoughtful determination. In fact, they are given jury instructions by the judge indicating that they must *leave their opinions about the case outside the jury room door.* What we wish the jury to do is reason as objectively as possible from given evidence to a conclusion. In short, we ask them for their judgment, not their opinion.

Distinguishing judgment from opinion is an important aspect of learning to reason and as such, an important understanding for teachers wishing to design and teach reasoning within points of view. The road one travels to form judgment is not the same road traveled to form opinion. The thinking that one engages in when forming a judgment is very different than the thinking that rendering mere opinion entails. Opinion is the product of estimation, impression and sentimental appraisal, while a judgment is the product of reasoning. Without being able to distinguish judgment from opinion, we often find ourselves on the wrong road when engaging in problem solving, decision making and exchanges of points of view; i.e. utilizing the wrong thought processes to come to conclusions, decisions, solutions or predictions. The consequences take the form of results, and the results can often be devastating.

Questions of Mere Preference

> The uncreative mind can spot wrong answers, but it takes a very creative mind to spot wrong questions.
> —Anthony Jay

We are often faced with questions that are evaluated subjectively and for which there are at least as many right answers as there are people asking and answering the questions. Within this realm falls opinion, or preferential response and mere intellectual appraisal. For example, questions as to where we might have dinner, or what kind of colors or music we like fall into this category. Questions of mere preference ask us for only subjective thinking and there is no need to reconcile our taste or choices with those chosen by others. Thus, we do not need to concern ourselves with forming judgment when dealing within this area of questions.

Questions Requiring Reasoned Judgment

> He who will not reason is a bigot; he who cannot is a fool; he who dares not is a slave.
> —William Drummond

In daily life the bulk of questions that face us don't ask us for simply our mere preference. Questions that require reasoned judgment are questions that call upon us to seek alternative points of view with a recognition of their strengths and weaknesses, use criteria to guide our thinking, understand what we do when we think, analyze points of view and learn to abandon our tendency towards self-deception and egocentric thinking. In developing a systematic, comprehensive approach to questions requiring reasoned judgment, we lay a foundation for good judgment—sound and verifiable decision making. This provides a foundation for greater understanding and is essential for human growth and interaction. Examples of questions requiring reasoned judgment are multifaceted and face us each day regarding such issues as abortion, affirmative action, immigration, foreign policy, domestic policy, health care, economics, politics, etc. Questions requiring reasoned judgment are not the same as questions regarding a preference for vanilla or chocolate ice-cream. This important distinction is essential for the teacher interested in designing reasoning activities for students.

Reference Reconciliation

> The greatest discovery of my generation is that human beings, by changing the inner attitudes of their minds, can change the outer aspects of their lives. . . It is too bad that more people will not accept this tremendous discovery and begin living it.
> —William James

Grasping the true strengths or weaknesses of our own thinking and the thinking of others asks us to step outside of our own point of view, to place our judgments on probation, so-to-speak, and be cognitively and attitudinally willing and able to enter into disparate points of view—thereby organizing the evidence and reasons in such a way, as stated earlier, to make the strongest case *against* what we believe. Yet to actually do this takes not simply cognitive ability but also a strong sense of intellectual courage as we seek to probe our own thinking in light of what others believe; it takes intellectual humility as we begin to understand that we have not figured out everything, that there are parameters to what we know; it takes an insight into when we might be reasoning selfishly or egotistically from our own point of view without the benefit of understanding how others view the world; and it takes a strong dose of empathy, as we actually begin to put ourselves in the shoes of others who do not agree with us and reason from their premises to their conclusions in the interest of understanding and fairminded critical thinking.

The necessity for understanding points of view can be found in any meaningful communication and healthy exchange of ideas. Furthermore, it is a conscious, self-motivated act that calls for our mental fitness and active participation in the formation of our own character. By requiring us to develop an open mind and to learn to suspend judgment, an understanding of point of view and the process of reference reconciliation enables and empowers us to analyze, integrate, digest and officiate our own knowledge and the knowledge of others in the interest of higher understanding and thus, is absolutely essential for any healthy exchange of ideas. For this process of empathic awareness, developing a dialogue and discourse of vicarious emotion as opposed to a toxic language of individualistic competition is essential. We learn to go beyond attacking the messenger to actively dialoguing about the message.

As much as understanding a point of view requires that we step inside the point of view of another, embrace its premises, and construct reasons to support it, it simultaneously requires that we step outside our own point of view, suspend our judgment and imaginatively respond to reasons and criticism from an opposing point of view, one that does not agree with ours. This process, what I term *reference reconciliation,* is first, one of fairminded recognition and second, one of critical integration as we come to see the strengths and weaknesses of opposing points of view as they relate to our own and vice versa. This process requires attitudes of humility or what can be termed an *emotional intelligence* that reasons empathically. In this way *reference reconciliation* is at once the process of metacognition, or the rethinking of ones' thinking to make thinking better.

Teaching Dialectical Reasoning: Learning the Process of Recognizing, Questioning, Analyzing, and Evaluating Points of View in the Interest of Developing One's Own Perspective

> The object of the education of children lies in not communicating the values of the past, but in creating new values for the future.
> —John Dewey

For those of us who wish to help students understand and officiate points of view in the interest of helping them develop judgment and character, it is essential we understand the process of thinking about points of view and the process of forming judgment. In order to effectively teach point of view to students, we must be clear as to what a point of view is, how to recognize it and eventually how to assess and evaluate it in the interest of truth and merit. Coming to know that there is a cognitive and affective process involved in acknowledging and refereeing points of view will help us both understand how to construct lessons for students as well as how to help students develop an awareness of this process.

Before beginning, let me make clear that this process as explicated is not a linear process. Although what follows may appear linear, i.e. first you do this and then you do that, this is not my intention. Thinking is a messy process of formulation that requires convergent and divergent thought patterns. My purpose is to simply indicate that there are things we think about when we consider a point of view and although these thoughtful considerations may not proceed in a linear fashion, it is essential to be aware of what one does when one examines a point of view in the interest of formulating judgment on a given issue, problem or decision. Finally, as we shall see later, a point of view can be broken down into components, or constitutive parts which can be understood relative to the entire system of thought.

The process of dialectical reasoning can be briefly characterized as follows:

Recognizing the point of view. The starting point of understanding a point of view must begin with its recognition. By recognition, we simply mean that one should be able to concretely, precisely and accurately depict the point of view—its argument, its conclusions, its premises and its reasoning. We should be able to state the point of view, reason from its evidence to its conclusions and, simply said, be able to empathically embrace it.

Questioning the point of view. Essential to an adequate understanding of a point of view must be the ability to question its logic for clarity and accurate understanding. This questioning should be undertaken not in the spirit of proving the point of view wrong, but to assure oneself that one has adequately embraced the logic of the point of view and truly understands it as a system of thought. This process is not simply cognitive but involves an emotional intelligence or affective attitudes of curiosity, imagination and independent thinking.

Analyzing the point of view. Once we are sure we understand a particular point of view, we analyze the point of view for purposes of seeking to understand its consequences, origin, how it assembles and marshals evidence; in doing so, we begin to compare and contrast that which we know or think we know about a given issue or circumstance in light of that which we are analyzing. As we analyze the point of view we begin to see its assemblage and congruity. This requires that we develop attitudes of perseverance and discipline as we seek to engage in the process of analysis.

Evaluating the point of view. The evaluation of a point of view cannot proceed until we have accurately understood what we seek to evaluate. At this stage we can now see the adequacy or inadequacy of the point of view we are analyzing, the soundness and validity of its arguments, and in doing so, we can come to form a judgment regarding the point of view—a judgment that is based on our understanding and analysis of the logic of a given point of view. This evaluative process involves the development of reasoning dispositions and attitudes of intellectual integrity as we are asked to evaluate our own point of view and that of others in accordance with shared standards.

Developing one's own perspective. At this stage, we are in the process of ferreting out from what we've been examining exactly that which is not logical or that which we believe doesn't fit. When we develop our own perspective critically, we are doing so dialectically, which means that we appropriate from those points of view that which we think is positive and at the same time reject and abandon that which we think is not adequate or reasonable. This process is one of synthesis—of negation and appropriation—as we seek to incorporate the most positive aspects of points of view in the interest of truth and merit. This process of course varies from situation to situation as we can also come to reject completely what we've been analyzing and evaluating or, on the other hand, incorporate various aspects. What is important is to understand that the development of one's perspective *in a critical manner* involves a dialectical understanding and willingness to fairly analyze and examine contrary points of view to those that we might hold, no matter how attached to our point of view we might be. It is at once a process of ideological birth and death as new ideas emerge from the old, and that which was or might have been, is laid to rest. And so, the development of judgment, or one's own perspective, requires intellectual attitudes of courage and self-efficacy—a confidence in our own judgment regardless of the difficulty or challenges in forming it.

How to Recognize a Point of View

Bigot *n*. One who is zealously attached to an opinion you do not entertain.
—Ambrose Bierce

Points of view can be understood by separating them into their constituent parts. That is to say, every point of view is a system that has a logic that fuels it. Understanding the constitutive parts of a point of view and the logic that fuels it helps us clearly, fairly, and precisely recognize the point of view. This recognition, as I noted, is the first step in dialectical reasoning; I cannot assess that which I do not know.

We can say that every point of view can be recognized and is constructed around the following constitutive parts:

A goal or purpose: Every point of view attempts to reason towards a goal or purpose. Every point of view makes claims that are purposeful in an attempt to accomplish something, whether it be to convince one of something or to convince one against something—whether the goal is to persuade us of a better way to do something, a way to perceive a new idea, or a way to think about something, every point of view is an act of attempted accomplishment towards conscious ends. When attempting to recognize the point of view one question I need to ask myself is, 'Can I see its vision, where it wants to go and what it attempts to accomplish?'

Questions at issue or problems to be solved: Every point of view is organized around some questions at issue or set of problems to be solved. In this context, I am using the word *problem* not as a pejorative term but to indicate an obstacle or obstacles that must be removed or overcome in the pursuit of our goals or objectives. These questions at issue, or problems, are constructed and entertained in order to accomplish the goals or purposes of the point of view. How we come to see or frame an issue or problem can determine if and how we will accomplish our goals. I would need to ask myself at a minimum, 'Regarding any given point of view in question, can I understand how this point of view frames issues or states problems?'

Information, data, and ideas: Every point of view relies on information, data, or ideas to make sense of the world. At times the information is demonstrable, experiential or anecdotal and often times it comes from secondary sources. However, each point of view regarding any issue must marshal information in the service of its purposes and thus seeks to classify, categorize and use this information to solve given problems or resolve specific questions at issue. When understanding a point of view, I would want to ask myself, 'Am I clear as to how the point of view uses information, i.e. what its sources are, how it classifies and assembles the information within the parameters of its arguments?'

Vocabulary and ideas: Every point of view uses language and expresses ideas through its symbols in the form of words; it attaches meaning to vocabulary in a way that conveys the central points it wishes to impart. Failure to understand the conceptual dimensions of a point of view and the language that it employs to convey meaning results in a failure to understand the point of view in general. So, one question I would need to ask myself would be 'Do I really understand how the point of view is using language? Can I clearly understand what it means by what it says and the definitions it offers for important terms?'

Assumptions or beliefs: Every point of view rests on what is taken for granted or what the point of view believes. All points of view, either consciously or unconsciously, rely on assumptions and beliefs. In fact, assumptions are really the springboard of all reasoning. Identifying the assumptions inherent in a given point of view is essential for accurate and clear understanding of how conclusions and solutions to problems and decisions are formulated along with the origin of its claims. Thus, I would need to ask 'What assumptions does the point of view rest upon? Am I clear as to what the starting point of reasoning is that fuels the point of view?'

Evidence: Every point of view either marshals reasons or evidence for what it believes or is noticeable by its lack of evidence and reasons. Being able to clearly and precisely iterate the evidence marshaled by a specific point of view is constitutive for understanding. Similarly, being aware that a point of view lacks evidence and what that evidence might be is fundamental in analyzing the point of view and eventually evaluating it. I would want to ask myself when attempting to recognize a point of view, 'What evidence or reasons are being marshaled in support of the positions, assumptions or claims adopted by the point of view? How is the evidence being assembled and presented?'

Conclusions, decisions, and actions: Every point of view comes to conclusions or inferences as to how we should act, solve problems and form decisions. Every point of view states or claims something about what is unknown based on what is known. These conclusions, decisions, inferences and actions rest on the assumptions that guide the point of view. When recognizing a point of view, 'What conclusions does the point of view come to and/or what solutions or decisions does it offer to problems? How does it come to these conclusions or inferences?'

Consequences: Every point of view has consequences for believing or not believing it, for accepting or not accepting it, either for the proponent of the point of view, for others, or for both. We should be able to trace out the implications of a point of view or engage in what I term *consequential thinking*. We should be able to ask, 'Has the point of view indicated consequences of one position or another? What are they? What consequences have not been stated that should be noted?'

Knowing that there are constituent elements to a point of view helps us begin the process of accurately and precisely identifying and recognizing the point of view for critical assessment and analysis. Without comprehension of the constituent elements of a point of view, we are often left without the tools necessary for critical understanding and it is precisely this lack of comprehension that proves to be lethal if we are truly interested in understanding what motivates our thinking and the thinking of others.

How to Question a Point of View in the Interest of Incisive Recognition and Metacognition

Aristotle could have avoided the mistake of thinking that women have fewer teeth than men by the simple device of asking Mrs. Aristotle to open her mouth.
—Bertrand Russell

Oftentimes points of view are vague, or not developed fully or completely. For a healthy dialogue and exchange of ideas, learning *internal and external* questioning techniques, i.e. to question one's point of view and the points of view of others, is crucial. Routinely raising root questions about what someone else thinks is a difficult process which has little or no respect in today's society. Many people feel threatened when asked for reasons and evidence for their frames of reference. They too often become defensive and close their minds. Many people look at questioning as a form of hostile interrogation as opposed to constructive inquiry and unfortunately come to believe that those who question their ideas and points of view are somehow attacking them, putting them on the spot or otherwise attempting to undermine their very being. Similarly, learning to ask oneself questions is simply not the norm for most people. Here, the assumption held by many is that those who question themselves regularly are overly introspective, introverted and downright weird. So, the result is that we shy away from questioning, both internal and external in favor of uncritical acquiescence.

We have the tendency to reduce the new to the old; we are not used to questioning our ideas, world view or consequent actions and decisions. If we were less than perfect, we would have already have changed, right? Yet developing and evaluating what we believe in light of what others believe illuminates the path to well-reasoned judgment. Therefore, learning to question one's point of view and the points of view of others is crucial for any healthy exchange of ideas and eventual judgment on a given problem or issue. Some internal and external directions for questioning that we could and should ask would be:

What is the origin of the point of view? Where did the point of view come from (mine or others)? How long has the proponent of the point of view known what he/she claims to know? Where did they learn what they think they know? Is the origin valid?

What evidence or reasons motivate the point of view? What evidence and reasons does the point of view (mine or others) offer for its beliefs? What are some of the reasons that people believe this point of view in favor of another point of view? Why?

How does the point of view in question conflict with other points of view? How does this point of view (mine or others) conflict with other points of view on the same issue? How would questions contained in another contrasting point of view be answered by the point of view being advanced?

What are the consequences for accepting as true, this point of view? What follows from the point of view? What would believing the point of view imply? What are the practical consequences or implications of believing this point of view?

How to Analyze a Point of View

Others will tell you to try to prove you are right. I tell you to try to prove you are wrong.
—Louis Pasteur

Because we cannot analyze that which we do not know, essential recognition and understanding of a point of view must precede analysis. The old adage, "one cannot disagree with a position one does not understand," assumes that understanding presupposes analysis and *judgment*. Simply stated, we must understand something before we can disagree with it, abandon it or reject it. Yet uncritically assuming understanding is the norm for many people. In contrast, as indicated repeatedly in this essay, critical thinking asks us to assure that we are fairly and accurately understanding and recognizing a point of view of another before engaging in analysis and evaluation of the point of view. In fact, probing the justification for one's own belief systems relative to another point of view would require that we formulate the strongest argument *against* what we believe; and this involves entering into and conceiving of points of view not keeping with our own. This process would involve a clear and precise understanding of opposing points of view, as I have iterated above, and then would advocate reasoning from the premises inherent in the points of view to their conclusions. It would require that we listen critically and actively to views expressed by others as opposed to listening uncritically and selectively; and it would demand that we keep our minds open to opinions, criticisms, and conducts not keeping with our own.

When we begin to analyze a point of view as a system relative to its constituent parts and then examine those parts relative to the whole, we can begin to uncover and expose its logic, its rationality, and the merits of its claims—in short, we come to understand it as a system of thought that is accessible through mental understanding. This is not to say that the process is a linear one, i.e. first we do this, and then we do that, etc. However, it is an attempt to understand that we cannot assess and analyze that which we do not know—that recognition and analysis must intertwine with, if not precede, evaluation. Furthermore, we must look to issues of clarity, precision, accuracy, breadth, justifiability, and fairness when attempting to analyze a point of view we have recognized. These intellectual standards will allow us to assure not only that the point of view is well stated, clear in its principles, and justified in its conclusions, but will also impose upon us the necessity to avoid our own biases and prejudices.

Once we have recognized a point of view, in essence encapsulated its premises, assumptions, conclusions, evidence, information, vocabulary, and consequences, we can then begin to assess and analyze its merits. Is the point of view clear in its goals? Does it marshal evidence for its claims and beliefs? Have the consequences or implications of the point of view been traced out? Is the information upon which the point of view relies relevant or irrelevant? Is the source of information reliable or unreliable? Are the questions and problems clearly defined? Are the arguments valid, i.e. do the conclusions flow from the premises? Are the reasons and premises true, and is the point of view sound? These are just some questions that we would want to ask as we set about the task of analyzing points of view and engaging in reference reconciliation.

How to Evaluate a Point of View

> Toward no crimes have men shown themselves so cold-bloodedly cruel as in punishing differences in belief.
> —James Russell Lowell

The process of evaluating a point of view is intertwined with its analysis. As we come up with answers to our analytical questions, we begin to evaluate the point of view. This can happen simultaneously with our analysis. For example, if the assumptions that make up the point of view are unsubstantiated or unclear, then we can evaluate them as such. If the information that informs the point of view is unreliable, irrelevant or overgeneralized, then we can evaluate the claims in light of the information. If the arguments are not sound or valid, we can comment on this through our evaluative assessment.

In evaluating a point of view, it is important that we attempt to suspend our judgment in the interest of fairminded examination—to learn to place our judgment on 'probation' so-to-speak. Are we evaluating a frame of reference or point of view from the confines of our own perspective or is the evaluation truly based on the merits of what is being put forth? Are we being fair to what is being represented to us or are we inadvertently and selectively slipping in our own biases and prejudices?

Developing Our Own Perspective

> A beautiful theory, murdered by a gang of brutal facts.
> —Thomas Huxley

In developing our own perspective we are engaging in the dialectical process of forming reasoned judgment. This process can be done uncritically, i.e. we can substitute opinion for judgment, pursuing or selecting positions on issues based on our own preferences, prejudices and biases; or, we can do it critically, which implies that we have in a fair way examined points of view we may not agree with on issues within which we have invested a great deal of emotional and cognitive capital.

The consequences of developing one's perspective on issues uncritically are clear: we would come to conclusions and decisions about issues based on our own self-serving, self-justifying belief systems regardless of reasons and evidence. To develop one's perspective critically, on the other hand, would require that we reason within various points of view towards conclusions, decisions or solutions based on the best reasons and evidence proffered; it calls upon us to retool, refine and hone our thinking to meet the exigencies of the given moment or current situation. This process is the road to reasoned judgment as opposed to the road to rendered opinion. It is a difficult road to traverse and realizes that issues of reasoned judgment that face the human mind have more than one point of view and to officiate them rationally one must engage in a process of critical thinking or fairminded reasoning.

Reasoning Opportunities: Designing Point of View Lessons for Primary Students

> We can teach anything to the child honestly, if we reason within the child's experience.
> —Jerome Bruner

We have discussed at length in this article about what a point of view is, how to reason within and among points of view, and the components that must be examined in order to recognize and understand a point of view. Now that we have a knowledge of the "dance" we call "understanding a point of view" and the "steps" involved in that dance, let's turn our attention to designing lessons for students that allow them to practice developing empathy while at the same time learning to reason their way to conclusions and decisions. This section will address how our understanding of point of view can be infused into the design of critical thinking lessons for students in primary grades. I have specifically chosen primary grades as the focus of our lesson discussion as I taught kindergarten, first and second grade for two years each, respectively. During that duration of time, I experimented in the development of lessons that intended to help students develop insights into the importance of reasoning and especially the importance of reasoning among and within different points of view. If this process can be accomplished with young students in the primary grades, I only leave it to the imagination of the middle school or high school teacher who wishes to incorporate these insights into their lesson plans.

When designing point of view lessons for students in any grade, let alone the primary grades, we must be careful that we reason within the experiences of our students. Dialectical reasoning can be taught successfully to students as young as five years old if the lessons are developmentally appropriate, relevant and personalized. When you think about it, children are constantly engaging in role playing whereby they personify the assumed characteristics and points of views of others. Capitalizing on such play is the creative responsibility of the teacher in search of that teachable moment.

One such lesson that I have used successfully with kindergarten and first grade students involves using powerful children's literature to introduce the process of point of view recognition, questioning, analysis, evaluation and perspective building to students. This lesson involves using the book *The Real Story of the Three Little Pigs* by A. Wolf as told to Jon Scieszka. In this delightful and important picture book for young children, the story of the three little pigs is retold from the point of view of the wolf. Although a cute and amusing story, the book offers more than simply entertainment; it represents a powerful tool and resource in the arsenal of the critical thinking teacher and student.

In this story, A. Wolf (the nom de plume of the Wolf), tells the reader that the story told by the three little pigs is simply not true. According to the wolf, the real story involves a cup of sugar and a sneeze. The wolf begins by telling the reader that he was at home attempting to make a birthday cake for his Granny (the book shows him in the kitchen with a bowl full of cake mix). However, according to A. Wolf, he ran out of sugar and had a dreadful cold that caused him to consistently sneeze. In an attempt to finish making the cake the wolf decides to go to his neighbors' houses to see if he could borrow some sugar to complete the cake. Of course, his neighbors are pigs.

At the first house he politely knocks but receives no reply. This is the house that is made of straw and resided in by the first little pig. When he gets no answer after his initial knock, his cold suddenly forces him to sneeze and low and behold, the house falls down, killing the first little pig. Well, since he is a wolf and since wolves eat pigs, he decides to make a meal of the dead pig and go to the second house in his search for sugar.

At the second house, made of sticks and occupied by the second little pig, he knocks once again in search of the sugar. No one answers at the house and finding himself sneezing once again, the house of sticks falls down and the second little pig is found dead in the rubble. The wolf again eats the pig (calling it a second helping) and proceeds to the third house.

The third house is the house made of bricks and resided in by the third little pig. After knocking on the door and receiving no answer, the wolf decides to go back home and abandon the idea of baking a cake in favor of making his Granny a card for her birthday instead. However, as he is about to leave, the third little pig insults the wolf's Granny by suggesting that she sit on a pin. According to the wolf, he became so incensed and irate that he began yelling and carrying on outside the house of bricks until such time as the last remaining pig called the police. The police arrived and removed the wolf, taking him to jail and incarcerating him. The wolf is last seen in prison stripes gazing out through the bars of his jail proclaiming that he has been framed and begging for a cup of sugar.

I divide my lessons into time segments for planning purposes. For example, I might divide this lesson into day one, day two and day three.

I like to begin this lesson by reading the traditional story of the three little pigs from the pigs' point of view. I want to be sure that students have accurately recognized and understood it. So, on day one as I read the story, I engage in an open Socratic discussion with students. I begin by asking them to clearly and precisely depict the pigs' point of view. Using a marker, I then visually chart or mindmap the story on graph paper, noting students' responses to questions regarding the pigs' point of view as I go along.

Once the story is complete and student responses have been depicted on chart paper, I then personalize and make the lesson relevant by asking students if they have ever had an argument, altercation or dispute with another student at school or, maybe with their siblings at home. Here, I am attempting to couch the lesson in the lives of my students while at the same time setting the stage for an eventual transfer of the lessons' insights. As students respond in the affirmative, I then ask them what they did to resolve the dispute. The usual response is that the students consulted an adult, either a teacher or loved one, to help them sort out the truth. When I ask them how the teacher or loved one figures out which side to believe, themselves or their classmates or siblings, I am met with blank stares. This is natural, as the students have no idea that they have a point of view or that there is a process to recognize and analyze it. I then introduce the concept *point of view* to students by saying, "When we tell our side of the story to someone, we can call a side of a story a *point of view*." Once the concept *point of view* is introduced to students, I then begin to use it regularly as vocabulary in dialogue and questioning. In this way, students come to understand the concept and transfer it and relate it to their own experiences.

On day two, usually after we've had a lively discussion regarding point of view, I then tell the students that I know the wolf. Further, I tell the students, "he asked me to tell you his point of view regarding the story of the three little pigs because no one has heard his side of the story." Before beginning the story, I ask the students if they think the wolf will tell the truth and almost all the students tell me that the wolf will lie. This is not unusual as students at an early age form assumptions about wolves that they get from cartoons or popular culture—assumptions that wolves are bad and mean animals out to hurt others. Ironically, these assumptions sometimes form students' first entry into perceiving some people or classes of people as "the other" or someone to be feared, as the wolf is often conceived of as different and thus something to be feared, hated or disdained. One of the clear metacognitive purposes of this lesson is to have students learn how to examine their own assumptions (in this case re: wolves).

Now that the stage has been set, the students are eager to hear the wolf's point of view and I thus proceed to read and discuss the Real Story of the Three Little Pigs with the students, depicting the story through graphic organizers or mind-mapping, similar to that which I did with the pigs—charting and depicting their thinking visually. Some of the questions I ask them are:

Why does the wolf wish to tell you his point of view?
What does the wolf want you to believe about the pigs? Why?
What is the problem according to the wolf?
What information is the wolf giving us and how do we know it is true?
What reasons does the wolf give for his actions?
What would be the consequences of believing the wolf?
How is the wolf's story different from the pigs'?

When the story is completed and I am assured that the students have understood the wolf's point of view, I then ask them how we might figure out who is telling the truth. They of course do not know, other than proclaiming in unison that the wolf is lying.

At this point I take out a cardboard box and tell the students that inside the box are things I found in the wolf's house that might help us figure out who is telling the truth. The students then unpack the box and find:

- An empty bag of sugar
- Cold tablets with three tablets missing
- A store-bought birthday card that says, "Happy birthday to my Grandma on her 80th birthday"
- A small baggie with various wadded-up pieces of tissue paper
- A box of unopened cake mix

At once I can see the "lights go on" as most students begin to grasp an understanding of what is transpiring. We then engage in further Socratic discussion regarding the items and what they might or might not prove.

During the discussion, I tell the students that we call these items *evidence* and then ask them what the evidence tells them. Once again, I am using the word *evidence* in discussion with them so as to reinforce their understanding of the concept within a relevant, problem-posing curriculum.

The following are actual and verbatim responses I have received from kindergarten and first graders throughout the United States where I have taught this lesson:

- *From all the evidence I think that the wolf is not guilty.*
- *From my point of view the wolf is guilty because if he took all the cold medicine his cold would have been better and he would not have sneezed.*
- *I think the wolf is telling the truth because of all the things we found.*
- *I think the pigs are telling the truth because the cake mix already had sugar in it and so why would the wolf have needed to borrow sugar.*
- *I think the wolf was lying because he said that he was going to make his grandma a card and the card he gave you was a store-bought card.*
- *I disagree with Dean, I think that the evidence shows that the wolf had a cold and so he needed sugar.*
- *At first I thought the wolf was guilty but now I think the he is telling the truth because of the cold medicine and tissues you found.*
- *I think the wolf is lying because in the book the cake mix was in the bowl and you have a full box of cake mix that is not opened and so the wolf couldn't be telling the truth.*

Once the lesson is over (usually day three) and the students have written about what we have done (or have drawn pictures if they cannot write), I then involve the students in metacognition by asking them (and not in these words, but words that they can understand) to think about their thinking. Here are just some of the questions I have used in this lesson:

- *What did we do to figure out who was telling the truth?*
- *Could you have figured out who was telling the truth if you did not know both sides of the story? What did you have to do to get both points of view?*

- *What was evidence and how did you use it to think?*
- *Did your thinking change when you thought about the evidence? How and why?*
- *Was the evidence important in your thinking? Why and how?*
- *What evidence could you use and what evidence was not useful? Why?*
- *Do you think that you know now how people figure out who's telling the truth when they are faced with two points of view or more? How?*
- *Why did I ask a lot of questions? Did you find you had questions? Did they help you? How?*
- *Did you change your thinking as a result of hearing both points of view? How and why?*
- *Do you think you can use what you've learned about point of view in your real life? How and why?*

By designing specific lessons that are interesting and fun while at the same time motivating and engaging students in a discussion and analysis of point of view, students begin to learn the process of recognition, questioning, analysis and evaluation in developing their own perspective. Furthermore, they are developing the ability to transfer these insights into their own lives in an effort to mediate and resolve disputes, analyze historical actions, form judgment, develop their own perspective, and critically examine claims in a search for truth. Enabling students by designing reasoning opportunities to critically think *about* and *through* points of view, we come to help students develop character and to understand the process for sound judgment.

Summary: What Students Have Learned

Human history becomes more and more a race between education and catastrophe.
—H.G. Wells

In teaching students the dance, so to speak, of how to reason dialectically, how to form their own perspective and how to understand point of view, we also teach students the steps to that dance. We teach them to develop a language for thinking and engage this language in fairminded discourse; we teach them to recognize and evaluate evidence; we teach them to examine their own assumptions and the assumptions of others; we show them the importance of questioning deeply and encourage inquiry through the questioning model; we help students understand the difference between relevant and irrelevant information; we introduce them to processes that allow them to verify sources of information; we teach them humility and the necessity of suspending judgment; we teach them how to analyze and evaluate arguments; we teach them to reason dialectically by helping them learn to evaluate perspectives and interpretations; we teach them how to recognize contradictions and explore implications and consequences; and through all of this, we help them develop courage and confidence in their own judgment. And if this was not enough, we teach them how to do this within the context of reading, writing, speaking, listening and role playing, thus providing opportunities for students to learn to more effectively read and write for a purpose; to more critically listen and speak to others; and to more actively become literate. Furthermore, we lay the pedagogical basis for sound, fairminded critical thinking at an early age thereby exposing students to these concepts early in life so that they might later develop into active and wise participants in the formation of democracy.

The task is formidable, for it involves embracing and teaching the process of reasoning; it is enjoyable and more powerful, because it is couched in children's play and as a result more transferable as an insight when grounded in the subjective lives of students; and, bedded in the reality of the child, the task becomes attainable and measurable.

The consequences and implications for teaching dialectical reasoning and reference reconciliation can be a movement towards a global and national citizenry empowered by empathic, fairminded discourse in every personal, social and institutional aspect of life. The consequences of not teaching this form of reasoning can be continued individualistic competition, egocentric reasoning, narrow-minded debate, irrational discourse and increasing intolerance and inhumanity—in short, catastrophe. The possibility is there—the choice is ours.

References

Albrecht, Karl (1987) *Brain Power: Learn to Improve Your Thinking Skills.* p. 68 New York: Simon and Schuster

Bruner, Jerome (1983) *In Search of Mind: Essays in Autobiography.* New York: Harper and Row

Scieszka, J. (1989) *The True Story of the Three Little Pigs.* New York: Viking Press

Making Critical Thinking Critical

Joe L. Kincheloe

A variety of animals pose as critical thinking programs from the highly sophisticated, socially contextualized and politically informed, to the psychologicalized, rationalized, and test-driven. I have always been perversely fascinated with the latter types, especially as they are institutionalized within the public schools and schools of education I've observed. I keep hoping such programs will just fade away, but, alas, at the end of the millennium they are healthy and thriving. All educators agree that it is important to teach students and teachers to think critically. According to this trite wisdom, teachers can be taught how to teach critical thinking in a few hours of special workshops. When critical thinking is taught in this manner, it is rarely conceived in the context of the unique demands of an educational practitioner.

In this psychologized, rationalized, and test-driven context the social and cognitive assumptions behind the notion of critical thinking promoted are ignored. Epistemological meta-analysis and the resulting political implications of the programs are often looked at as foreign concepts in these contexts. Shirley Steinberg's and my work in post-formal thinking (Kincheloe and Steinberg, 1993; Kincheloe, 1993; Kincheloe, 1995; Kincheloe, Steinberg, and Hinchey, 1999; Kincheloe, Steinberg, and Villaverde, 1999) posits that in order to teach critical thinking teachers need first to be capable of a post-Piagetian, meta-analytical, discursively aware form of cognition in relation to a variety of disciplines and knowledge forms. This post-Piagetian, or post-formal thinking, is a self-reflective form of thought that attempts to move beyond the logical base of Piagetian formalism by employing subjugated ways of knowing, critical theory, and postmodernist critique.

Practitioner ways of knowing are unique, quite different from the technical, scientific ways of knowing traditionally associated with professional expertise. Professional expertise, as Donald Schon maintains, is an uncertain enterprise as it confronts constantly changing, unique, and unstable conditions. Teachers never see the same classroom twice, as teaching conditions change from day to day. The students who reacted positively to a set of pedagogical strategies yesterday, respond differently today (despite William Bennett's assurances of "what works"). Schon's practitioners relinquish the certainty that attends to professional expertise conceived as the repetitive administration of techniques to similar types of problems. In the post-formal reconceptualization of critical practitioner-thinking the ability of practitioners to develop research strategies that explore the genesis and efficacy of comfortable assumptions and implicit objectives is extremely important (Schon, 1983).

In education, post-formal teachers become teachers-as-researchers who question the nature of their own thinking as they attempt to teach critical thinking to their students. What are the limits of human ways of knowing? Where do we begin conceptualizing post-formal modes of teacher thinking that lead to a metaperspective, to empowerment? Drawing upon our critical postmodern system of meaning, we cannot help but anticipate ways of knowing and levels of cognition that move beyond Piagetian formalism. Adults do not reach a final cognitive equilibrium beyond which no new levels of thought can emerge; there have to be modes of thinking that transcend the formal operational ability to formulate abstract conclusions, understand cause-effect relationships, and employ the traditional scientific method to explain reality. We know too much to define formality as the zenith of human cognitive ability (Arlin, 1975).

It is the issue of critical empowerment, the ability of individuals to disengage themselves from the tacit assumptions of discursive practices and power relations in order to exert more conscious control over their everyday lives, that psychologized models of critical thinking fail to address. Rational, accurate thinking emerging from modernism's one-truth epistemology produces not only a congregation of nervous right-answer givers and timid rule followers, but a rather mediocre level of education unrelated to any ethical effort to constructively use our ability to reason. The technicist efforts to cultivate higher order critical thinking among teachers too often involved removing prospective practitioners from their lived worlds in order to control the variables of the situation. As a result, thinking is sequestered in artificial laboratory settings where passion and authentic feelings of love, hate, fear, and commitment are scientifically removed. Cartesian-Newtonian models of the rational process of critical thinking are always culturally neutral, always removed from the body and its passions. These modernist models assume that a practitioner can be removed from his or her embeddedness in a physical context without affecting cognition (Hultgren, 1987; Bobbitt, 1987; Bowers and Flinders, 1990; Hinchey, 1998; Cannella, 1997).

This separation of various contexts from cognition constitutes a large part of what is wrong with psychological critical thinking programs. Whether we are teaching high school math, elementary language arts, or teacher education, the approach is the same: break down the information to be learned into discrete parts that can be easily memorized. Thus, cognitive theories, grammatical rules, vocabulary, math computation skills, the "causes" of the Civil War, are all to be "learned" in this way. As long as the curriculum is conceived in a technical way with prespecified facts to be learned, with improvement of standardized tests the goal of instruction, with little concern granted to connecting school and life, with no debate over the role of learning in a democratic society, then critical thinking programs will stupify (Macedo, 1994) more than they will enlighten.

Take the way modernist science has taught us to teach reading. Mastery learning programs break reading skills into subskills such as beginning consonant sounds, vowel sounds, ending consonant sounds, consonant blends, and vowel diagrams. Teachers learn to teach these in a structured, sequenced manner until students pass the mastery test on each subskill. Again, the common sense, linear methodology seems to satisfy everyone's demands. Upon deeper examination, however, problems begin to materialize—even on the superficial level on which such programs are assessed.

Researchers have found that in the first few years of such programs, reading skills *scores* among early elementary students increase. However, by the time the children are in the sixth grade, reading levels not only begin to decrease, but students were not reading. Although students were scoring high on achievement tests, the examinations measured only what early grade teachers had taught—the subskills. Reading or language arts classes had revolved mainly around worksheets or dittos on the subskills. Very little actual reading was taking place. Students had learned the fragmented curriculum well. They had indeed learned the isolated subskills and had reflected that knowledge on the standardized tests. Even so, they were not reading for knowledge, enjoyment, or meaning—they were not even reading. The reading program had committed a fatal modernist error: it had assumed that the parts add up to the whole. As with most human endeavors the whole was far greater than the parts (Shannon, 1989).

Uncritical, Critical Thinking

It has been in this epistemological context that our psychologized critical thinking programs—or "uncritical critical thinking" has been developed, Trapped within a modernist logic, uncritical critical thinking was hyperrationalized, reduced to a set of micrological skills that promote a form of procedural knowledge. In its reductionism this uncritical critical thinking removed the political and ethical dimensions of thinking. Students and teachers were not encouraged to confront why they tended to think as they did about themselves, the world around them, and their relationship to that world. In other words, these uncritical critical thinkers gained little insight into the forces that had shaped them, that is, their consciousness construction. In addition, the mainstream critical thinking movement was virtually unconcerned with the consequences of thinking, viewing cognition as a process that takes place in a vacuum. Thinking in a new way always necessitates personal transformation; indeed if enough people think in new ways, social transformation is inevitable. The nature of this social and personal change was not important to uncritical critical thinking advocates.

Uncritical critical thinking advocates were unable to transcend the boundaries of formal thinking as they reduced thinking to the micrological skills, they taught a fragmented version of scientific thinking (the highest expression of formality). Students were taught to differentiate, to group, to identify common properties, to label, to categorize, to distinguish relevant from irrelevant information, to relate points, to infer, and to justify—usually in isolation from any scientific or larger conceptual problem. It can be argued that such an approach to critical thinking actually obscured mm than it exposed by hiding its hyperrationality behind its scientific appearance.

Though its intentions were well founded, the movement never realized that critical thinking is more than a cognitive skill to be mastered, that it is not the province of only the gifted, that teacher education must teach critical thinking in the context of reflective practice. Uncritical critical thinking always saw higher order thinking as a process separate from the environment of the school. Proponents never saw the critical, emancipating dimensions of thinking that are inseparable from the democratic way students, teachers, and administrators interact with one another (Kincheloe and Steinberg, 1998). In the uncritical context educators did not have the conceptual tools to understand the complexity of critical thinking for empowerment. One lesson that critical analysis has taught us is that the self and the conscious process are ambiguous and contradictory entities pushed and pulled by a plethora of forces. The idea that critical thinking can be taught without rigorous historical study, linguistic analysis, and a deep understanding of knowledge production is naive (Kincheloe and Steinberg, 1998).

Moving toward Empowerment: "Critical Critical Thinking"

So what is "critical critical thinking"? Authentically critical thinking moves in an emancipatory direction with an omnipresent sense of self-awareness. Moving in an emancipatory direction implies a concern with the development of a liberated mind, a critical consciousness, and a free society. Teachers as critical thinkers are aware of the construction of their own consciousness and the ways that social and institutional forces work to undermine their autonomy as professionals (Ashburn, 1987; Hultgren 1987). Emancipatory teacher thinking sets the self "in question." Self-images, inherited dogmas, and absolute beliefs are interrogated, teachers begin to see themselves in relation to the world around them, to perceive the school as a piece of a larger mosaic. Teachers begin to see an inseparable relationship between thinking and acting, as the boundary between feeling and logic begins to fade from the cognitive map—a map redrawn by feminist cartographers.

Indeed, cognitive style holds specific and ideological consequences. We cannot think about thinking without considering the power dimensions of the act—the *empowerment* of higher orders of thinking. For teachers to think in an emancipatory manner involves empowered actions and practices activities that contribute to the best interests of students, community members, and other teachers and conduct that enables those affected to employ their intelligence and ethics. Thus, the move to "critical critical thinking" involves the transcendence of the notion that thinking is merely a cognitive psychological activity. This may be the key to understanding the static flatness of uncritical critical thinking, As both a psychological and social activity, critical critical thinking is perceived as "in process," ever in a state of being constructed. For example, teachers cannot think about the curriculum outside of a social context. If they do, they are deceived by the political innocence of a body of agreed-upon knowledge being systematically passed on to students by an ever-evolving, but always neutral, instructional process. We know too much to be seduced by the never-aging sirens of political neutrality. As a deliberate process, the curriculum is always a formal transmission of *particular* aspects of the culture's knowledge. Do we teach women's and African Americans' history in eleventh-grade social studies? Do we read Toni

Morrison and Alice Walker in twelfth-grade literature? These are sociopolitical questions—that is, they involve power.

Thinking affects social practice; it is never detached. How we think about teaching works to change or maintain the status quo. Descriptions of the world do not rest, they do not retreat to a sociological easy chair, They are part of the commerce of the world; as they define it, they change it. Thinking is always a major strategy in the cultural battle. If such is so, then conceptual matters can never be sequestered in the psychological domain. Cognition in a critical postmodern context becomes sociocognition.

What I am calling critical critical thinking, I refer to elsewhere as post-formal thinking. In speaking and writing about this cognitive theory I try not to concretely define post-formalism but to continuously construct it and observe it in the individuals I encounter around the world. To define it would imply that it was a discrete stage with universal features. Such definition would fall back to the totalizing inclination of modernism, its tendency to capture meaning. The postmodern encounter with post-formal thinking induces us to "do" post-formal thinking, to dive into the post-formal water. As such, it will remain elusive, a prisoner-at-large resistant to the trap of consistent meaning. The way it is defined will always involve the interaction between our general conceptions of it and its interactions with its ever-changing experiences, the new contexts in which it finds itself. As Heidegger once put it, thinking is not so much a cognitive action as it is a "way of life." Thinking, he concluded, is how human beings remember who they are and where they belong.

Remembering who we are and where we belong involves the ability to make informed choices, to engage in critical critical thinking. Post-formal teachers and students following the concerns of Heidegger, employ critical thinking to choose between competing theories and curricular and instructional strategies. Without the ability to make critical preference, teachers are disinclined to teach their students critical critical thinking. Students are cognitively and ethically deskilled, as they find themselves unable to distinguish work of quality from drivel. In this situation students consider schooling normal when it immerses them in busy work and mindless rote-based, test-driven exercises. Of course, they lose interest in learning.

The Theoretical Basis of the "Critical" in Critical Thinking

Critical pedagogy and the critical theory on which it is based raise one of the central issues in post-formalism's critique of mainstream articulations of critical thinking: whose interests are served by particular psychological and educational perspectives, Such a question, of course, drags mainstream psychology kicking and screaming into the political arena, the sphere of society that involves the struggle for the organization and distribution of power. Proponents of critical critical thinking are always concerned with the way this political dynamic operates, the way various institutions and interests deploy power in the effort to survive, shape behavior, gain dominance over others, or in a more emancipatory vein, improve the human condition. Realizing that power is not a central force in the psycho-social process, proponents of critical critical thinking understand that humans are the historical products of power. Men and women do not arise outside of the process of history; our identities are fundamentally shaped by our entanglements in the webs that power weaves (Samuels, 1993; Thiele, 1986; McLaren, 1994).

A critical thinking informed by critical pedagogy is concerned with the specific nature of these entanglements, the way power shapes subjectivity in general and classroom practices in particular. Viewing these processes of power as having naturalized themselves to the point of invisibility, a critically informed education wants to expose them for all to see. In this context the post-formal critique pays special attention to the critical pedagogical analysis of the relationship among knowledge, authority and power (Giroux, 1994). Traditional educational philosophies viewed pedagogy as a body of techniques and skills used to teach a designated core of subject matter. Because of such a definition, pedagogy has been viewed with condescension within the academy. Post-formalists maintain that the critical rearticulation of pedagogy propels it to a central position in higher education, social theory, the humanities, and psychology. Thus, critical thinking in this context becomes not only a school practice but a cultural practice that exists wherever power produces knowledge, shapes values, and constructs consciousness, These pedagogical and power-related features are inseparable from both an understanding of educational psychological processes and the post-formal quest to develop a democratic cognition.

Paulo Freire (1970), operating in this critical tradition, spoke frequently about "reading the world." In this context Freire was referring to these power dynamics, as he moved his students to make connections between social and educational knowledge and the political forces that shaped it. An understanding of power's complicity in the production of society's validated knowledge, its educational knowledge in particular, is essential information for racially, ethnically, and economically marginalized students who are trying to figure out why they are deemed "slow" and "incompetent" in the schools they attend. With an understanding of the role of power in education and the knowledge of school, they begin to make sense of what happens when the cognitive process they are taught is not critical. A dramatic and hopeful transformation occurs when marginalized students grasp this power-related dynamic, a change of consciousness that allows them a critical x-ray vision to see through psychological evaluations of their *lack of* ability (Macedo, 1994; Marfin-Baro, 1994).

Thus, individuals informed by a critical view of power appreciate its ability to produce or construct the ways their worlds, their everyday lives operate. Power's production of knowledge and identity, they come to realize, shapes who can do what to whom. Such recognitions are seen by critical thinkers as a source of empowerment, a dangerous knowledge that provides individuals the tools to defy the dominant power bloc (Fiske, 1993). Post-formal delineations of power team from these theoretical articulations and for us attention on the intersection of macro-political and micro-individualist power dynamics. In this framework post-formal critical thinkers carefully analyze the macro-forces of subjugation in society such as the political economy of class elitism, patriarchy, white supremacy, and technical rationality/decontextualized reason and their impact on individuals and groups operating in diverse contexts and conditions. At the micro-level, post-formalists examine consciousness and unconsciousness and the ways human agents subvert and resist the macro-forces of power in their lived realities. The production of pleasure is often an important feature of the macro-micro intersection and is accorded the attention it deserves. Cultural texts such as TV, movies, video games and music, for example, have become increasingly important in a critical pedagogical context as they embody the interactivity of power and person in the struggle for critical consciousness.

The Frankfurt School of Critical Theory which provided the notion of "critical" that informs our notion of critical thinking worked in the 1920s to forge a theoretical fusion of Marx and Freud. In this amalgam Theodor Adorno, Max Horkheimer and Herbert Marcuse attempted to understand the relationship between the psyche and socioeconomic and political forces. How did this relationship operate, they asked, to impede popular support for political movements dedicated to freedom, democracy and justice, No emancipatory politics, the Frankfurt scholars assumed, is complete without a political psychology that traces the effects of particular political arrangements on human consciousness and vice versa. In the course of their analysis the critical theorists came to the conclusion that the growth of disciplinary expertise and the rationality that accompanies it has not led to a sophisticated understanding of consciousness, moral growth or human happiness. Indeed, the influence of this "irrational rationality" of disciplinary expertise has often served the interests of dominant power blocs by repressing human self-direction and undermining critical critical thinking. While the Frankfurt School did not achieve final success in their effort to reveal the connections between the psyche of the political, they did establish a line of inquiry and a mode of theorizing that remains extremely valuable to post-formal critical thinking at the end of the twentieth century (Alford, 1993; Smart, 1992; Elliot, 1994).

As advocates of post-formal critical thinking follow upon the paths blazed by the Frankfurt School, they come to the stark realization that educational psychology is isolated from the critical theorists' concern with both the political and the process of critical consciousness formation. The study of the complexity that characterizes the production of subjectivity seems to be lost in mainstream educational psychology to the point that such issues cannot even be discussed in the discipline's conferences and literature. While the Frankfurt School was concerned primarily with the insights of psychoanalysis (Freudian) in its marriage of the political and the psychological, post-formalism seeks the analyses of a postmodernized psychoanalysis as well as a socially-situated cognitive psychology in its efforts to reap the political and educational benefits derived from the development of critical thinking. Post-formalists realize in this context that power helps shape the choices that determine the types of aptitudes and cognitive abilities individuals develop. Not only do humans become the sort of beings they are as consequence of their location in the web of power relations, but such political dynamics even define the characteristics educational psychologists designate as higher-order thinking (Wartenberg, 1992). What is labeled critical thinking, thus, is not simply socially-influenced, it is politically inscribed and constructed in part by the nature of one's relationship to power.

Though grounded on the work of the Frankfurt School, critical theory and its educational offspring, critical pedagogy, have continually evolved. Buoyed by the rediscovery of Italian social theorist Antonio Gramsci and his hegemony theory, the critical tradition has profited from its encounter with feminism and postmodernism/post-structuralism over the last quarter of the twentieth century. While these theoretical innovations and their relationship to the development of a post-formal critical thinking are necessary understandings, it is important to recognize these transitions in critical theory and pedagogy. Social theory in the mid 1970s embraced new understandings of ideology and subjectivity. No longer was power/ideology viewed as producing a distortion of "authentic reality" as seen by a "true consciousness." The evolving social theory challenged the possibility of critical scholars ever telling the "whole truth."

Scholars in the new paradigm would have to be content with providing partial explanations of phenomena from their particular vantage points in the web of reality. Thus, post-formalists critique the authoritative pronouncements of mainstream educational psychology about the nature of critical thinking. In its stead they offer no objective, final revelation about the eternal nature of such cognition (Walkerdine, 1988). Their call to democratize the beast is open-ended, motivated by an effort to diversify its meaning and admit more marginalized people into the community of the "cognitively anointed." In part the call is an admission that we don't exactly know what critical thinking is and never will; our only alternative is to simply keep looking for and collecting manifestations of it that meet the standards of our historically constructed value judgments. Such uncertainty, post-formalists assume, is preferable to the antidemocratic, ethnocentric tyranny of mainstream psychological certainty.

Within the terrain of ideology, hegemony, and questions of oppression critical social theory has become far more sensitive to meaning making. In this context the new theory studies the process by which significations and representations are deployed to maintain asymmetrical power relations. These processes become far more significant in an age of electronic media where pictures play an increasingly important role. One does not have to look very far in the late 199N to observe these meaning making processes at work in media. Representations of African Americans as threatening, irresponsible criminals flood TV shows and movies. School movies use African American youth as signifiers for urban decay, crime, and school disruption, in the process shaping the public's perceptions in a manner that induces them to blame the victims of racism for the intensification of racial inequality.

At the same time the new social theory gains a more sophisticated view of hegemonic signification and representation, it also opens new possibilities for resistance and emancipation of the oppressed. As the Eurocentric scientific delineation of history, the world around us, and the nature of reason is called into question as merely one of many cultural delineations, peoples living on the ethnic, cultural, racial, class, religious, and sexual margins gain the possibility of emancipation from bondage to the "one true way of being." As I have written elsewhere (Semali and Kincheloe, 1998), local knowledges and rationalities gain a new space to assert themselves in settings previously restricted. The emancipation referenced here is not the early Frankfurt School's notion of reclaiming an authentic, non-socialized self, but a more humble situated emancipation. Such a process is aware of the inevitability of social construction and the persistence of ambiguity and uncertainty but at the same time the possibility of local rationalities and the promise of new ways of thinking and being (Mumby, 1989; Vattimo, 1991; Alvesson and Willmott, 1992).

In an era where social criticism is often viewed as irrelevant, critical pedagogy provides a valuable if often ignored resource for educators, psychologists, and other cultural workers. Such criticism is especially valuable in the critical vacuum of educational psychology as post-formal critical thinkers point out the contradictions between the field's liberal rhetoric and the regressive consequences of its actions. As critical scholars map educational psychology's contributions to inequality, competition as motivation, and a lack of caring, they deconstruct the political encodings in terms such as "quality," excellence," "ability," and "failure." Focusing on the way such unexamined dynamics serve the interests of dominant groups, critical thinking itself becomes a central feature of the effort to democratize intelligence. It is important to remember that at the time of psychology's birth the field represented itself as a force for human liberation and the healing of human suffering. As critical scholars post-formalists believe the discipline should be measured by these claims and thus be held accountable for the ways it has furthered race, class, and gender oppression.

As an institution that categorizes, classifies, and assesses cognition, educational psychology must become more aware of the political consequences of its power to proclaim normality, pathology, or sophisticated cognition. Any attempt to reclaim critical thinking must enable psychologists to trace the imprint of unexamined sociopolitical assumptions on what are provided as objective descriptions of an individual's aptitude. Here, post-formalists argue that mainstream educational psychology becomes an ideology that is, a producer of meaning, that maintains dominant power relations. Thus, the post-formal task of reconceptualizing critical thinking becomes an act of resistance, a counter-hegemonic struggle to challenge psychological "authority via expertise." Educational psychology, in the words of Ulrich Beck (1992), becomes not a liberating force but a producer of "social risks" that threaten the well-being of particular individuals-a long march from its humanistic origins. The technical rationality of the discipline with its standardized methods, narrow linear thinking, distance from naturalistic context, and universal application of techniques and assumptions has failed. Because such a rationality refuses to consider the sociopolitical role of critical thinking, it produces a bureaucracy of rule-following technocrats (Tomlinson, 1988; Levin, 1991; Schleifer, Con Davis and Mergler, 1992; Abercrombie, 1994). Such functionaries study the mechanical parts of the watch but have never thought about the nature of time.

Sheltered and isolated by its allegiance to this technical rationality, uncritical critical thinking is naive concerning the complex process of self-production. Instead of placing this dynamic at the heart of critical thinking where it belongs, mainstream educational psychology and the pedagogy it supports have ignored the effects of changing socio-cultural conditions, political efforts to position voters and consumers, and the libidinal dynamics of identity construction to name merely a few aspects of the process. Critical analysis of the field seems to indicate that for the most part educational psychology has not learned the simple lesson that the actions of individuals are limited by conditions *not of their own making*. Such an understanding connects critical theory with Vygotsky's appreciation of the social aspect of cognition. Contemporary critical theory extends the insights Vygotsky garnered in the 1930s in a way that provides a far more sophisticated appreciation of the "social" in the socio-cognitive, the critical in critical thinking.

Critical scholars argue that psychology's capture by this technical rationality produces an epistemology that assumes reality is perceived similarly by everyone. Because what we know is inextricably tied to a contextually shaped conceptual framework, different people will hold different perceptions of similar events. The recognition of this phenomenon holds dramatic implications for teachers working in elementary and secondary classrooms. Different students with divergent frames of reference will understand not only specific lessons in varying ways but will conceptualize the entire school process in profoundly contrasting manners. In childhood education and developmental psychology, this feature takes on special importance in light of the language and material effects of developmental appropriateness. Assuming that everyone perceives schooling in a similar manner and that all students are operating on a level playing field, developmental appropriateness is riddled with monocultural, gender, and class-based presuppositions about behavioral norms, cognitive styles, and educational goals. When students operating outside of white, middle/upper middle class boundaries do not match these culturally-inscribed expectations, they are deemed incompetent and provided with "remediation" to make them more "orderly" and "structured." They are deemed incapable of critical thinking.

If a central feature of educational psychology involves the analysis of why children fail then an understanding of these critical assertions is necessary for practitioners. How does the concept of achievement come to be defined in this culture? Why are there race, class, and gender dimensions to who gets defined as high and low achievers, critical and deficient thinkers? To critical observers these would seem to be sonic of the major inquiries of the discipline. Questions such as these in an educational psychology, directed subdiscipline such as special education are often ignored. Once again technical rationality focuses the field's attention on the "how to" questions of special education teaching, not the socio-cultural questions of how are decisions made to track particular students into special education (Elliot, 1994; Fiske, 1993; Nooteboom, 1991; Polakow, 1992; Tomlinson, 1988). The technique-obsessed rationality that drives such educational approaches is incapable of viewing schooling as a cultural process where student processes of meaning-making shape the way they respond to the demands teachers present them. Until educational psychology accepts this critical assertion there is little probability that intelligence will be democratized, that mainstream articulations of critical thinking will be challenged, and that critical thinking is a goal that a wide range of students from diverse backgrounds can achieve.

Teaching Post-Formal Critical Thinking: Re-Thinking Reason

Post-formal teachers operating with a sophisticated understanding of critical-critical thinking, the politics of knowledge and their relationship to the lifeworld of everyday experience, are ready to take part in the revolutionary process of reconceptualizing comfortable Western notions of reason. Post-formal theory is grounded on the understanding that reason is a social construction, culturally mediated by signs, symbols, and codes. In this context, Cartesian-Newtonian reason is not trans-historical and trans-cultural but a sophisticated form of meaning-making. The traditional scientific aim of its own rational universalism is rejected with its abstract reason divorced from experience and its concern for adjusting individuals to reality. This dynamic of adjustment reveals itself in functionalist theories that reinforce the legitimacy of the status quo rather than engaging students in a critique of its shortcomings. Mainstream educational psychology fits in this functionalist context, as it identifies deficiency and/or pathology in the marginalized student. The possibility of cultural mismatch or conflicting social values among the culture, of school, the psychological criteria for assessment, the mainstream definition of critical thinking and the student, is rarely considered.

The post-formal re-conceptualization of Cartesian-Newtonian reason challenges the mainstream educational psychological construction of autonomy and isolated self-direction as the ultimate manifestations of the reasonable individual. In this context the abstract individualism of modernity inscribes cognitive theory with a validated set of procedures for attaining rational autonomy, a.k.a., formal critical thinking. Known, of course, as the scientific method, these procedures provide modernist educational psychologists with the yellow brick road to rigor, context-freedom, protection for the bias/distortion of subjectivity, and truth. The teaching that emanates from these assumptions assumes that the purpose of instruction is to impart this procedural form of uncritical critical thinking and to measure students' capacity to employ it. As post-formal teachers rethink reason, they embrace intimacy and interpretation rather than distance and proof. In this context such teachers value the personal knowledges of students and the ways understanding draws individuals together. Such an emphasis is not a retreat to irrationality but an effort to push the boundaries of reason beyond a limited set of procedures and the confines of abstract principles.

In this critical pursuit, post-formal teachers seek to engage their students in the understanding of the world in general and everyday life in particular both in relation to one another and from as many vantage points as possible. A central feature of post-formal critical thinking's expansion of reason involves the ability to uncover new perspectives, new angles on the world, everyday life, and self. In this context students and teachers learn to contextualize in new and exciting ways. In a post-formal classroom studying the Gulf War students would study not only U.S. accounts of the conflict, but Iraqi perspectives. They would interview gung-ho U.S. Army veterans, war protestors, Iraqi victims, and observers from Africa and Latin America. Students would analyze the war in a geopolitical context, a multinational economic context, an environmental context, and a medical context. The role of the post-formal teacher would involve devising new contexts and new perspectives from which to explore the meaning of the war. Moral and ethical questions would be raised and student interpretations of the event and analysis of its personal meaning in their lives would be encouraged.

As students studied the war in a variety of contexts, they would simultaneously engage in a meta-analytical cognitive analysis of contextualizing itself. Such an analysis would help students understand that post-formalism frees us to conduct inquiry in ways that match the special needs presented by specific contexts. Such a position concerning knowledge production is emancipatory in the way that it frees us from the limitations of Cartesian-Newtonian procedural thinking. It also illustrates the inseparability between research method and cognitive strategy, a relationship rarely noted in mainstream cognitive and educational psychology's construction of critical thinking. Such insights induce democratically grounded post-formal educators to become researchers of unique manifestations of cognitive sophistication, of new forms of intelligence. In these ways we can begin to insert the critical in what passes as critical thinking.

References

Abercombie, N. (1994). Authority and Consumer Society. In Re. Keat, N. Whiteley, and N Abercombie (Eds.) *The Authority of the Consumer*. New York: Routledge.

Alford, C. (1993). Introduction to the special issue of political psychology and political theory. *Political Psychology*. 14 (2), 199–208.

Alvesson, M., & Willmott, H. (1992). On the idea of emancipation in management and organizational studies. *Academy of Management Review*. 17 (3), 432–64.

Arlin, P. (1975). Cognitive Development in Adulthood: A Fifth Stage: *Developmental Psychology*, 11 (5), 602–606.

Ashburn, E. (1987). Three crucial issues concerning the preparation of teachers for our classrooms: Definition, development, and determination of competence. In E. Flaxman (ed.), *Trends and Issues in Education*. 1986. Washington, DC: U.S. Department of Education

Beck, U. (1992). *Risk Society: Towards a New Modernity*. Trans. M. Ritter, London: Sage.

Bobbitt, N. (1987) Reflective Thinking: Meaning and Implications for Teaching. In R.G. Thomas (ed.), *Higher Order Thinking: Definition, Meaning and Instructional Approaches*. Washington, DC: Home Economics Education Association.

Bowers, C.,&Flinders, D. (1990). *Responsive Teaching: an Ecological Approach to Classroom Patterning of Language, Culture and Thought*. New York: Teachers College Press.

Cannella, G. (1997) *Deconstructing Childhood Education: Social Justice and Revolution*. New York.

Elliot, A. (1994). *Psychoanalytic Theory: An Introduction*. Cambridge, MA: Blackwell.

Fiske, J. (1993) *Power Plays, Power Works*. New York: Verso.

Freire, P. (1979). *Pedagogy of the Oppressed*. New York: Herder and Herder.

Giroux, H. (1994) *Disturbing Pleasures: Learning Popular Culture*. New York: Routledge

Hinchey, P. (1998). *Finding Freedom in the Classroom: A Practical Introduction to Critical Theory*. New York: Peter Lang

Hutgren, F. (1987). Critical thinking: Phenomenological and critical foundations. In R. G. Thomas (Ed.) *Higher-order Thinking: Definition, Meaning and Instructional Approaches*. Washington, DC: Home Economics Education Association.

Kincheloe, J. (1993). *Toward a Critical Politics of Teacher Thinking: Mapping the Postmodern*. Westport, CT: Bergin and Garvey.

Kincheloe, J. & Steinberg, S. (1993). A tentative description of post-formal thinking: The critical confrontation with cognitive theory. *Harvard Educational Review*, 63 (3), 296–320.

Kincheloe, J. (1995). *Toil and Trouble: Good Work, Smart Workers and the Integration of Academic and Vocational Education*. New York: Peter Lang.

Kincheloe, J., & Steinberg, S. (1998). *Unauthorized Methods: Strategies for Critical Teaching*. New York: Routledge.

Kincheloe, J., Steinberg, S., & Hinchey, P. (1999). *The Post Formal Reader: Cognition and Education*. New York: Garland Press.

Kincheloe, J.,Steinberg. S., & Villaverde, L. (1999). *Rethinking Intelligence: Confronting Psychological Assumptions About Teaching and Learning*. New York: Routledge.

McLaren, P. (1994). *Life in Schools: An Introduction to Critical Pedagogy in the Foundations of Education*. White Plains, NY: Longman.

Macedo, D. (1994). *Literacies of Power: What Americans Are Not Allowed to Know*. Boulder, CO: Westview.

Martin-Baro, I. (1994). *Writings for a Liberation Psychology*. A. Aron and S. Corne (Eds.), Cambridge, MS: Harvard University Press.

Mumby, D. (1989) Ideology and the social construction of meaning: A communication perspective. *Communication Quarterly*. 37 (4), 291–304.

Nooteboom, B. (1991). A postmodern philosophy of markets. *International Studies of Management and Organization*. 22 (2), 53–76.

Polakow, V. (1992). *The Erosion of Childhood*. Chicago: University of Chicago Press.

Samuels, A. (1993). *The Political Psyche*. New York: Routledge.

Scheifer, R., Con Davis, R. & Mergler, N. (1992) *Culture and Cognition: The Boundaries of Literacy and Scientific Inquiry*. Ithaca, NY: Cornell University Press.

Schon, D. (1983). *The Reflective Practitioners: How Professionals Think in Action*. New York: Basic Books.

Semali, L. & Kincheloe, J. (1998) *What Is Indigenous Knowledge? Voices from the Academy*. New York: Garland.

Shannon, P. (1989). *Broken Promises: Reading Instruction in Twentieth Century America*. Granby, MA: Bergin and Garvey.

Smart, B. (1992). *Modern Conditions, Postmodern Controversies*. New York: Routledge.

Steinberg, S. & Kincheloe, J. (1998). *Students as Researchers: Creating Classrooms that Matter*. Bristol, PA: Falmer Press.

Thiele, L. (1986). Foucault's triple murder and the modern development of power. *Canadian Journal of Political Science*. 19 (2), 243–60.

Tomlinson, S. (1988). Why Johnny Can't Read. Critical theory and special education. *European Journal of Special Needs in Education*. 3 (1), 45–48.

Vatimo, G. (1991). *The End of Modernity*. Baltimore: Johns Hopkins University Press.

Walkerdine, V. (1988). *The Mastery of Reason: Cognitive Development and the Production of Rationality*. New York: Routledge.

Wartenberg, T. (1992). Introduction. In T. Wartenberg (Ed.), *Rethinking Power*. Albany, NY: SUNY Press.

Eight Critical Points for Mathematics

Peter M. Appelbaum

How am I to think of "critical thinking" in my classroom? I find this an overwhelming task at the current juncture in mathematics education. Once finding solace in the National Council of Teachers of Mathematics *Standards'* (NCTM 1989, 1991, 1995) support for problem solving, reasoning, communication, and assessment that features these general goals, I now find myself caught in the cross-fire of a turf war among students' expectations for a skill-based lecture format, parents' desires that range from a delight in the "reform" movement to horror at the open-ended assignments coming home, standardized tests that have not yet caught up with reform, and a media-amplified backlash reminiscent of the seventies' Back-to-Basics. I cherish the central place of mathematics in the school curriculum and note the legacy of mathematical associations with critical thinking—having heard numerous clichés throughout my life that refer to mathematics as contributing to clarity of thought, an appreciation for logic, and a propensity to analyze and generalize arguments and presumptions. Yet I also note with concern the historical inconsistency of any sort of "transfer of learning" of these skills to non-school experiences. And I further recognize the role of mathematics in perpetuating an ideology of "reason" that can contribute to regimes of truth and power rather than to a project of social justice (Appelbaum 1995, 1998; Mellin-Olsen 1987; Swetz 1987; Walkerdine 1987).

> There has probably never been a time in the history of American education when the development of critical and reflective thought was not recognized as a desirable outcome of . . . school. Within recent years, however, this outcome has assumed increasing importance and has had a far-reaching effect on the nature of the curriculum. (Fawcett, p. 1)

Thank *goodness* such attention was paid to critical thinking back in the thirties when Harold Fawcett's dissertation on his geometry class was printed as the NCTM yearbook. Sixty years later, we surely should be able to recognize innumerable examples of Fawcett's attributes of a student "using critical thinking well;" such a student:

1. Selects the significant words and phrases in any statement that is important, and asks that they be carefully defined.
2. Requires evidence supporting conclusions he or she is pressed to accept.
3. Analyzes that evidence and distinguishes fact from assumption.
4. Recognizes stated and unstated assumptions essential to the conclusion.
5. Evaluates these assumptions, accepting some and rejecting others.
6. Evaluates the argument, accepting or rejecting the conclusion.
7. Constantly reexamines the assumptions which are behind his or her beliefs and actions. (Fawcett, pp. 11–12, paraphrased)

The fact that this list is referenced as vital to our understanding as recently as 1993 (O'Daffer & Thomquist) would presumably attest to over a half-century of accumulated wisdom regarding how students studying mathematics involve themselves in a process described by Costa (1985) and Ennis (1985) as effectively using thinking skills to help one make, evaluate, and apply decisions about what to believe or do. . . .

One problem is the continued under-theorizing of critical thinking in an individualized or egocentric and antisocial politics of education that echoes another early twentieth-century formulation often quoted—Robert Hutchins.

> It must be remembered that the purpose of education is not to fill the minds of students with facts . . . it is to teach them to think, if that is possible, and always to think for themselves (quoted in O'Daffer & Thomquist, p. 39).

An observation I want to stress in this essay is that I no longer construct "critical thinking" for myself as thinking "skills," and find the notion that I "teach" critical thinking a barrier to successful experiences in my classroom. I prefer to take my students as critical thinkers who enrich their abilities and deepen their conceptions of themselves as thinkers through our efforts in class. This is an extrapolation from recent transformations of "problem solving" in mathematics. In 1980, the National Council launched Problem Solving as the number one "basic skill" for the eighties (a clever response to the Back-to-Basics movement). Horror of horrors: we found problem solving curricula sequencing the various problem solving skills and strategies added on to an already crowded smattering of mathematics; a whole new realm of opportunities for some students to feel good about themselves and others to "learn" that they are no good at solving problems. By the nineties, we have the *Standards'* presentation of problem solving not as a skill to be explicitly taught, but rather as the context through which all mathematics should be learned. Having tried this out, I am moving on to "critical thinking" as the context rather than the objective of my classroom curriculum.

A claim to be made again and again is the haphazard association of mathematics with any sort of rationality or clarity of thought. The links we make are based on a cultural convention of mathematical activity in schools as opposed to any universal quality of mathematics that the subject exemplifies (Appelbaum 1995; Hersh 1997; Pinxten et al. 1983; Rotman 1993). This claim has recently been well made in different terms by Heinrich Bauersfeld (1995). As Bauersfeld tries to research children's thinking, "certain problems arise with the structuring of the internal process":

> How does a child learn to correct an inadequate habit of constructing meaning? Teachers can easily correct the products, but there is no direct access to the individual (internal) processes of constructing. Thus, on the surface of the official classroom communication, everything can be said and presented acceptably, but the hidden strategies of constructing may lead the child astray in other strategies or in the face of even minor variations. (p. 285)

When it comes down to it, writes Bauersfeld, ". . . there is no help from mathematics itself, that is, through rational thinking or logical constraints, as teachers often assume. Mathematics does not have self-explaining power, nor does it have compelling inference; for the learner there are only conventions" (p. 287). For me, any claim to critical thinking is not unleashed by the mathematics; it is an attribute of the classroom activity, or a description of pedagogical dynamics.

Yet another driving feature of my current understanding of critical thinking is the dangerous pleasure it affords as an "objective" toward which I steer my students and for which I reward them. In the words of Alfie Kohn (1993), "a brief smile and nod are just as controlling as a dollar bill; more so, perhaps, since social rewards may have a more enduring effect than tangible rewards" (p. 31). I now work at reminding myself that critical thinking is not something my students need to be tricked into performing, but rather a process they will go through as human beings as long as my organization of classroom activity does not stifle it, reward it, or distort it.

It is necessary, according to Erna Yackel (1995), "for teachers to understand that students' activity is reflexively related to their individual contexts, and that the teacher contributes, as do the children, to the interactive constitution of the immediate situation as a social event" (p. 158). Alan Schoenfeld (1989), meanwhile, collects research to support the notion that mathematics can be taught in a problem-based way so that students experience the subject as a discipline of reason developed because of the need to solve problems and for intellectual curiosity. Jack Lochhead (1987), on the other hand, stresses attitudes over methods, encouraging us to have students choose or construct their own problem solving techniques, rather than follow a specific method; students are forced through a structure to choose and evaluate their method. And the ever-quoted "bible" of contemporary mathematics education, the NCTM's *Curriculum and Evaluation Standards* (1989) chimes in:

> A climate should be established in the classroom that places *critical thinking* at the heart of instruction . . . To give students access to mathematics as a powerful way of making sense of the world, it is essential that an emphasis on *reasoning* pervades all mathematical activity. (p. 25)

So, how am I to think of critical thinking in mathematics? I imagine curves of motion through space, each of which is a trace of the above approaches, and of which each has particular moments of critical change. In geometry we sometimes speak of "critical points" of a curve, and as I look back over my shifting pedagogy I can identify such points in the flow of my classroom life, points at which the flow has a sudden shift in acceleration toward a critical thinking classroom. What follows is a list of eight critical points in the historical trace of my teaching/learning strategies, each of which invites considerations of how to enrich critical thinking in the teaching and learning of mathematics in schools.

1. Treat Mathematical Actors as Mathematical Critics

I used to have my students invent their own procedures and algorithms and to always search out another way to do a problem. The result was presentation of multiple perspectives on a single situation. This helped to establish mathematics as a humanly constructed technology of meaning which I hoped would lead to two results: (a) a view of oneself as a maker of meaning; and (b) a view of mathematics as made by people, and thus subject to the same critique as other human endeavors, according to criteria of value.

Now I recognize that it is not enough to provide a forum of presentation or solipsism. Dewey admonished that a democracy provides not just access but the opportunity to be *heard*. Students in my class not only explain their strategy or procedures. They now have to use another person's strategy or procedure in a similar problem/situation, and participate in a discussion that notes the strengths and weaknesses of each. Students are asked to identify a situation in which they would use each strategy offered (for example, to explain to a younger child, to impress a town council member during a presentation on a local issue, to calculate most quickly, to be most sure of their result. . . . Now my students perceive mathematical thinking through multiple perspectives and can articulate a plausible reason for selecting each perspective over others in particular contexts of use.

For example, we once needed to determine how many bags of concrete mix to purchase if one bag would fill two square feet of area (three inches thick was the recommendation), and the area was a rectangle measuring three feet by five feet. Kudan suggested eight bags, because $3 \times 5 = 15$ and $15/2 = 7\frac{1}{2}$, and he figured he would need to have to buy whole bags. Marlee came to the same conclusion by reasoning in terms of a ratio: $1:2$ is equivalent to $7\frac{1}{2}:15$. Xandie drew a picture of a three by five rectangle, drew lines at every foot to create a fifteen square grid inside the rectangle and proceeded to color in two squares at a time—counting up to seven—which left an empty square; the empty square called for another bag, making the total eight bags. Pearline skip-counted by twos on her fingers until she got to fourteen, and then figured another bag would make eight.

Students discussed their solution strategies. The group noted that Xandie's and Pearline's methods were similar in that they counted the bags needed, one visually and one numerically. The students liked Marlee's ratio approach the best because it seemed the simplest to do, even though it was the most challenging to understand why it worked. Kudan's strategy seemed fastest and the most reasonable one to use in a situation where the numbers involved might be cumbersome. In another problem, if the numbers were something like 53 feet by 294 feet and 3 inches, and a bag covers 7 and a half square feet, they felt that the counting strategies would be too confusing, and the ratio too difficult to solve. This group of students went on to work through another similar problem using all four strategies each, including in their journals thought on what audience would most appreciate each strategy as an explanation.

2. Make a Choice, Pursue It, and Consider the Consequences

I used to structure my activities to include a collection of critical thinking skills, in order to facilitate my students' development and refinement of these skills: comparing, contrasting, conjecturing, inducing, generalizing, specializing, classifying, categorizing, deducing, visualizing, sequencing, ordering, predicting, validating, proving, relating, analyzing, evaluating, and patterning (O'Daffer & Thomquist).

Now I no longer view my job as a trainer in skills. I instead recognize that my students come to me with varying inclinations to use skills of critical thinking in school contexts. I presume that critical thinking is a trait of human experience. I can take advantage of this trait and make critical thinking the context through which mathematics is learned. I provide open-ended situations in which students use the above skills of critical thinking to draw a mathematical conclusion or accomplish a mathematical task. I ask the students to design the questions and investigations themselves. Student then must *choose* one question or investigation, work together based on their selections, and report to the classroom community as they see it would make an impact. Here they must choose as well. We discuss whether their choices of question, investigation, timing and format of reporting were good ones, and how they made these decisions.

My class was once investigating calculator patterns. We selected a starting number from 0 to 9 and an adding constant from 0 to 9. Students would enter some starting number and add to it the constant number; then repeatedly adding the constant number, patterns emerged in the one's digits on the calculator screen. After initial explorations, ideas for investigation were collected in a class discussion: odd versus even constant or starting numbers; the relationship between the constant and the length of the resulting pattern; the effect of a starting number on a particular constant chosen; and so on. Students chose to work in groups based on which investigation seemed most interesting or promising to them.

Another day, we explored which four-sided shapes could make a square shadow when held up to a light source. Groups investigated the relative importance of angles, parallel sides, lines of symmetry, and distance from the light source. Several groups split into two research teams that either worked abstractly or preferred an experimental approach, cutting out shapes and tilting them against a light source to see the shadows produced. This was a great activity that led to many insights in geometry. But most fascinating was the class's conclusion that teams working abstractly were able to understand the significant issues more readily than the people who had worked with the actual shadows.

3. Obsess About Functional Relationships

I used to collect data in explorations and support students' identification of patterns in the data, encouraging them to search for more than one pattern or to articulate more than one rule or description of the same pattern.

Now my students are pressed to go further by recognizing how changes in one or more categories of data are related to changes in other categories. In an investigation of the behavior of bouncing balls, students studied the fact that the ratio of the height a ball is dropped from its return height is consistent and a special property of a ball (this ratio is called a "coefficient of restitution"). Research groups collected data on weight, circumference of the ball's equator, density, and heights of bounce, comparing data across these different categories of measurement. Another group explored heights at which the ratio no longer held, depending on the different characteristics that had been measured.

On another day, this same class was studying water drops. After measuring the rate of absorption of a drop of water for different materials, one group switched to maximum number of drops a material could absorb. By changing their variables, they were able to convince the class of the importance of their research for athletic clothing, sanitary napkins, and Band-Aids.

Analyzing a survey of interest in new bike racks versus new stall doors for the second floor bathrooms, my class noted confusion over how race was defined in their survey. These students suggested that affirmative action forms and surveys unwittingly perpetuate an image of "minority" by lumping together some groups into one big category while dividing other groups into specific categories. (For example, Dominican-American and Haitian-American were important distinctions in this school, whereas Italian-Americans, Polish-Americans, recent Russian immigrants, and some Hispanic students would all identify themselves as "white.") Class members felt that the "minority" status of some groups should be questioned.

Strategy games also offer an opportunity to understand the relationships among variables. Mancala is a game I often use: it involves moving "stones" in and out of "pots." Usually there are four stones in each pot to start, and a typical board has six pots on each player's side. Playing the game with standard rules offers numerous opportunities for strategy and decision discussion, especially when we expand the conversation by shifting the goal of play: to win, to lose, to keep the game lasting as long as possible, to "tie." But we can also study how changes in variables, the number of stones in each pot to start, the number of pots, the direction of move on each turn, effect the strategies for a game "well played."

4. Problematize the "Answer"

I used to have students share the different ways they obtained an answer, having them offer their strategy for arriving at an answer as an argument for why people should accept their answer. Later, they would express how they got their answer without using any numbers or shape names in their story. Then they would explain why their answer was important in terms of the question asked.

Now, I encourage students to offer several possible answers based on their calculations. They explain to each other how they might come to an answer despite the seeming universality of their computations. They write up or present in play form a decision involving a choice of three or more answers or actions based on their calculation that dramatizes the complexity of choosing with conflicting criteria.

Returning to the concrete problem discussed above, each strategy came to the same numerical calculation, $7\frac{1}{2}$. Students suggested eight bags; until they were encouraged to problematize their answer. Perhaps they should buy fifteen bags and share with a friend who also needs concrete. Perhaps the company cleverly packages bags for two square feet knowing that anytime people have an odd number of square feet they round up and buy extra mix; let's buy only seven bags and sacrifice a tiny bit of thickness.

Sometimes my class becomes members of a game design team. The Property Management people ask them to consider using one twelve-sided dodecahedron die instead of the usual two six-sided cubic dice, since there is an overstock on the dodecahedron dice. In their game, players who roll a six or higher move forward, while those rolling less than six move backward. Students can use a variety of methods to determine that players will move forward more often with the two cubic dice. Yet the decision still remains—Will it be a better game with players moving forward more often, or just a shorter game?

Problematizing the answer can also be done by making the answer into a question. I start with the answer and ask what might lead to it. Instead of asking for the average of a list of numbers, I give the average and ask for several sets of numbers that could have that average. The square shadows activity is like this as well; given a square shadow, what might be the shape?

5. Problematize the Pedagogy

I used to offer options for learning a particular topic or skill. Sometimes I would arrange centers based on multiple intelligences; sometimes I would use jigsaw cooperative learning techniques around key components of a unit.

Now I present the teaching of a particular topic or skill as a controversy among educators. I have students experience at least three different ways that people have thought of (I avoid a binary continuum/happy medium situation) and have students evaluate the approaches (a) for themselves, (b) according to what they perceived as the logic of mathematics, and (c) how it helps them connect to things in their life.

For a unit on percent, students were asked to critique an area model of percent, base-ten blocks described as fractions of the "whole" square flat, money as percent of a dollar, and a ratio model during their bouncing ball investigation. A follow-up activity studying meat labeled "low fat" led students to suggest that such labels were deceptive marketing ploys because even "low fat" meat by weight is extremely high in fat by volume. It just happens that fat takes up lots of space and weighs hardly anything when compared with meat. Class members prepared explanations for parents and family members according to the model of percent they thought would best communicate their ideas to the particular audience.

Another study of percent involved some students interviewing a professional (a carpenter, a baker, a rug layer, a taxi driver), while others researched non-fiction materials in the school library; and, still others read books written for them by former students. Class discussion focused on how the pedagogies differed, and how the pedagogies influenced interpretations of the meaning of percent. Students then created their own books, puppet shows for younger children, and rap songs and manuals for older children, on percent; they discussed presentation as effecting the representation of percent as an idea. (For a discussion of such curriculum as "postmodern," see Gough 1998.)

6. Understand Mathematics as Rhetoric

In the past I would collect examples of the use of mathematics in newspapers and on television. These would prompt investigations in my class, based on graphs, charts, and other statistics. Students would gain an appreciation for the role of mathematics in everyday life, and pursue their own studies of the use of mathematics in different sections of newspapers, and in magazines they read themselves (videogame magazines, *American Girl*, etc.).

Now I ask my students to study how the mathematics is represented and to consider why the author chose a mathematical representation over other possibilities. We consider the difference in scales on a graph, choices among graph and chart types, units of measure, and the placement of mathematics in the argument.

Recently, we were discussing an economic plan presented by a candidate running to reelection. Obtaining platform papers from the local party office, some students noted the prominence of mathematical language and models used for prediction based on equations. Their report to the class facilitated a discussion regarding the mere need to stuff an economic plan with mathematical rhetoric and imagery just to impress the audience with seriousness. The group offered two alternative summaries of the plan that did not use equations or numerical facts but instead generalized the main points of argument in the plan. One summary seemed lacking in content, but the other seemed to them and the rest of the class to be potentially as convincing as the mathematical jargon.

7. Realize Apprentice Mathematicians and Citizens as Objects of Mathematics

I used to make sure my students experienced decision making as authentic creators of mathematics as well as in the role of mathematically literate citizens. In the first context, I imagined my students as apprentice mathematicians learning a craft. In the second context, they behaved more like discriminating members of a democratic community, forming opinions about environmental, consumer, health, and political issues with the help of mathematical thinking.

I now add a third position toward mathematics (Weinstein, 1996). We study the ways in which mathematics is used to turn ourselves into objects of study. Last year we examined district standardized test scores and reports on them in the local newspapers. Students interviewed adults in their neighborhoods about their impressions of the scores and the local schools. The principal agreed to be interviewed about the school's scores and how she felt they effected discussions of the curriculum among the teachers.

Recently the connections between theoretical and experimental probability were introduced through a project on market research. Groups of students chose a product and surveyed schoolmates regarding their preferences. A major component of insight during this project was when students noted that they could shift a large number of people toward a second or third choice by varying the relative price for each. Links were drawn to the appearance of "choice" in stores and the likelihood that consumers are led to buy products in order to clear out stock or for other marketing needs. Conjectures about ways in which marketing decisions could be manipulated were tested through further market research surveys.

In these projects we also talk about issues of representative samples. I often bring in examples of notorious mis-predictions based on non-representative samples (such as the effects of heart medications on women being misunderstood for many years when studies only included male patients), the inaccuracies of political polls, and the magnifications of error when one uses a sample to estimate a quantity for a larger population.

8. Perform Celebratory Archaeology

I used to assess student understanding and performance with a variety of assessment strategies, including tests, performance tasks scored with rubrics, portfolios of work selected as exemplary by students and clinical interviews.

I still use these, but find it crucial for students to see for themselves that they have learned particular skills and concepts, and that they can apply these in new contexts. We carefully look over a period of time and collect lists of what students find important, facts they can organize in more than two ways, and conjectures or arguments they believe are central to a summary of the material learned. Finally, we collect a "good list" of investigations they wish they could pursue if they had more time (and perhaps will as part of optional future work), conjectures they think they could "prove" to someone else, and questions for further discussion. Important here is our discussion of criteria for including something on these lists, and the need to keep the list to a meaningful length.

This list of critical points is my way of organizing what I have learned about critical thinking in my classroom, both conceptual and the skill-based critical points of pedagogy for mathematics education. I interpret my teaching practice as making the political more pedagogical because my practice embodies political interests that are emancipatory in nature. I treat students as critical agents, make knowledge problematic, utilize critical and affirmative dialogue, and make the case for struggling for a qualitatively better world for all people (Shapiro, 1993).

> In part this suggests [taking] seriously the need to give students an active voice in their learning experiences. It also means developing a critical vernacular that is attentive to problems experienced at the level of everyday life, particularly as they are related to pedagogical experiences connected to classroom practice. (Shapiro, p. 277)

I do not expect all readers to agree with me. Indeed, many people want to clutch the (false) certainty of mathematics as a scaffold to critical thinking, while others believe that strong basic skills in mathematical calculations are a prerequisite to their *later* application in critical thinking. I am proposing that we turn this around. Starting with the critical thinking that our students bring with them, we create experiences through which we can recognize occasional instances of apparent certainty and through which we can develop conceptual understanding that leads to a cultivated collection of calculation skills. But more than this is the *presence* of a kind of *critical insight* (Shapiro 1993), an awareness that pervades the ideology of surface description (in which our world is named in particular and distorting ways).

My pedagogical starting point is not the individual critical thinking student, but the critical insight of individuals and groups in their various cultural, class, racial, historical, gendered, and other settings, in which diverse problems, hopes, dreams and fears become particular to individual students. In my practice, I do not search for the perfect critical thinking lesson. What I do is rethink my current lessons and units (Paul, et al., 1990) in terms of the critical points of practice I have listed above.

Are my students "less gullible, more logical and more critical in their thinking," as Harold Fawcett asked himself back in the thirties? And if so, will my list of critical points be packaged, sealed, and marketed in your local teacher store (Tanner, 1985)? I certainly hope not. I write with the thought that you too will write and that I will read what you have written. You will describe what you do, in order to make meaning of your teaching, confronting how you came to be like this, and reconstructing how you might do things differently (Smyth, 1989; Kincheloe, 1993).

In my own experience, I was able to construct a meaning by performing a standard move in mathematics: Widen the context. I found that I could teach a critical thinking classroom by listening to the critical insight of my critical thinking students. I stopped narrowing my attention to what *I* should do and placed what I do in the context of how everybody in that room is thinking. What and how *are* they thinking? I have stopped searching for lessons that teach critical thinking and instead document for myself the ways in which my students exhibit critical insight in a mathematics class. Am I *allowed* to give up certainty, indubitability, timelessness or tenseness? Am I unfair? Hersh (1997) ends his work, *What Is Mathematics, Really?*, by raising the same issue: When we drop restrictions like certainty or timelessness it is like breaking out of the restrictions of the real number line in algebra.

> "Dropping the insistence on certainty and indubitability is like moving off the line into the complex plane. . . . We don't throw away all sound sense. The guiding principles remain: intelligibility, consistency with experience, computability with philosophy of science and general philosophy." (Hersh, p. 249)

A humanistic philosophy of critical thinking in mathematics respects these principles. The turf wars of mathematics education in the late nineties are witnessing a negotiating team: Critical points in a humanistic approach to critical thinking in mathematics.

References

Appelbaum, Peter M. (1995) *Popular Culture, Educational Discourse, and Mathematics* Albany, NY: SUNY Press.

Appelbaum, Peter M. (1998) Target: Number. in *The Post-Formal Reader.* Joe Kincheloe and Shirley Steinberg (Eds.) New York: Garland.

Bauersfeld, Heinrich (1995) "Language Games" in the Mathematics Classroom: Their Function and Their Effects. in *The Emergence of Mathematical Meaning: Interaction in Classroom Cultures*, Paul Cobb & Heinrich Bauresfeld (Eds.), pp. 272–292. Hillsdale, NJ: Lawrence Erlbaum.

Costa, A.L. (Ed.) (1985) *Developing Minds: A Resource Book for Teaching Thinking* Alexandria, VA: ASCD.

Ennis, R.H. (1985) Goals for Critical Thinking. in *Developing Minds: Adolescence Book for Teaching Thinking*, A.L. Costa (Ed.) pp. 54–57. Alexandria, VA: ASCD.

Fawcett, Harold (1938) *The Nature of Proof* (NCTM Yearbook) New York: Columbia University Teachers College Bureau of Publications.

Gough, Noel (1998) 'If This Were Played Upon a Stage': School Laboratory Work as a Theatre of Representation. In *Practical Work in School Science: Which Way Now?* Jerry Wellington (ed.) London: Routledge.

Hersh, Reuben (1997) *What Is Mathematics, Really?* New York: Oxford University Press.

Kincheloe, Joe (1993) *Toward a Critical Politics of Teacher Thinking: Mapping the Post-Modern* Westport, CT: Bergin & Garvey.

Kohn, Alfie (1993) *Punished by Rewards: The Trouble with Gold Stars, Incentive Plans, A's, Praise, and Other Bribes* Boston: Houghton Mifflin.

Lochhead, Jack (1987) Thinking About Learning: An Anarchistic Approach to Teaching Problem Solving. in *Thinking Skills Instruction: Concepts and Techniques*, Marcia Heiman and Joshua Slomianko (Eds.), pp. 174–182. Wash., DC: NEA.

National Council of Teachers of Mathematics (1989) *Curriculum and Evaluation Standards for School Mathematics* Reston, VA: NCTM.

National Council of Teachers of Mathematics (1991) *Professional Standards for Teaching Mathematics* Reston, VA: NCTM.

National Council of Teachers of Mathematics (1995) *Assessment Standards for School Mathematics* Reston, VA: NCTM.

O'Daffer, Phares G. and Bruce Thomquist (1993) Critical Thinking, Mathematical Reasoning, and Proof. in *Research Ideas for the Classroom: High School Mathematics*, Patricia S. Wilson (ed.) New York: Macmillan/NCTM.

Paul, Richard, A.J.A. Binker & Daniel Weil (1990) *Critical Thinking Handbook K–3rd Grade: A Guide for Remodeling Lesson Plans*. Rohnert Park, CA: Center for Critical Thinking and Moral Critique, Sonoma State University.

Pinxten, Rik, Ingrid van Dooren & Frank Harvey (1983) *Anthropology of Space* Philadelphia: University of Pennsylvania Press.

Rotman, Brian (1993) *Ad Infinitum: The Ghost in Turing's Machine . . . Taking the God Out of Mathematics and Putting the Body Back In*. Stanford, CA: Stanford Univ. Press.

Schoenfeld, Alan (1989) Mathematical Thinking and Problem Solving. in *Toward the Thinking Curriculum: Current Cognitive Research*, Lauren Resnick and Leopold Klopfer (Eds.), pp. 83–103. ASCD Yearbook. Alexandria, VA: ASCD.

Shapiro, Svi (1993) Curriculum Alternatives in a Survivalist Culture: Basic Skills and the "Minimal Self" in *Critical Social Issues in American Education: Toward the 21st Century*, H. Svi Shapiro & David Purpel (Eds.), pp. 288–304. New York: Longman.

Smyth, J. (1989) A Critical Pedagogy of Classroom Practice. *Journal of Curriculum Studies* 21 (6): 483–502.

Swetz, Frank J. (1987) *Capitalism and Arithmetic: The New Math of the 15th Century* La Salle, IL: Open Court.

Tanner, Laurel (1985) The Path Not Taken: Dewey's Model of Inquiry. *Curriculum Inquiry* 18 (4): 471–479.

Walkerdine, Valerie (1987) *The Mastery of Reason: Cognitive Development and the Production of Meaning* New York: Routledge.

Weinstein, Matthew (1996) Towards a Cultural and Critical Science Education. Paper presented at the annual meeting of the American Educational Research Association. New York, New York, April.

Yackel, Erna (1995) Children's Talk in Inquiry Mathematics Classrooms. in *The Emergence of Mathematical Meaning: Interaction in Classroom Cultures*, Paul Cobb & Heinrich Bauresfeld (Eds.), pp. 131–162. Hillsdale, NJ: Lawrence Erlbaum.

Storytelling in the Classroom: Crossing Vexed Chasms

Greg Sarris

I begin my American Indian literature course by telling a story told to me by my Pomo elders. I then ask students, usually at the next class meeting, to repeat the story as they heard it. Invariably their stories tell them more about themselves than about the story or about the speaker and culture from which the story comes. Here students can see how they are approaching the story and begin to explore unexamined assumptions by which they operate and which they use to frame the texts and experiences of members of another culture. This storytelling (about a story) engenders a reflexivity that pervades, or establishes the groundwork for, further study of American Indian texts. Below I present the story I tell so that I can discuss student responses to the story and assumptions inherent in the responses.

> Now let me tell you a story. It is a story from this land, told to me by a Kashaya [Pomo] elder. When I was young, growing up in Santa Rosa, just about a hundred miles north of here, I heard many of the old-time stories. In the Kashaya language they are called *duwi dici-du,* literally "telling about Coyote" or "Coyote stories," about the time when animals were still people.
>
> Sometimes late at night the old-timers would tell these stories; sometimes just to talk, it seemed, and other times because something in the story had a particular message for us. Maybe because of something we did or said. But the stories are only to be told in winter. So now, in telling this story [during spring months], I am breaking a rule. I'll just fix the story so it's not the same.
>
> This time Coyote was admiring the stripes on Junco's face. "How do I get stripes like that?" he was asking. He stood there looking at Junco, seeing those stripes, envious as Coyote often is of what others have. Junco-Junco is a bird, a tiny bird, grayish brown in color with face stripes—he laughed. He said, "Well, Coyote, you can't have these stripes. They are for me, they are my design."

Coyote huffed. "There must be a way I can have them." "Well, if you won't tell anyone," Junco said, "I'll tell you how to get stripes. You won't want to do it anyway, not when you find out what it is you have to do."

"But I do," said Coyote. "I'll do anything."

"Well, then, this is it." Junco rolled his eyes in mock disgust, as if irritated by Coyote's persistence. "You must take the marrow from your bones and then mix it with a little water. Stir and then apply evenly on both sides of the face."

"How do I get the bone marrow?"

"Break a bone, suck it out."

And that is just what Coyote did. He hiked his leg over a thick log, and then with a good-sized rock in his hand, he came down *Swoosh* on that leg. Just like that, crushing his leg, cracking the bone wide open. "Ouch! Ouch!"

"Ha! Ha!" Junco called and flitted through the brush. "Ha! Ha! You fool. Greedy sucker, you believe anything anyone tells you." Coyote looked up, but by this time, Junco was long gone, clear over in Ukiah Valley somewhere. Coyote's leg began to swell and fester. Before long, infection set in, and a stench wafted through the air drawing the attention of buzzard, crow, and condor. Several other birds came also, all of them hungry for rotten flesh. They began to dive, swoop down on Coyote. He swung at them, fought madly, and in the end, found himself with only a handful of feathers. He found he had feathers from each bird.

What am I going to do with these feathers, he was asking himself. I should sweat, pray that the birds don't haunt me with these feathers. And by sweating, I can heal my infection also. So he went into the sweathouse and planted each of the feathers in a circle. He built a good fire of manzanita wood. He prayed, sang songs. Then he got too hot and went out to cool off. Suddenly, while he was lying outside under some brush, he heard voices, people all speaking different languages, coming from down inside the sweathouse. What is that, he was thinking. And upon re-entering the sweathouse, he found the people, all different from one another, sprung from each of the different feathers. They went out [of the sweathouse] each going in different directions, destined for places all over the earth. The Kashaya people stayed right there. They are made from the feather of crow. Sometimes they are referred to as Crow Feathers, even to this day.

My goodness! Coyote thought. But he was so thirsty he had to go for water. He was starving, too. He stumbled upon a grasshopper den and scooped up as many grasshoppers as he could. Then, with a sharp digging stick, he began to dig a hole in which to toast the insects. Unbelievably, while digging, he hit water, causing a geyser that squirted up and went everywhere in streams and rivers, until it reached the ocean and lay still and salty. Into that water [ocean] Coyote threw a manzanita stick which became a trout; after that, a piece of madrone which became a salmon, a turtle for abalone, and for whale a bear. "Now the people will fish to eat," he said. The water looked eerie, just lying flat with whale's back up and out of the water, so Coyote caused it to ebb and flow. "Do like this," he was saying, gesturing with his arms. "Make waves."

That's how people said it was done, these things. Those who were watching and passed the story down through time. How Father God did these things. It goes on. . . . Coyote did many foolish things. Once I heard a woman tell the story differently. Well, actually, it was another part of the story—about when the earth was flooded and the people ran to the highest mountain and turned into trees. Well, that's all I can say today. See you next time. [A version of this story also appeared in Robert Oswalt's *Kashaya Texts*. It was told by Herman James, a Pomo elder.]

I record my version of the story so that after the students have presented their versions they can hear how they rearranged and omitted certain features of the story. The version above was transcribed from the latest recording, and, during the subsequent class meeting, students' stories proved consistent with those of former students. Always most striking is the omission of contextual information. If information reporting the story's genesis, Kashaya generic classification, or rules associated with the telling itself is presented at all, it is always within a narrative that begins and ends with Coyote. Students see narrative and context of production as extricable, independent from one another, and draw lines governed by preconceived notions of narrative.

Another interesting feature of the students' stories is their assiduous attention to detail and plot. As they put their stories together in groups, I witness lengthy discussions about whether or not it was a piece of manzanita that became a trout, or whether Coyote unconsciously tripped upon a grasshopper den or knew exactly there the den was. Certain details, however, are rarely acknowledged. The clause about Father God seldom appears because, according to students, "a Christian concept did not seem Indian." One consequence of the close attention to detail is an overabundance of etiological explanation. While the students sense the story is about creation, and while the story itself contains etiological tags and does concern creation, the Coyote's actions do not necessarily precipitate the formation of the world as we know it, as most of the students' stories would have one believe. On the contrary, the story indicates that Coyote was functioning, living his life, in a world that already existed, a world where people sweated, used digging sticks, and feasted on grasshoppers. The salient feature of the Kashaya Pomo language is the verb, and if the story were told in Pomo, it would become quite clear how action and not subject becomes thematized, something that is suggested by a close examination of the story even as it is told in English. However the students, who, I must admit, didn't have the opportunity to inspect the story until after their own retelling, totally neglected this thematization. Nonetheless, they see that cultural biases influence interpretive acts, and when issues of language and translation are raised in the future, they are much more sensitive to how a translation may itself be an interpretation. Students then continue to approach this literature dialogically, confronting, and attempting to talk across, the spaces between their world and that of an American Indian text.

I started with this example of storytelling in the classroom because it illustrates how storytelling might promote critical discourse about texts, but also because this example, and my brief discussion of it, should help clarify the old and still pervasive misconception of critical thinking as something devoid of cultural and historical contexts. Before returning to the subject of storytelling as a method for encouraging critical discourse, I think it imperative to consider this mis-conception and its implications in the classroom.

Richard Paul, a leader in the Critical Thinking Movement, suggests that in teaching critical thinking teachers, must enable students "to see beyond the world views that distort their perception and impede their ability to reason clearly." Critical thinking should, according to Paul, "empower [the mind] to analyze, digest, and rule its own knowledge, to achieve fair-mindedness and critical exactness" (2–3). This is in ways an attractive notion, though hardly a new one. Kant's conception of rationalism as pure thought, that process which Kant believed releases one from "immaturity," or "that state of will that makes us accept someone else's authority to lead us" (qtd. in Foucault 34), assumes that rationality is in itself something transcendent, devoid of the history and subsequent bias that has largely created the subject who is using it. As Foucault pointed out, this rationality became inextricable from the social and political circumstances of the time. Various sciences, which had slowly been developing in the past two hundred years, suddenly became legitimate and bloomed in that they had a purpose not just to explain functions of the government and human species, but, more importantly now, to explain how government and human species might be used for the purposes of that same government and its constituencies. Each activity in its own specific way demanded reflection on how it could best be accomplished (32–50). The prince, concerned with a well-governed polity, (or, as it was called in the eighteenth century, a well-policed state) had to have a scientific—or rational—sense of his people and the environment. As we now know, what was rational for Machiavelli's prince was not necessarily so for the people or the environment. Although Paul distinguishes self-serving critical thinking from strong sense critical thinking, his language of "rule," "command," and "critical exactness" could foster this sense of critical thinking as something separate from historical and social contingencies. Understanding, and not control, is the goal of critical discourse, and this understanding is dynamic, dialogical in nature. A more clearly stated purpose for critical thinking might be to foster a process or attitude which enables the individual to, as Gramsci says, "'know thyself' as a product of the historical process to date" (324). Such a process can only come about when that history and assumptions about that history are challenged. Knowing thyself and knowing the other, then, are interdependent.

As the exercise with the Kashaya Pomo story illustrates, critical discourse and any activity that predicates interpretive acts depend largely on the thinker's tie to a given knowledge base and belief system and on the linguistic features associated with the belief system. If critical thinking or so-called rationalism does not at the same time point to its intrinsic limits, to its tie to the cultural and political realities, that shape thinkers as 'knowledgeable subjects, a system that excludes difference, culturally or otherwise, is likely to be perpetuated. Teachers and students are led to believe that some people think critically and that others do not, so that those of us who have it, that is, critical thinking, must teach it to those of us who do not have it. What is taught is more likely to be a set of cultural norms associated with modes of a specific and culturally based type of critical thought. And the subjects examined are those within a given knowledge base established and maintained in very specific ways. We get caught in and perpetuate a kind of vicious cycle where those students who don't think the way we do reinforce for us, just in their inability to think in a manner we call rational, the need for us to teach them. Intentionally or not, critical thinking is taught as a normalizing device. All that could engender strong-sense critical thinking—that which would challenge given assumptions and enable students and teachers "to see beyond the world views that distort their perception and impede their ability to reason clearly"—has been effectively excluded.

This perceived split between life experience and critical thought complements a chasm that many students experience between life experience and other classroom activities. What students find in texts and from classroom discussions often has little to do with what they know from home. Both material and nonmaterial elements of the students' homes may be absent from the classroom or manifested in different and unrecognizable ways. The foreign world of Dick and Jane continues in college with a sociology professor's definition of the nuclear family as that family comprised of father, mother and siblings. The culturally diverse student, and many other students for that matter, are forced to negotiate the discrepancies between home life and that which is found in the classroom. Too often students become disaffected, unable to deal with the conflicts; or they successfully learn to operate from one side of the chasm, repressing their life experience as it may interfere with what is happening in the classroom. These latter students accept the words and ideas of texts and professors as authoritative and tend to see their lives in terms of the texts, never considering the possibilities of seeing the texts in terms of their lives.

Of course, much has been said lately about the disaffected and alienated student. Discussions of reader response and interpretive communities, fostered by Stanley Fish and a host of others, have pointed to the power and potential of students' subjective response as readers. They argue that the reader is socially and politically charged, that what the reader brings to the text depends on the circumstances of her experience. It has become increasingly difficult to dismiss student difficulties as mere cognitive dysfunctions; such attributions, now more thoroughly contextualized, have lost their objective value. A student's difficulty in the classroom is just as likely to be social, and ultimately political, in nature. In a paper presented at the 1987 MLA convention and entitled "Literate Cultures: Multi-Voiced Classrooms," Madorie Roemer provided a list of models that could be helpful in recognizing and incorporating subjective response in classroom activity. She pointed to the work of Thomas Newkirk (specifically "Looking for Trouble: A Way to Unmask Our Readings" in *College English,* Dec. 1984) who, in Roemer's words, "has made the problem we have in confronting a poem the basis for our understanding of that poem. He allows readers to see how their own readings enact a recessive process of revision and redefinition, amending interpretations as they proceed" (6). She notes the work of Kathleen McCormick, Gary Waller, and Lois Fowler in the new *Lexington Introduction to Literature,* which again uses various strategies to make the reader conscious of herself as a reader. Attempting to make interpretive acts the central subject of study in her classes, Roemer uses John Berger's *Another Way of Telling* "directing students' attention at once to the 'readings' we perform in so simple an act as the recognition of an event depicted in a photograph" (7).

But in using any of these models one cannot assume that the reader's response, and what constitutes that response, is present, or will necessarily emerge. Many people, for instance, point to dialogue, specifically dialogue of the sort Paulo Freire uses as a basis for establishing *conscientizcão—"learning* to perceive social, political, and economic contradictions, and to take action against the oppressive elements of reality" (19). The "dialogical teacher" uses dialogue that enables students to reach "a perception of their previous perception" (108). But dialogue can become a circumscribed mode of discourse that excludes, often unknowingly, the student's experience, given a chasm between life experience and classroom activity, which is likely to be exacerbated by the perceived authority of the teacher and a knowledge base determined and maintained by dominant cultural norms. Dialogue does not guarantee *conscientizacão;* a dialogue can in fact just as easily be seen—as an allegory, telling the story of a story of power relations between teachers and students and between certain "bright" students and other "not-so-bright" students. If students are responding, dialogically or otherwise, from one side of the chasm, that of the classroom, are we getting that which could make for a difference that makes a difference? Can all of us, students and teachers, be engaged in strong-sense critical thinking?

The presence of this chasm must be considered, then, especially in light of a student population that is increasingly diverse culturally and linguistically. The chasm itself suggests criteria by which we might assess, or think about, the models we use to foster critical thinking in the classroom. First, the model or method must engage the life experience of the students. Here, of course, much depends on the sensitivity of the instructor and precisely how the model or method is utilized in a given classroom context. Second, the model must enable students to scrutinize their experiences or what constitutes their assumptions. Eliciting subjective responses is not enough; in order to make students conscious of what they bring to the classroom, they must be able to hold their response up for scrutiny, say against given texts and other stories, so that they can enter into critical dialogue about their relationship to texts and other ideas. Cultural variance is a means here and not an end. An experience is not expressed so that it might simply be validated, but so that it might inform, and be informed by, other experiences. In satisfying these criteria two chasms are crossed: 1) that between life experience and school experience, and 2) that between either blank acceptance or mere subjective responses to information and critical reflection about information.

In the broadest sense, it is people's stories that tell them the most about themselves. Stories become an important device individuals use to interpret to each other their experiences—experiences with work, school, a text, their families. Helen B. Schwartzman has observed that, within organizational settings, "stories are a pervasive social form . . . that can generate organizational activity (not just comment on it) and interpret and sometimes transform the work experience" (80). Stories are not simply representational ; as representations they reveal the nature of interpretive acts. Schwartzman studied the stories of staff members in a community mental health center and found the stories to be "a form for individual interpretation, construction, and reconstruction of events [that] provide individuals and the organization with a way to create and then discover the meaning of what it is they are doing and saying" (91). In his discussion of Zuni storytelling, Dennis Tedlock shows that, if given a fixed text and the opportunity and encouragement to revise and retell the text, people will use their individual experience as a means to interpret and comment upon the fixed text. The Zuni storyteller, recounting the oral narrative *Kyaklo an' pennane (The Word of Kyaklo),* changes the story from one occasion to the next, as the storyteller considers his audience and what they know or do not know, or realizes something about the story for the first time. Tedlock writes that "The interpreter [as storyteller] does not merely play the parts, but is the narrator and commentator as well. What we are hearing is the hermeneutics of the text of Kyaklo" (236).

Likewise what I hear in my American Indian literature courses is the hermeneutics of the text of Coyote and Junco; students not only see their stories as interpretations, but, in seeing as much, discover also what constitutes their interpretations and how that shapes the distance between their world and that of the story as I first told it. Thus, the two criteria established above have been met: students have engaged their experience, here in the mere re-telling of the story, and they have been able to discover, in a critical fashion, what underlies their assumptions about narrative and Indian culture as my version of the story was played back against their own.

The students in my American Indian literature courses have been predominantly middle-class whites, certainly not Kashaya Pomo. Their stories, as I have pointed out, display certain kinds of assumptions associated with their experiences. What began as a dialogue across white middle-class American culture and that of Kashaya Pomo culture became a larger dialogue across other texts and American Indian cultures associated with those texts. The dialogue, and of course the exercise that prompted the dialogue, instills a reflexive attitude, causing students always to consider what they might be doing to texts as readers. Again, it must be remembered that this was one kind of storytelling exercise, suited for one kind of subject matter. As a group, the students were generally accustomed to texts from a culture that reflected their own values and assumptions, albeit in various and sometimes foreign ways, and reading did not foster the kind of disparity between their world and that of a text, at least not the sort that was discovered between their world and that of the Kashaya Pomo. I created an exercise to hoodwink them. But in other classroom settings, those I am interested in writing about here, such an exercise would not work, at least not in the same ways. The culturally diverse student is faced with quite the opposite scenario: what is taught in the classroom—what she reads—emerges from a knowledge base and a set of cultural norms that are often quite foreign. And in the culturally diverse classroom, there may be a multitude of knowledge bases where the features and subjects of one base may or may not overlap those of another. How might storytelling enable these students to talk back to material that is foreign in many ways? How might storytelling engage students from several different cultural backgrounds?

The Saddle Lake Experience and Beyond

In the spring of 1984 1 was asked to design and teach a writing course for a group of Cree students who would be selected from the Saddle Lake Reserve in Alberta to participate in a tribally funded summer educational advancement program held at U.C. Santa Cruz. At the time, I directed the U.C. Santa Cruz Student Affirmative Action/Educational Opportunity Program Writing Center and taught writing courses designed for the campus' ethnic minority and low-income students. I thought material from these courses might interest the Cree students, and I sent away to Canada for public documents on Native Education that I thought could prompt critical discussion. Despite my best intentions, I found that after three weeks, with only two weeks left in the program, I succeeded in little more than encouraging personal anecdotes from the students.

The class posed many challenges from the start. The students were more homogeneous in this class than in any class I had taught; they were from the same reserve, and, in one way or another, were related to each other. At the same time, I had high school seniors and college freshmen who were from seventeen to twenty-six years old. Most had "stopped out" of school at some point, something not unusual on a reserve where only 15 percent of the students finish high school, and four of the eight women in the class had children. These students were cautious, reluctant at first to speak in class. I felt good that we could finally talk, but at this point, after three weeks, it was clear that we had made little progress in terms of critical writing and reading. Their papers remained purely anecdotal and uncritical, like classroom discussions, or full of vague unsubstantiated claims coined in that all too familiar pseudo-academic prose.

I remember an eighteen-year-old woman who agreed with me that her ideas needed to be developed and that much of her language was vague.

This woman was a senior who had "stopped out" twice, once when she was twelve because she "couldn't relate to school anymore," and again when she was fourteen to have a baby. She had written about alienation in the classroom, a topic we had been discussing for over a week. "I guess I need to find more stuff on it in the library," she told me, "and use a dictionary for those words." While we sat in my office discussing alienation, the student kept experience—what constitutes her as a reader, writer, and thinker, and could illuminate any notion of alienation—far away, like something left in the dorm, locked away with the rest of her luggage. Lest a teacher jump too quickly with suggestions about how this student might engage her personal experience, it should be remembered that the chasm here is likely to be protective. Teenage pregnancy, poor grades, and being over-weight signal failure in some way; all are difficult enough to live with, let alone discuss with a teacher or in a classroom of peers. And has the cross-cultural dynamic been considered here, where assumptions and expectations that inhere in classroom activities are not likely to be Cree? Yet the fact remains that this student's story could not only provide her a powerful critical tool for engaging texts and ideas, but could, in the process, expose the forces which inculcate failure and alienation—the same forces that keep her experience outside the classroom.

Not long after the conference with this student, I found myself again listening to a flurry of stories about discrimination and alienation in the classroom environment. (We had been discussing selections from Maxine Hong Kingston's *The Woman Warrior* and Richard Rodriguez's *Hunger of Memory.*) The students were volunteering stories, mostly second-hand accounts, providing "right examples" of discrimination and alienation. In many of these anecdotes I descried moments of conflicting cultural problems that once examined might open larger and more critical discussions. But it was at that point of contact, or critical inquiry, that these students would retreat from discussion. Of course, I knew that much of what underlay the issues of discrimination and alienation in terms of the students I personal responses was morally and emotionally charged. So my hands were tied; too much questioning, besides displaying my likely ignorance and insensitivity, was likely to suggest to the students a power move on my part for more "right answers."

Then one student told of a teacher who sat a Native girl in the corner with a coloring pad and crayons while other students worked on computers. When this student, then a teaching assistant, asked why the Native girl was in the corner, the teacher replied, "Oh, she's not really interested. She's from out in the bush, you know. She never says much. She's more creative."

More hands shot up. We moved from one story to the next. Frustrated, I attempted to ground the discussion, at least momentarily, by returning to the story of the Native girl. I thought perhaps we could ask some questions about her circumstances in that classroom, perhaps ponder her future as a student.

"What is going to happen to that girl?" I asked.
The immediate response: "She'll drop out."
"Let's tell her story," I suggested, not knowing what to expect. "Let's take it from the time she is put in the corner to the time she drops out." The hands went down.
Silence.
"Let's just make it up, each person tell a part of her story. I'll start." I kept talking now just to fill the void I had created. "She will begin to get confused and hate her parents for sending her to school," I said, "to a place where she feels different." Eventually a tentative voice: "She'll feel lonely and frustrated, like she has no one to understand her."
Another student followed: "When's she's about nine or ten, she'll find some other kids who feet like her. Probably Native kids. They tell each other they are O.K., what they do is cool."
Then another: "By the time she's twelve, she starts skipping school."
"She's probably getting high now, too. Dope and drinking."
"She feels good she has someone like her to be with."
"But at the same time she hates school—and her parents, maybe. All of the kids are mad, pissed off mostly."
"Not when she's high. She feels good when she's high."
"She has a boyfriend by this time and might get pregnant. She's, oh, I'd say about fourteen or so now."
"Well then, she's not going to school very much and doesn't even realize it."
"So it's like nothing when she drops out. No biggie."
"She might get a job, that's if she's living in the city. Ain't any jobs on the reserve."
"Or she might stay home and take care of the baby."
"She's going to be frustrated, bummed out, either way."
"My boyfriend was frustrated. He was drinking and got killed in a car accident last Christmas. On the reserve. But I been raising our baby by myself anyway, for four years now."

By speaking in the first person, this last student—the student who had been in my office—indicated the kind of synthesis that might have taken place, not just for her, but for other students as well. Here was more than an anecdote that complemented a given idea; the anecdote, or in this case, the collective story, born of personal experience, informed that idea. To what extent the students were at that moment conscious of what had happened I did not know. I never attempted to interrupt the awesome silence that followed the rendering of this story.

It was at the next class meeting that I saw what had taken place. The students expressed anger. They also felt exposed. "We've been made to feel stupid all along and we believe it," they kept saying. Luckily, they trusted me and continued speaking. "Teachers make us want to drop out and they [government officials and other non-natives] say we're dumb. See, 'Natives are stupid, can't take care of themselves.' They never listened to us from the start." Another student historicized the problem thus: "The first white man gave us infested blankets [with smallpox]. His people are still with us, getting our children, finishing us off in the schools." The students sensed how their own voices had been thwarted. They talked boldly now from a position of self-determined strength.

We had not yet tested what we were saying against other ideas and texts about discrimination, but I felt we were well on our way. I pointed to the power of personal knowledge in the classroom and how that knowledge can help us make connections with ideas in books, can help us know why we may not understand ideas the way a teacher does, or can help us see why a teacher cannot understand the students.

For that class meeting, I had asked the students to read a series of government documents regarding Native Education. "What did you think of the Section V Preamble on Native Education?" I asked in a rather quick and arbitrary shift to the day's business. I quoted the lines:

> That [deplorable state of Native Education in Alberta] is not totally the fault of the educational system.
> There are other reasons: historical, social, economic and a reluctance on the part of some Natives to fully appreciate the significance of education for their over-all advancement. (Public Policy Statements, 116)

The loud excitement quieted to a mere mumbling. I pointed to another line that noted Native people suffered from "a legacy of intolerance" (151) and the inherent irony in the lines that followed claiming that "there is a danger that the increasing involvement by Natives in their own education may result in a growing isolation of Native people" (151). Looking back, I am certain my use of the word "irony" and other such terms did little to promote conversation.

In sheer desperation, I told a story. I played the devil's advocate. I posed as an administrator of public education and talked about my experiences with Natives and how I came to the conclusions stated in the lines above. A woman who was older and more outspoken challenged me with another story. She did not speak in the first person—perhaps the story was not hers per se—but it was a story she knew well. She told about a Native girl's experience in school, about the books the girl had to read, and about her struggles at home where a grandmother insisted that above all else the girl remain Cree and know the language of her ancestors. Already, like her grandmother, this girl felt vulnerable before government officials and refused to talk openly about her conflicts "so it looks like we don't fully appreciate the significance of education for our overall advancement." Another student, a much younger woman, related a story about an older sister who graduated from college with a teaching credential and ended up as a hairdresser in her home. "They won't hire Natives as teachers in the school. On the reserve my sister has to wait for one of the government teachers to retire. How can I be motivated? What am I to appreciate?" "Yeah," a young man blasted, "what does overall advancement mean?"

I defined "overall advancement" as I understood it from my position as a government official. "No," this last student argued, "you did not listen to the first story. How does your definition take into account our culture and our desire to keep it? When we hear our elders talk of tradition as the only thing we have left, take a look around and it's true. And then the schools want us to forget that—that and the whole ugly history of what's been done and is still being done right in the classroom. Like she [the student who spoke of infested blankets] said. Now maybe you know what a chasm is for us Natives and why we 'don't appreciate the significance of education for [our] overall advancement.' How can you know? We just told you we don't talk much to officials."

Now they were talking to an official, or at least seeing that they could. I countered again, but I was quickly losing ground. My short-sightedness was exposed not just as a proxy for a real government official, but as an American familiar with only the Bureau of Indian Affairs and other American Indian institutions. The students made subtle distinctions between the two systems based on what I had assumed and projected from the American model(s). They talked openly about the discrepancies between what I assumed and how the Canadian system actually works and affects the lives of Natives. Here the students discerned assumptions inherent in a story and how those assumptions predicated thinking and decision-making. Their own stories—what they knew from their lives—became the essential ingredient for critical reflection and insight. The other shoe had dropped: they had not only brought forth their stories, but they now had held them up to another story in order to understand better that story and their own.

These students felt empowered; they found that by engaging their life experience they operated from a position of strength. They found that texts—oral stories, fiction, government documents, movies, advertisements—are alive, filled with interpretations based on certain assumptions, and that they could actively engage, or, as they said, "talk back," to these texts. Storytelling became a means for critical inquiry, not just about the texts, but simultaneously about the students' relationships to them. When a text stumped us, we resorted to stories to point out the gaps between ourselves and the texts. Sometimes the stories pointed to an unfamiliarity with complex and subtle language usage. This unfamiliarity had again to do with certain kinds of experience or lack of it, and when the students understood as much, when their stories pointed to language usage in the broader academic and political context, they felt challenged to understand and make use of the various rhetorical strategies encountered.

I remember a particularly vivid story about Joan Didion, about what she looked like and about what people she wrote for looked like and how they talked, "using big words and long, long sentences." The student who told this story created a scenario where Joan Didion and a Native woman discussed the Saddle Lake Reserve in Alberta, just north of Edmonton. The Didion character discussed exteriors—the architecture and the condition of the houses, cars, the local store and gas station—in complex sentences. In simple, more direct language, the Native woman talked about day-to-day life, her concerns for her children, the struggle to make ends meet, and the excitement of winning a bingo game. Language usage told much about the speaker's world and the type of knowledge she possessed about that world. Those big words, those essays "I can't relate to" no longer provoked fear and withdrawal, but a challenge, a curiosity about a story yet untold. We made whatever was problematic a starting point, just as Newkirk does when teaching poetry. I began to note too a smoother, more effective blending of the anecdotal and critical in their writing. Students became aware of how in many instances they were using an interlanguage, a language somewhere between their own and that which is acceptable in the academy. Their prose was indicative of their efforts to mediate different kinds of discourse.

Excited by this successful experience with storytelling, I was anxious to experiment in my writing courses, where I might have students from as many as ten different cultural backgrounds. That fall, in the middle of a discussion of Richard Rodriguez's "Going Home Again: The New American Scholarship Boy," I had the bright idea that we should try storytelling. The students disagreed with Rodriguez's assertion that the culturally and linguistically diverse student needed to "almost mechanically acquire the assumptions, practices, and style of the classroom milieu" at the expense of the home culture in order to succeed. They argued with personal anecdotes that began with the typical, "Well, for me . . ." No one really considered how or why Rodriguez came to his conclusions, or, for that matter, how their own stories disproved his conclusions.

"Each of us tell a part of Rodriguez's story," I suggested. "From the beginning so we can see what his life was like and how he might have made certain decisions about it. Picture yourself as him, how you might have done the same." But a Chinese woman started by telling a story about a Chinese girl, a story which the next student, a Chicano, had a hard time following. "We all have different stories," the students protested. Obviously, collective storytelling would not work here in the same way it had for the Cree students who shared a common history and set of cultural norms. When a Cree student told a story about Cree life, or even about a text from a Cree perspective, the other students could readily identify with the story and comment on it. Here, the Chicano student could not follow the experience of the Chinese student. I had also been wrong in assuming that, because the students disagreed so strongly with Rodriguez, a story reconciling his point of view would force them to consider their own stories in a more critical light. By making up a story, they did not necessarily have to engage their own experiences.

Improvising, I then asked the two students to tell a story illustrating how they came to conclusions different from those of Rodriguez. To ensure detailed accounts and to allow the other students time to reflect on what was being said, I suggested the two speakers tell their stories in parts, each telling about the "early life" part of the story before moving on to the next part. Each storyteller, and other members of the class, could stop then and listen to the other's story. This way, the stories could be held up to one another and to the original text. I encouraged the storytellers to invent from their own experience. The following is what we heard:

> First student: Ming kept thinking she sounded funny when she talked. Her voice was too soft, she thought. It was true because the teacher always asked her: "Speak up." She thought she sounded funny, worse when she tried to speak loudly. It made her accent come out. Everybody was saying the word "cool." She sounded funny saying that. She practiced at home. In front of the mirror she'd make her mouth shape [out the word] like the other kids.

> Second student: No, the thing that bothered Jose most was the food. You know . . . what the other kids were eating at lunchtime. In those boxes, you know, the ones with Mickey Mouse painted on them. . . . The other kids have sandwiches, peanut butter and jelly, stuff like that. Jose, he is carrying his father's old work pail and canteen and he pulls out a tamale. "What's that?" someone says. On the other side of Jose is a Mexican who knows what tamales are, but he does not help

Jose. He [the other Mexican student] is a pocho; he says nothing, acts like he doesn't know what a tamale is either.

What became interesting as the two stories progressed was the ways in which they were similar to Rodriguez's story, something the students had not anticipated. A chasm did exist between home life and school life, only here the dividing mechanism was located in the company of peers, not in the teacher. The students' stories better informed them of their own positions even as the stories informed the text. Richard Rodriguez's scholarship boy sacrificed the culture of what follows the storytelling(s). If students are to scrutinize their stories so that their stories might inform, and be informed by, other experiences found in texts, teachers must be careful not to let difference, or otherness, be transformed into sameness. Schwab notes the tendency within interpretive communities to assimilate difference by projecting, or recreating texts to fit preconceived notions, as in the case of my students with the story of Coyote and Junco. She notes that assimilation can happen in two directions: "the assimilation of the text to the reader's subjectivity and the assimilation of the reader to the text's subjectivity" (115). In the latter instance, a reader or, in this case, listener may identify imaginatively with a text so that the distinction between her world and that of the text becomes blurred barring any recognition, and understanding, of difference. Of course, it is hoped that storytelling and the discussions that follow storytelling will expose such tendencies when they occur, and it is here the teacher must work, recognizing the potential of chasms between home life and school life to foster assimilating tendencies, to illuminate conflict and difference rather than dissolve them. Discussions that follow the storytelling event are problem-exposing in nature, not problem-solving. It is the story, after all, that made the difference.

What I have offered here are three stories about storytelling strategies, each suited to a different classroom environment: middle-class non-Indian students studying American Indian literature, Canadian Cree students reading American texts and Canadian government documents, and culturally diverse American students reading material by a host of culturally diverse American writers. Different strategies will undoubtedly be more suitable for different situations. The three stories I have related illustrate, I hope, the potential for storytelling to empower and engage culturally diverse students while providing, in turn, a context for strong sense critical thinking for all of us, students and teachers alike, such that the nature of our shared reality, and our relationship to it, is made more visible and less intimidating. My stories are models of, not necessarily models for, using storytelling to foster critical discourse. But it is interesting to me how even these three stories always prompt more stories.

References

Berthouex, Susan J. and Robin S. Chapman, "Storytelling: A Way to Teach Non-Native Students. "*Non-Native and Nonstandard Dialect Students.*Urbana: NCTE, 1982, 37–43.

Foucault, Michel. *The Foucault Reader.* Ed. Paul Rabinow. New York: Pantheon Books, 1984.

Freire, Paulo. *Pedagogy of the Oppressed.* Intro. Richard Shaull. New York:Seabury, 1970.

Gramsci, Antonio. *The Prison Notebooks: Selections.* Trans. and ed. Quinton Hoare and Geoffrey Nowell Smith. New York: International Publishers, 1971.

Marcus, George E., and Michael M. J. Fischer. *Anthropology as Cultural Critique.* Chicago: U of Chicago P, 1986.

Oswalt, Robert. *Kashaya Texts.* Vol 36. Berkeley: U of California Publications in Linguistics, 1964.

Paul, Richard. "The Critical Thinking Movement. "*National Forum* (Winter 1985): 2–3.

Pomo Elders, esp. Essie Parrish and Mabel McKay. Personal communication. Santa Rosa California and vicinity. 1958–.

"Public Policy-Statements on Native Education. "Committee on Tolerance and Understanding. Edmonton: Government of Alberta, 1984.

Rodriguez, Richard. *Hunger of Memory, the Education of Richard Rodriguez, An Autobiography.* Boston: Godine, 1982.

Roemer, Madorie Godlin. "Literate Cultures: Multi-Voiced Classrooms. "MLA Convention. San Francisco, 27 Dec. 1987.

Saddle Lake Summer Course. U.C. Santa Cruz. Santa Cruz, California. 1984.

Schwab, Gabriele. "Reader-Response' and the Aesthetic Experience of Other-ness." *Stanford Literature Review* (Spring 1986): 107–136.

Schwartzman, Helen B. "Stories at Work: Play in an Organizational Context. *Text, Play and Story: The Construction and Reconstruction of Self and Society.* Ed. Edward M. Bruner. Washington: American Ethnological Society, 1984. 79–92.

Tedlock, Dennis. "The Spoken Word and the Work of Interpretation in American Indian Religion. "*The Spoken Word and the Work of Interpretation.* Philadelphia: U of Pennsylvania P, 1983. 233–246.

Writing I Course. *Crossing Cultures.* U.C. Santa Cruz. Santa Cruz, California. 1984.

The Role of Service-Learning in Critical Thinking

Nancy P. Kraft

Imagine a school where seventh grade children are involved in an integrated project that addresses issues of homelessness and poverty and culminates in students' active involvement in organizing a food drive, working in a local soup kitchen, and making the community aware of the larger political, economic, and social issues surrounding poverty, hunger, and homelessness. This is the promise of service-learning. But in order for service-learning to raise this kind of critical consciousness in children and youth and to provide a transformative experience that spurs them to social action, it needs to be grounded in critical pedagogy processes that encourage reflection and a sense of empathy for others' situations. The key to making this happen is to create a community of learners where the students and teachers jointly investigate, through collaborative critical inquiry, issues that are of relevance to them in their lives and of broader social significance.

Critical thinking, or inquiry, is a skill that necessitates one to engage in processes of questioning beliefs, values, and assumptions that one holds about virtually everything. Yet common practice in schools, in Ira Shor's (1992) words, is to "answer questions rather than question answers." Paulo Freire (1970) has labeled this approach a "banking" education where teachers deposit information and skills in students' memory banks. Consequently the role of students is nothing more than parroting back previously deposited information. This method is especially prevalent in most compensatory education programs where the purpose is to remediate socalled disadvantaged students through drill and practice activities, rather than engaging in guided inquiry that enables them to critically question and reflect on issues that have some social meaning and significance for themselves and others in similar situations.

If our intent is to instead link learning to social action through developing students' critical thinking capacities, then what kind of practices are needed in schools to enable and encourage critical thinking? What teaching and learning practices are most likely to ensure students' abilities to engage in critical thought and discussion? What kinds of roles will teachers and other adults in schools have to assume to foster and nurture critical thinking in students? And what about the students themselves—what roles will they have to assume in order to hone these kinds of questioning skills?

This chapter seeks to answer these questions through: (1) re-conceptualizing education that is grounded in a philosophy of service-learning; (2) differentiating and critiquing alternative ways to view critical thinking; (3) illustrating how service-learning is a vehicle to encourage and enable students' critical thinking; and (4) examining what conditions are necessary in schools to foster students' critical thinking skills.

What Is Service-Learning

Educational practices that are grounded in approaches emphasizing relevance and authentic learning experiences such as service-learning have the potential to transform classrooms into centers of inquiry and students into active, rather than passive, learners. Service-learning is an approach to education that educators are using to create more authentic learning opportunities for students. According to the Alliance for Service-Learning in Education Reform (1993), service-learning is a method:

a   under which students learn and develop through active participation in thoughtfully organized service experiences that meet actual community needs and that are coordinated in collaboration with the school and community;
b   that is integrated into the students' academic curriculum or provides structured time for students to think, talk, or write about what they did and saw during the actual service activity;
c   that provides students with opportunities to use newly acquired skills and knowledge in real-life situations in their own communities; and
d   that enhances what is taught in school by extending student learning beyond the classroom into the community and helps to foster the development of a sense of caring for others.

Service-learning can take many forms depending upon community needs, student interests, and the curricular objectives of the program. All service-learning programs have certain commonalities: they integrate service with learning and feature "reflections", or student discussion and writing about their experiences. Examples of service-learning that have the potential for student involvement in social action include the following:

Students may work on **citizenship issues**, such as:

- researching voting procedures in their hometowns;
- conducting a survey of political candidates to reflect their opinions on a variety of issues; and/or
- organizing a voter registration drive.

Students may work on **environmental issues**, such as:

- designing and building a nature trail;
- developing and maintaining a community garden;
- testing the water quality of a local stream or reservoir; and/or
- presenting a proposal to the state legislature for clearing up a polluted water supply.

Students may work on **educational activities**, such as:

- tutoring younger children;
- teaching conflict resolution skills to other students;
- researching and designing exhibits for the local natural history museum;
- preparing oral tapes of books for the blind; and/or
- producing telecasts or newspaper articles for the local media on topics of concern.

Students may help **community agencies**, by:

- constructing special equipment or resources like wheelchair ramps for neighborhood homes or Braille instructions for sight-impaired parents who attend school functions;
- assisting English language learners with application forms;
- cooking meals for shelters or for those who are not able to leave their homes; and/or
- installing smoke detectors for those who need them.

Students may work with **senior citizens**, by:

- writing and producing biographies;
- collecting information to design an historic fair;
- conducting research about cultural heritage; and/or;
- creating collages that highlight significant life events in both the students' and seniors' lives.

Service-learning that is connected to the academic curriculum is integrated, coherent, and based on the belief that learning comes to life for students only when it is intimately connected to their experiences and the lives of real people. Structuring time for students to think, talk, and write about their service-learning experiences lends authenticity to the learning experience. It allows students to use their minds while encouraging them to engage in critical inquiry that requires them to reflect and process information and ideas in ways that transform their meaning. It gives schoolwork intrinsic value beyond achieving success in school, since there is a connection between the knowledge acquired and the larger social context in which the students live.

Effective service-learning programs provide structured opportunities for students to apply academic theory to real-world practice. While active or experiential learning does not necessarily guarantee that students will become critical thinkers, the potential is there. A basic tenet of service-learning requires students to reflect on their experience, discuss how the service experience ties back to their academic learning, assess how they have impacted the community through their work, and identify how their experience affects their future studies and career ambitions. Service-learning can be a vehicle through which students begin to understand concepts such as community revitalization and economic development and learn how they can use their skills and education for social action to better the community (and eventually the world) in which they live. The community values the students' contributions and students feel a sense of pride in their work.

Service-learning is not synonymous with community service. Community service, in and of itself, is beneficial to students and the community. However, service becomes far more powerful in its effects when a deliberate linkage is made with academics and learning opportunities. Service-learning combines community needs with student interests and learning needs, and gives students opportunities to learn new roles, think more critically and analytically, and apply knowledge and skills in a systematic way.

In addition to these factors outlined by the Alliance, Billig and Kraft (1997) add that service-learning is a method that should be supported by regular assessment to provide feedback and guide improvement. To accomplish this they believe that assessment has three purposes:

1   as an indication of how well students are comprehending and applying knowledge, skills, and attitudes;
2   a means to determine how well teachers are facilitating learning and connecting content to students in meaningful, relevant and authentic ways; and
3   to provide input and establish what kind of programmatic changes are necessary to accomplish program goals.

Alternative Views About Critical Inquiry

As more and more schools are beginning to integrate service-learning into their curriculum, several key points need to be considered to make service-learning a viable approach that enables the kind of critical inquiry with the potential for social action and change. Critical thinking, however, has been viewed from various perspectives with several popular conceptions existing in schools. One is that critical thinking is an outcome of schooling. This idea of critical thinking is limiting because it negates the very nature of what it means to engage in critical thinking—it can never be finished in some final, static manner. Instead, it is a way of life that encourages one to challenge or be critical of universal truths or total certainty.

Another perspective that is popularly touted in schools has students engage in a process of logical reasoning that may or may not alter students' perceptions or beliefs about social reality. Critical thinking of this nature typically asks students to conceptualize, apply, analyze, synthesize, and/or evaluate information gathered from, or generated by observation, experience reasoning, or communication. This practice of critical thinking is nothing more than cognitive activity that asks students to engage in logical reasoning or to scrutinize arguments for assertions unsupported by empirical evidence. This mode of critical thinking does not necessarily challenge the student to analyze the information from a variety of perspectives—from the perspective of the assumptions underlying one's beliefs and behaviors—and much less from the perspective of race, class, or gender and power relationships in society.

This way of thinking about critical thinking does not alter the very basis of belief systems, as students and teachers, alike, may not even be aware that there is an alternative way of thinking about the information that is couched in a larger political, social, economic, historical, and cultural context. While thinking of this nature entails much more than the mere acquisition and retention of information alone, it is generally an uncritical reflection on the information under consideration. In this mode, schooling and the education that occurs there is more about socializing students into a way of thinking about and viewing the world.

Another perspective, that is the focus of this chapter, is a process of critical thinking that enables students to question the very basis of their own beliefs, values, and assumptions, and has the power to change the way that students' view themselves and the world. According to Brookfield "it involves calling into question the assumptions underlying our customary, habitual ways of thinking and acting and then being ready to think and act differently on the basis of this critical questioning" (1987, p. 1). It also goes beyond questioning self to questioning others, social reality, and the world, or in other words, challenging the importance of context. In Freirian terms this way of thinking has been characterized as enabling students to read the world rather than merely being able to read the word. Service-learning as a means to enable students to read the world involves teaching them how to engage in critical inquiry. Thus, critical thinking becomes a process that encourages students to pose essential critical questions such as the following, identified by Bigelow, et. al. (1994) in Rethinking Our Classrooms:

- Who benefits and who suffers;
- Why is a given practice fair or unfair;
- What are its origins;
- What alternatives can we imagine; and
- What is required to create change?

They go on to state that through this kind of inquiry, students learn to think about the many facets of experience including advertising, cartoons, literature, legislative decisions, job structures, newspapers, movies, agricultural practices, and school life. Questioning of this nature enables students to understand how, why and who constructs knowledge and power.

In this manner, thinking critically is more than merely conceptualizing, applying, or analyzing information and making meaning of that information as it relates to one's experiences. Instead, critical thinking also involves an analysis of the surrounding people and community and an analysis of the visible and invisible messages of the world. It is a process of encoding the power structure and our role in these processes (Freire and Macedo, 1987). Critical thinking recognizes that what students learn in school does not take place in a vacuum; but rather includes the entire social, economic, cultural, political, and historical context that shapes one's position and existence in the world. In this manner, thinking critically is essential to creating and maintaining a healthy democracy. It is only through this type of inquiry that the potential for social transformation and action exists.

How Service-Learning Enables Students' Critical Thinking

One of the primary tenants of service-learning is that students engage in processes of reflection on and about their service experience. In many service-learning programs the practice of reflection means having your students think about the experience they have had, the meaning of their experiences, and how the experiences impacted their lives and the lives of other people. When service-learning programs are grounded firmly in academics, reflection serves an even broader purpose of reinforcing cognitive processes of thinking and brain functioning. Research suggests that working effectively at a challenging task requires significant amounts of reflection—a critical part of brain functioning (Diamond, 1995).

John Dewey believed that reflective thinking is the key to making experiences educational in that it links observed and experienced facts with ideas. The experiential learning cycle developed by Kolb illustrates the relationship between reflection and understanding (1984). The four parts of his cycle include:

- concrete experience where learners involve themselves fully and openly;
- reflective observation where learners are able to reflect on and observe experiences from many perspectives;
- abstract conceptualization where learners create concepts and integrate observations in logically sound theories; and
- active experimentation where learners use theories to make decisions and solve problems.

Kolb believed that learning, change, and growth occur through a process starting with experience, followed by observations and reflection on that experience, and then in-depth analysis to understand and modify behavior and/or choose new experiences. Reflections lead to change and are therefore a basic element in learning.

Reflection consists of two steps. First, it involves a process of students surfacing their tacit knowledge or beliefs and assumptions about their experiences. Second, it requires critical evaluation of the knowledge, beliefs, and assumptions to help students gain insights into their meaning systems that influence and shape their beliefs. Ultimately, the practice of reflection serves to help students either develop new knowledge, concepts, beliefs, and values, or affirm their existing beliefs. These two steps are imperative in order for students to benefit from their service-learning experience in ways that challenges them to think more critically about their involvement and how that involvement impacts themselves and others.

In this mode, service-learning has the potential to alter and change students' beliefs and value systems. But whether this occurs will be dependent on the ways in which service is structured and reflected on to compliment learning in the classroom. As illustrated in Table 1, the service component in service-learning has been conceptualized as either promoting the value of students engaged in charitable acts or helping them realize that they are capable of effecting real and meaningful change (Kahne and Westheimer 1996). Depending on the underlying goals (i.e., charity or change) of the service-learning experience, they believe that service-learning has the potential to impact students morally, politically, and intellectually. If the service-learning experience fosters charity rather than change, the emphasis in the moral domain is more likely to be about giving rather than caring. In the political domain, charitable service-learning experiences instill in students a sense of civic responsibility, i.e. experiences that demonstrate the value of altruism and the dangers of exclusive self-interest. In contrast, service experiences with an underlying focus toward change help students understand what it means to participate in a democracy and political and social activism. In addressing how service-learning can potentially impact a person's intellectual dimensions, they believe that service-learning grounded in change is more likely to foster transformational experiences for students than service-learning postured as charitable experiences.

Table 1
Service-Learning Goals

	Moral	Political	Intellectual
Charity	Giving	Civic duty	Additive experience
Change	Caring	Social reconstruction	Transformative experience

Source: Kahne, J. and Westheimer, J. (1996). "In the service of what? The politics of service-learning," *Phi Delta Kappan*, 77(9), 593–599.

Quality service-learning programs are those that help students engage in higher-order thinking. Transformation, however, will only occur when critical inquiry is combined with action. A process of critical inquiry that helps students surface their tacit beliefs and assumptions and evaluate these through reflection, has the potential to move students' thinking in ways that question and challenge thinking grounded in the status quo.

The simple kinds of reflections that sometimes occur in school, requiring students to engage in reflective writing and keeping journals as a means to document personal learning discoveries, often do not support academic or intellectual growth. Neither does reflection of this nature challenge basic assumptions and alter belief systems. Standards for determining the intellectual quality of student learning and reflection are those that require students to think, to develop in-depth understanding, and to apply academic learning to important, realistic problems. Standards for promoting a sense of caring requires critical thinking that brings into question beliefs and perceptions as well as enabling a sense of critical consciousness raising.

Following are two examples that have the potential to transform students' beliefs. The first illustrates how biases and stereotypes of elderly and poor persons can be challenged and eliminated when students are required to engage in critical thinking and reflection as part of their service-learning experience. The second example challenges students to become political activists in questioning community attitudes toward people of color through practices concerning the burial of community residents.

Example 1: Service-Learning Focused on Elderly Issues and Concerns

Middle school students from a suburban and predominantly middle class neighborhood took on a project that involved reading stories to and interacting with elderly residents in a nearby nursing home. Every other week the students visited the home and spent an hour reading to residents and listening to them share stories of their past and childhood experiences. To prepare the students for this experience and to integrate this experience into a curriculum unit that focused on the relationship between elderly and the impact of economics on lifestyles the teacher asked his students to reflect on the questions, "What is old? How are elderly treated in this society? and What is the relationship between one's financial status and growing old?" Listing students responses to these questions on the blackboard gave the teacher many ideas of ways he could address their responses and underlying beliefs and stereotypes they had about elderly and the elderly poor through the science, social studies, math, and language arts curriculum using an integrated, coherent curricular approach.

As the middle school science curriculum focused on nutrition, living systems and physical change, students researched caloric needs of individuals at different stages of life and how body systems change during the aging process, looking specifically at common ailments creating physical challenges for elderly persons. In social studies, students studied the relationship between income level and access to quality medical services and nutrition programs. They also compared and contrasted perceptions of elderly persons across several cultures, both those represented by the student make-up of the school and those of elderly residents living in the adjacent inner city. In addition to these, students studied social issues such as loss of autonomy, independence, and the impact of limited incomes. They also researched how government programs and policies impacted elderly in different social strata and the effects these policies had on elderly who were poor. Another assignment had students critically view television programs to assess how popular culture and the media represents elderly and the poor. Based on all their research, the students developed a survey to assess the prevalence of these issues among elderly persons in their own neighborhoods. The resulting data were tabulated and aggregated by ethnicity categories and then represented and interpreted through a variety of means such as pie charts, bar graphs, and narrative analysis. Survey results indicated differentials in access to health care and a quality of life for elderly residents dependent on a person's socio-economic status.

This unit about the effects of economics on elderly lifestyles culminated with student's writing papers that illustrated their own understandings of the impact of economic conditions on lifestyles, especially those of the elderly. Students brainstormed ways to counter negative portrayals of elderly in this society and how to raise others' social and critical consciousness concerning the issues they had uncovered through their own investigations. Several students chose to submit these to the local paper where they were published in the editorial section. While the original intent of the project was for students to be involved in service to elderly citizens, the way the teacher structured learning and reflection resulted in a transformative experience for students. Their involvement in this project helped students come to view elderly from a more compassionate and respectful perspective now that they realized the breadth and depth of physical and emotional challenges confronting elderly citizens. Students also took an active interest in supporting and advocating for social issues that impacted the lives of elderly in their own community.

Example 2: Service-Learning Focused on Community Issues

The second example caused students to question and challenge community attitudes and values toward people of color through their participation in a project focusing on the restoration of a cemetery in their community. In this southern town, there were several cemeteries, one of which had been allowed to deteriorate. In visiting the cemetery and noting the names and dates of death on the headstones, students realized that people buried in this cemetery were early residents of the community who had been buried there in a fifty year period following the civil war. To determine who these early community residents were, the students researched local newspaper archives and conducted interviews with living relatives who were still residents of the community. To their surprise, the students came to realize that all the people in this particular cemetery were Afro-Americans and many of them had been prominent citizens in the community who had made major contributions. Their research also revealed segregation practices and early attitudes toward people of color in the community.

After engaging in lengthy research, students decided to write stories about these early residents and publish a book on local history and contributions of early residents. Since the social studies curriculum for students in the primary grades focused on an understanding of community, these middle school students wrote books that second graders could read and understand about local history. Because this school was bilingual, with French as the second language, students translated the books into French as a way to hone their own language skills and reinforce French language skills for primary children.

Their involvement in this service-learning project helped the students to understand the negative effects of segregation in the community and enabled them to better understand the issues surrounding the civil rights movement in their social studies unit and in their community. Continued discussion led the students to political action in petitioning the city council to spend resources on restoration of the Afro-American cemetery, as had been the case with the cemetery on the other side of town, where early white residents had been buried. Being successful in their campaign to restore the cemetery, students also sponsored numerous activities to raise sufficient money to replace headstones that had been destroyed or missing. This on-going project, that continued to expand into other areas of community involvement, exemplified curriculum integration, pulling in all subject areas—math, reading, social studies, science, language arts, music, and art. The project also led to critical consciousness raising among students and community members alike, in questioning and challenging the allocation of community resources toward differentiated ethnic groups in the community. The ultimate benefit of the project was in validating people of color who had been active and productive members of the community and whose contributions would have gone unnoticed had it not been for these students who were involved in this project of giving to these former community residents "voices from the grave."

To maximize learning, as illustrated in these examples, service-learning should require students to engage in deeper, reflective analysis and processing of learning experiences. To maximize critical thinking, reflection should call into question those practices and/or policies that impact peoples' lives' often in negative ways. Reflection is a cognitive process that fosters critical thinking, problem solving, synthesis, interpretations, and evaluation—all skills considered within the realm of complex and higher order thinking. A process of reflection will help bridge learners' past experiences and existing mental structures. As Meyers points out, this will lead learners from concrete operations to more abstract, reflective ways of thinking. He argues, "whenever teachers build bridges between concrete, everyday ideas and more abstract, academic concepts, they are fostering critical thinking (1986, p. 77)." To nurture critical thinking and effective reflective activity, reflection should be continuous, connected, challenging, and contextualized, as shown in Table 2 (Eyler, et. al, 1996).

Table 2
Principles for Effective Student Reflection

Continuous	Must be an ongoing part of a learner's education and service involvement over the course of his/her educational career. Should include reflection before the experience, during the experience, and after the experience.
Connected	Links service to the intellectual and academic pursuits of the students. Academic pursuits add a "big picture"context to the personal encounters of each isolated service experience and help student s to search for causes and solutions to social problems.
Challenging	Requires intervention on the part of a teacher or colleagues who is prepared to pose questions and propose unfamiliar or even uncomfortable ideas for consideration by the learner.
Contextualized	The environment and method of reflection corresponds in a meaningful way to the topics and experiences that form the material for reflection.

Source: Eyler, J., Dwight, E. G. Jr., and Schmiede, A. (1996). *A Practitioner's Guide to Reflection in Service-Learning: Student Voices & Reflections*, Nashville, TN: Vanderbilt University.

In order to foster the kind of critical thinking that reflection can bring about, teachers would have to work with students to develop their reflective thinking skills. This is generally accomplished by having students respond to open ended questions, write in journals or learning logs, or by participating in a debriefing or sharing session about their experience. Many techniques could be used to nurture this kind of reflective thinking, among which is the use of Socratic questioning as a reflection strategy. This is an excellent process because it probes student's reasoning and thinking abilities. Eyler, J., et al. suggest other ways that students can be encouraged to engage in reflection (1996). These include the following:

- **Reading:** case studies, books about social issues, government documents, professional journals, and classic literature;
- **Writing:** journals and logs, reflection essays, self-evaluation essays, portfolios, analysis papers, case studies, grant proposals, press releases, drafting legislation, letters to others (students, clients, self, and/or politicians), published articles (newspapers, newsletters, journals), and volunteer/agency training manuals;
- **Verbal exercise:** focus groups, informal discussion, formal class discussions, presentations, talking to other students, recruiting other volunteers, teaching a class, cooperative learning, story telling, individual conferences with faculty or project sponsors, and legislative testimony;
- **Projects and activities:** simulations, conducting interviews, art journals, role playing, collecting photos and/or creating slide presentations, watching movies and videos, presentations (involving dance, music, or theatrics), planning public relations events, analyzing or creating budgets, and program development.

Student involvement in service is a powerful experience. When service is coupled with learning and formal opportunities for reflection students can have tremendous benefits. McPherson (1989) identifies the following outcomes of reflection:

Effective problem solving: By examining experiences, students discover ways to handle real life problems more effectively both in their service projects and in other areas of their lives;

Lifelong learning skills: Students develop a greater ability to learn from experience by reflecting on positive and difficult experiences;

Increased sense of personal power: Through examination, students can clarify their goals and develop a variety of ways to accomplish them;

Higher level thinking: Reflecting on service encourages students to deal with the root causes of complex issues. Students learn to look for the big picture and to analyze and synthesize what they have learned;

Academic skills: In addition to skills needed for the service project itself, reflection acts as a vehicle to link a broad range of academic skills to the students' direct experience;

Celebration: When students think about the high points and the benefits of service, they feel a sense of renewal and accomplishment;

Improved service: Students discover ways to improve the quality and quantity of their service as they examine the effects of their behavior; and

Improved program: Both teacher and students receive important feedback on strengths and weaknesses of the program.

In addition to these, reflection from a critical perspective leads to feelings of empathy and feelings of compassion toward others' reality and conditions. It is only through reflection of this nature that the potential for transformation exists.

Conditions Necessary to Foster Students' Critical Thinking Skills

The kind of critical thinking that has been discussed in this chapter is not readily practiced or easily accepted in schools. While school outcomes often refer to instilling in students a capacity to engage in critical thinking, this kind of critical thinking is one that generally does not enable students to critically reflect on their own beliefs, values, and assumptions, let alone societal norms that often perpetuate an inequitable status quo. Thinking of this nature appears to be too disruptive at all levels of the system—it often is easier to accept the status quo rather than to challenge and advocate for change. Another reason this kind of thinking does not happen so readily is because of hegemony or the dominant and "accepted" way of looking at the world. A hegemonic view of the world is informed by one's ideological perspective. If an individual's worldview has never been challenged or questioned, one may not be aware that an alternative perspective exists or one may be unwilling to question belief systems.

Yet, if one of the goals of education is to provide opportunities for children and youth to become independent and critical thinkers, then the system needs to allow teachers to be independent and critical thinkers as well. Teachers, in turn, need to model critical thinking as well as teach students how to be critical, and encourage and welcome their questioning through providing ample opportunities for them to engage in reflective analysis concerning the service and the linkages between service and learning. Conditions that are supportive of this kind of critical thinking activity include: (1) a risk-free environment that welcomes and encourages questioning and reflection; (2) giving students a sense of ownership in defining what the service-learning experience and reflective process should entail; (3) valuing reflection and allotting the necessary time to engage in continuous reflection; (4) viewing reflection as a central activity to education and what it means to be educated—moving away from the practice that there is a "right" answer; and (5) a commitment from teachers to value student judgment.

One of the first ways to start encouraging reflection and critical thinking of this magnitude is to encourage and solicit participation by students in creating a democratic classroom where students have voice in their learning experiences. Democratic classrooms are those where students are actively engaged in collaborative critical inquiry as the focus of the curriculum. In these classrooms, students take more ownership and responsibility for their own learning. Apple and Beane suggest the following conditions to help foster democracy in the classroom:

- the open flow of ideas, regardless of their popularity, that enables people to be as fully informed as possible;
- faith in the individual and collective capacity of people to create possibilities for resolving problems;
- the use of critical reflection and analysis to evaluate ideas, problems, and policies;
- concern for the welfare of others and "the common good";
- concern for the dignity and rights of individuals and minorities; and
- an understanding that democracy is not so much an "ideal" to be pursued as an "idealized" set of values that we must live by and that must guide our life as a people (1995, pp. 6–7).

Reflection and inquiry about knowledge and its relationship to the human experience assists students in making connections between what happens in school and in their own lives. Connecting the work of school with the life of communities, as exemplified through service-learning, has the potential to help students become revitalized as learners and make sense of human experience.

Democratic planning at both the school and classroom levels should be a genuine attempt to honor the rights people have to participate in making decisions that affect their lives. If one of the purposes of schooling, and programs using a service-learning approach, is to enable students to become active citizens and prepare them for participating in a democracy, then the best way to teach them to prepare for that role is to let them experience it on a daily basis in the classroom setting. Kohn (1996) believes the best way to teach decision making is to allow students to make decisions—starting in the classroom.

Other authors have recommended the kinds of conditions that are needed as part of the curriculum and learning process that will ensure reflective thinking which, in turn, is more likely to enable collaborative critical inquiry. Bigelow et al. (1994) in *Rethinking Our Classrooms* recommend situating teaching and learning practices in the following components: (1) grounded in the lives of students; (2) critical; (3) multicultural, antiracist, pro-justice; (4) participatory, experiential; (5) hopeful, joyful, kind, visionary; (6) activist; (7) academically rigorous; and (8) culturally sensitive. In a similar vein, Shor (1992) identifies a range of classroom values that should influence the process as well as the curriculum of schooling. In order to encourage the kind of critical thinking emphasized in this chapter he believes that education should be participatory, affective, focus on problem posing, situated, multicultural, dialogic, desocializing, democratic, researching, interdisciplinary, and activist.

Brookfield believes that one of the conditions necessary to foster critical thinking is to first have critical teachers (1987). Borrowing from Paulo Freire, he identifies the characteristics of competence, courage, risk taking, humility, and political clarity as necessary for teachers to be considered "critical." In defining these further Brookfield says

> Competence in communicating clearly with people and in managing group activities democratically is needed to ensure that people understand that alternative interpretations of the world are possible and that participants have a chance to explore these fully. Courage is needed to withstand the resistance to challenging assumptions that teachers who try to nudge learners away from their uncritically accepted ways of looking at the world are bound to encounter. Courage is also needed in those times when teachers face condemnation and criticism of their efforts by outsiders, and when they have to combat attempts to prevent them from engaging in this activity.
>
> Risk taking is at the heart of all creative and exciting teaching, implying as it does that teachers as well as learners are fully engaged in the education transaction. A willingness to risk experimentation in one's teaching is an important aspect of modeling change and promoting critical openness in learners. Humility is essential to teachers, lest they slip into the all-too-seductive (but appallingly arrogant) role of omniscient guru of critical thinking. Political clarity is a more controversial concept. What is politically self-evident to one person is heresy to another. To Freire, political clarity is the ability to break free from distorting per-

spectives imposed by oppressive groups so that we can see the inequitable and hierarchical relationships in society clearly and fully (pp. 81–82).

If educators are to engage students in critical thinking, then a different method of teaching will be required—one that moves away from the transmission or banking model that is so prevalent in schools, to a critical

Table 3
Two Contrasting Theories of Learning:
The Banking Assumption and the Critical Assumption

The Banking Assumption	The Critical Assumption
Students need to be taught what to think and this can best be done by "banking" information into the student.	Students need to be taught how to think not what to think and this is best done in an environment of inquiry where teacher is midwife as opposed to banker.
The quiet classroom, where students are bent on particular tasks is a class that resonates real learning.	The quiet classroom is generally a classroom where few learn and is too often regimented, authoritarian, and teacher based. All learning is based on communication and all communication is based on dialogue. Without collaborative dialogue there can exist few genuine opportunities to learn.
That basic skills can be taught divorced from reasoning and reduced to preformulated repetitious tasks that are orchestrated at a future time in the service of thinking.	That basic skills cannot be reduced to formula or repetition and must be taught within the context of an interdisciplinary problem posing curriculum that calls for utilization of the skills in the service of reasoning.
That learning is essentially an autodidactic activity that takes place privately as opposed to publicly.	That learning is a public, communal, dialogical, and dialectical endeavor that is done in collaboration with others and that no learning is autodidactic.
If students have no questions it is probably because we as teachers did such a good job banking that they understand what they are learning.	If students have no questions they are probably not learning. All reasoning requires dialogical reasoning, which in turn requires Socratic questioning.
An educated person in today's society is a repository of facts and details; the *Jeopardy* contestant or whiz kid of the 1950s. Essentially educated people are people who have stored a lot of information.	An educated or literate person in today's society is not a *Jeopardy* contestant or repository of content, but is a person who can reason or come to well-founded conclusions based on reasoning. This requires a new notion of what it means to be educated as we seek to help students develop insights and principles and strategies of thinking.

model of teaching and learning. Weil (1996) differentiates between these two teaching models as illustrated in Table 3. As is evident, in comparing and contrasting these two modes of education, critical teaching has the potential to transform students through connecting their individual and collective experience to broader social issues relevant to their lives. Critical teaching can create meaningful and authentic learning experiences that are powerful and energizing for students.

Conclusion

Service-learning, as a philosophy, approach and method that connects students in real and authentic ways to their families and communities, holds the promise and potential to transform schools into arenas that encourage and enable students' critical thinking skills. For this to occur, however, several things are necessary. First, teachers and students alike will have to assume new roles. It is imperative that teachers view themselves as facilitators of learning, orchestrating meaningful learning experiences for students and that they welcome and encourage students' questioning and search for truth. Students, likewise, need to be open to new experiences and willingly engage in processes of reflection that challenge and call into question the very basis of their belief systems. Second, the process of reflection that accompanies service-learning activities needs to be carefully thought out and structured so that students engage in reflective judgment (as opposed to reflective observation) and/or reflective action if they are to learn and benefit from the service-learning experience.

References

Alliance for Service-Learning in Education Reform. (1995). *Standards for School-Based and Community-Based Service-Learning Programs*. Alexandria, VA: The Close-Up Foundation.

Apple, M. and Beane, J. (Eds.). (1995). *Democratic Schools*. Washington, DC: ASCD.

Bigelow, B., Christensen, L., Karp, S., Miner, B., and Peterson, B. (1994). *Rethinking Our Classrooms: Teaching for Equity and Justice*. Milwaukee, WI: Rethinking Schools, Ltd.

Billig, S. H. and Kraft, N. P. (1997). *Linking IASA (Improving America's Schools Act Program) and Service-Learning: Planning, Implementation, and Evaluation Guide*, Denver, CO: RMC Research Corporation.

Brookfield, S. D. (1987). *Developing Critical Thinkers: Challenging Adults to Explore Alternative Ways of Thinking and Acting*, San Francisco, CA: Jossey-Bass Publishers.

Cummins, J. and Sayers, D. (1995). *Brave New Schools: Challenging Cultural Illiteracy Through Global Learning. Networks*, New York: St. Martin's Press

Diamond, M. (1995, July/September). The significance of enrichment. *The In Report*.

Eyler, J., Dwight, E. G. Jr., and Schmiede, A. (1996). *A Practitioner's Guide to Reflection in Service-Learning: Student Voices & Reflection*, Nashville, TN: Vanderbilt University.

Freire, P. and Macedo, D. (1987). *Literacy: Reading the Word and the World*, South Hadley, MA: Bergin & Garvey.

Freire, P. (1970). *Pedagogy of the Oppressed*. New York: Seabury.

Kahne, J. and Westheimer, J. (1996). *"In the Service of What? The Politics of Service-Learning," Phi Delta Kappan*, 77(9), 593–599.

Kohn, A. (1996). *Beyond Discipline: From Compliance to Community*. Alexandria, VA: ASCD.

Kolb, D. A. (1984). *Experiential Learning: Experience as the Source of Learning and Development*. Englewood Cliffs, NJ: Prentice-Hall.

McPherson, K. (1989). *Service-Learning Concept Paper (draft)*. Unpublished paper. 2034 N.E., 104th, Seattle, WA.

Meyers, C. (1986). *Teaching Students to Think Critically: A Guide for Faculty in All Disciplines*. San Francisco: Jossey-Bass, 1986.

Shor, I. (1992). *Empowering Education: Critical Teaching for Social Change*, Chicago, IL: The University of Chicago Press.

Weil, D. (1996). *Two Contrasting Theories of Learning: The Banking Assumption and the Critical Assumption,* Guadalupe, CA: The Critical Thinking Institute.

Inviting Youth into Civic Action

Jenice L. View

ABSTRACT

We are all too familiar with images of disaffected, angry, or passive youth. Anguished adults ask: "What does it take to get young people involved in our civic culture? At what age are young people likely to become involved in civic action?[1] How do the theories for linking classroom education to civic action work in practice?" A recent research and demonstration project in a Washington, DC public school suggests that middle school students welcome difficult social studies material and, in an environment of adult power-sharing, can transform this understanding into civic action of their own design. In particular, the nine African American girls that actively participated in the afterschool program transformed historical and current information into civic leadership through engagement with a critical teaching process. Most telling was the conclusion that an environment of mutual respect seemed more important than curriculum and the instructor's teaching experience in mobilizing student action.

Summary

The research question posed by this study was:

> Does a critical method of teaching history to middle school students affect their desire and improve their ability to apply historical lessons to contemporary civic challenges?

The goal of this exploratory study was not to demonstrate causality but to observe and, perhaps to discover connections among the variables that would permit a conditional response.[2] This question was particularly interesting given the stated intentions of critical pedagogy theory to (a) change teaching practice, improve student learning, and overcome social inequities, and (b) the typical resistance by schools to making classrooms into social change laboratories. In short, my goal was to help middle school students find meaning in their academic work that was neither pegged to some abstract promise of a better future, nor divorced from their current social, political, and economic realities. Instead, I hoped to facilitate (without being directive) a conscious connection between information and action that allowed student creativity to blossom.

The four assumptions underlying the research question were that:

- adults are responsible for the successful outcomes of students;
- the "best" education is that which promotes an understanding of social injustice and which invites students to promote equity and to remedy injustices;
- middle school students can be effective agents in their own learning process in such a way that leads them to social action regardless of their race, ethnicity, class, gender, or prior school performance; and
- the learning of a specific history—taught in a particular manner— would produce ideas (if not action) generated by students for transforming existing conditions.

From January to June 1996, I served as researcher/instructor[3] of the Takoma History and Civic Action Project (THCAP), an afterschool program for students in grades 6–8. Using an original curriculum and a variety of instructional methods, which included cooperative learning, Socratic seminar, Small Group Activity Method, and experiential learning, I worked with thirty-one students. Two of the participating students were Latina, two were Caribbean American and the rest were African American, and there was nearly an equal number of boys and girls initially. Meeting three afternoons per week for two hours each session, students studied current events and the history of their families, school, community, and city, applying these lessons to local concerns. Throughout the semester, students engaged in a variety of hands-on learning experiences including oral history interviews, field trips, and background research for public presentations. The last four weeks of the semester, students were charged with the task of designing and executing their own civic action project.

By the end of the semester, the nine most active participants were African American girls, with a secondary group of ten to twelve students including five boys, two of whom were Caribbean American, and one Latina who participated in many of the THCAP activities.

One research observation suggests that students with a greater sense of personal power and a predisposition to civic action are more likely to avail themselves of opportunities to act than students who feel more helpless. However, this evidence does not support the stereotype that only "smart," or "middle-class," or "politically aware" students seek or exercise such opportunities. The students with good grades in THCAP were not always the best leaders if they lacked strong interpersonal skills. The more affluent students were not always more exposed to or aware of civic information if they were also sheltered from the grittier aspects of urban living. For some students, hands-on learning proved unfamiliar and scary. A student's success in the program—evidenced by active involvement, leadership, and follow-through—did not seem linked to family education, socioeconomic level, or preferred learning style. In fact, students who might be typecast as less likely to join such a program—students with academic, literacy, language, and social difficulties—often were the leaders among their peers.

The first step toward youth civic action, then, seems to be the willingness of adults to give youth an inch. Adults tend to chastise young people for not caring about their communities or to direct them to participate in community service because it is "good for them." Perhaps, instead, when we allow them to practice citizenship in a real-world context, they become active citizens. For individual teachers who seek to link schooling and student activism, there are never enough examples of *how* to put theory into practice, nor enough analyses of the outcomes of student civic action. This article documents such an applied research effort. The first part of the article presents the research observations, including the eight factors that seemed to have bearing on student outcomes. This is followed by the theoretical context for the work. The final section suggests the implications of this research on teaching practice.

Research Observations[4]

The core group of nine African American girls provide the bulk of the evidence for this study, although observations of the secondary group of ten to twelve students, and of the ten peripheral students also inform the results.

The factors that seemed to have the most bearing on student desire and ability to apply historical lessons to contemporary civic challenges were: their sense and expression of personal power; the extent to which I shared power with students; student predisposition to action; and student perceptions of a sense of community within and outside of THCAP. Factors that seemed to have lesser or inconclusive import were: the involvement of parents and school adults; the external rewards of participating in the THCAP; my level of skill; and the historical and civics subject matter.

The pledge which governed the program from the initial weeks was as follows:

- We are individuals with a purpose—We are working to improve ourselves, our school, and our community using our intelligence and creativity. We know that we are strong enough and smart enough to make a difference.
- We are committed to working together—We know that there is strength in numbers and that each of us brings unique talents to this effort. We will honor what is special in each of us.
- We are able to work through our differences in a non-violent way— We know that any time two or more people get together, there can be disagreements. We are creative enough and mature enough to express anger non-violently and solve our differences.[5]

Each session opened with snacks, informal conversation, inspirational music, and a review of the day's goals. Over the course of the semester, students took five field trips, interviewed eight visitors, received introductory training in certain skills, and made four public presentations based on what they learned through small and large group projects. The Project also received financial support (totaling $80) from the local grocery store and from some of the parents to defray the cost of snacks. Most program costs, such as art supplies and photocopying, came out of pocket. Highlights of the program included:

- *Registering 19 high school seniors to vote;* Learning and practicing some of *the basic skills of public speaking* from a past president of a local Toastmasters club;
- *Researching the history of Takoma School*, drafting a list of school problems and potential solutions, and preparing an oral presenta-

tion at a PTA meeting, including display boards of Takoma's Past, Present and Future;

- *Testifying at a public hearing* about the conditions of the school and the need for more school funding;

- Attending a press conference and then visiting the inner *offices of the Congressional representative* followed by visits to the House and Senate galleries;
- Conducting a *community mapping tour* to document community boundaries, businesses, organizations, problems, and resources.
- Visiting *the office of the community newspaper* and learning the basics of reporting, advertising, layout, and paste-up;
- *Interviewing a city council member* about the state of the city;
- *Interviewing a public affairs radio talk show host* about media and the city;
- Engaging in a discussion with a panel of long-time teachers and community leaders about *the history of citizen activism in the Takoma community;* and
- *Meeting with organizers for Stand for Children*, the national mobilization for children's issues sponsored by the Children's Defense Fund.

The final student project consisted of a week-long afterschool goodie sale that generated $246. Students used over half of the money to purchase six books for the school library and four heavy-duty brooms for the custodial staff. I used the remaining funds to subsidize an end-of-the-year outing and to purchase gift books as merit awards for the students who worked on the final project. All participating students received a certificate of appreciation at the end of the school year.

The evidence that supports the research conclusions emerged largely from eight major categories of observation during the six months of the program. Listed in order of importance, these categories are:

- Personal power;
- Power-sharing with students;
- Student predisposition to action;
- Sense of community:
- Adult involvement;
- Rewards;

- Instructor skill; and
- Subject matter.

Personal Power

Students demonstrated their sense of personal power by openly reflecting on the consequences of their actions, by taking risks, and by taking initiative in the context of feeling safe and autonomous. In particular, safety from physical harm and from humiliation were essential to taking actions and generating ideas.[6] The two domains in which students expressed personal power were within the confines of the afterschool program and in "public" spaces.

Personal Power Within the Afterschool Program

Several factors affected students' sense of personal power in this domain: safety, risk-taking, interpersonal skill, and reflection.

Safety. Feelings of safety took many forms. In the initial weeks of the program, the ending time of the program (5:30 p.m.) was a barrier to full participation for those students traveling home long distances in the dark, and an asset for students who needed to wait afterschool for an adult escort home. The program was a place for some students to avoid specific afterschool conflicts and/or general boredom.[7] One student seemed to suffer from clinical hunger and used the program as a way to get fed. Five sibling pairs participated in the program largely because younger siblings (grades K to 5) had fewer afterschool outlets; family tensions that spilled over into the sessions created less emotional safety for the older sibling, but overall the older siblings were able to temporarily transfer responsibility for their youngers to the instructor. During field trips, students would stay close enough to me to ask questions or hear instructions or commentary (maintaining physical safety), but would often be slightly removed, having formed affinity groups of two or three (maintaining emotional safety). When the field trips required auto transportation, some students received strict instructions from their parents to ride only in my car.

Risk-taking. Tied closely to safety is the ability or willingness of students to take risks. Several times throughout the program, students said, "Okay, I'll try it" whether the "it" was public speaking, working in teams with unfamiliar students, or interviewing long-time teachers. Students who were more likely to take calculated risks were more likely to stay with the program. They were also more likely to express personal power.[8]

Interpersonal skill. The challenges to student cooperation ranged from the benign (welcoming new members to the group) to the significant (budding romances) to the hysterical (high-strung emotions; long-standing animosities). Respect for self, for each other, and for authority was a recurring theme for students.[9] Students with highly developed interpersonal skills were able to navigate or diffuse conflicts, and to galvanize the ideas and efforts of others.[10] For example, one student floated easily among the various cliques within the large group and while quick to identify injustices, was also quick to offer solutions, and to mediate disputes.

Reflection. Early in the program, students called for more discipline of other students and for rules. This call was countered with appeals to self-discipline. Without the usual devices for motivating students—such as grades and disciplinary action—I encouraged students to develop their own code of behavior (see the Pledge on page 98). The degree to which students were able to think before acting seemed to be a partial determinant of the frequency of rule-breaking.[11]

Personal Power in the "Public" Sphere

The "public" sphere was any place outside of the afterschool classroom where students were likely to encounter adults or older students. This arena was an important laboratory for student personal power because there were no pre-conceived expectations that the middle school students had worthy ideas or merited a hearing by these adults and high schoolers. Success in negotiating the public sphere seemed a good indicator of the students' ability to create effective civic action. Traits such as initiative and autonomy were manifestations of personal power in the public sphere.

Initiative. Students who volunteered to extend assignments in new directions were more likely to influence task outcomes. These students overcame expressed fears to address older people outside of the program. In one case, a female student who said she did not have any experience with public speaking, offered to give the introduction when students made a major PTA presentation. A Latina, she incorporated into her remarks concerns about the school's multicultural population that other students had overlooked.

During the community mapping walking tour, students began to run toward an open-air fire in the high school field. A male passerby discouraged them, saying that they might be falsely accused of starting the fire. Rethinking their actions, three students approached neighborhood adults, asking them to call 911. One student offered his name, "in case the police need a witness." In addition to being an assertion of personal power in the public sphere, these actions suggested that the purpose of the walking tour—to identify, to identify with, and to take responsibility for the whole community—resonated for students in that moment.

A third example of personal power occurred during the voter registration activity. Initially, THCAP students expressed tremendous fear about speaking before two 12th grade government classes, even though they agreed with the concept. Reading from a fact sheet on voter registration that I created and that was revised by THCAP students, they took turns making arguments for registering. As fellow public school students with the ability to exercise their franchise, the high school students watched a short video and were pressed by THCAP students to complete registration forms; nineteen students complied. However, the personal power of THCAP students was revealed more forcefully during the class discussion period when the middle schoolers corrected some of the misconceptions about voting and registering expressed by the seniors. And during the lunch period, THCAP students took the initiative to distribute fact sheets and registration cards throughout the cafeteria, and to urge high schoolers to register. They were unsuccessful in securing any additional registrants, but expressed annoyance with the high schoolers (many of whom threw away the flyers) rather than attributing any fault to themselves. Initially intimidated, the THCAP students were cocksure by the end of the day.

Autonomy. Free of classroom confines and heavy administrative oversight, students felt greater flexibility and creativity in their efforts. Students often said, "Hey, we can . . .!", contrasting the afterschool program with attempts within the regular classroom to test the same ideas. One example was the fierce passion of two aspiring journalists, one male and one female, to create a school newspaper. They complained that one of the teachers, a former professional journalist, refused to help them with the idea. When I approached the teacher with the idea, he insisted that student writing skill needed improvement and there needed to be more institutional (financial) support available before he would consider such an undertaking. Following the THCAP field trip to the Takoma Voice community newspaper, the two students and five others worked hard to organize themselves into a reporting team. The effort did not get off the ground, largely due to leadership battles between the male and female student and to inconsistent attendance. However, students were permitted ample room to debate and experiment with the idea.

Power-Sharing with Students

The two domains in which I tried to consciously share power with students were interpersonally, and programmatically. In both domains, the

greater the frequency, the consistency, the duration, and the formality of the power-sharing "episodes," the more positively students responded.
Interpersonal Power-Sharing. At the outset, students were invited to propose ideas for disciplining themselves using the pledge; apportioning snacks; and forming small work groups. The only values that I insisted on were non-violence and cooperation.[12] Within the boundaries of the pledge, students stretched themselves to assume command of the program. Most who stepped over the bounds of propriety were simply asked, by other students or me, to refocus on the pledge. Three students (two female, and one male) who committed gross disruptions such as petty crime and blatant disrespect were asked to leave the program immediately. Two male students were asked to leave after demonstrating consistent lack of self-control, long after other female students had urged me to do so.[13]

My interaction with students was self-consciously open.[14] To emphasize the voluntary nature of participation, students were not penalized for missing sessions or assignments, even if this posture risked conveying indifference. Instead, I asked peers to state how an absence or failed commitment affected group work and urged students to take responsibility for group outcomes. Parents who were strict disciplinarians expressed concern that I "let those kids talk to [me] that way," because students were free to (respectfully) challenge adult authority.[15] The ever-changing room set-up permitted easy movement, the creation of large circles and small group working areas, and the sense that the space "belonged" to everyone. The conscious use of body language evolved more slowly: I became aware that students were less attentive when I sat in a circle with students than when I stood up—to the point of raising hands to ask questions rather than blurting them out. However, "power postures" were used sparingly, again to permit students freedom of movement.

One observation of interpersonal power-sharing was surprising. The typecasting of students prevented some of them from exercising leadership when given the opportunity to do so. "Good" (or, cooperative) girls seemed constrained by their habits of obedience to authority,[16] and "bad" (or, boisterous) boys seemed equally flustered by the open reception to their energy.[17] In each case, students seemed frustrated that the student-centered environment forced them to direct their actions toward one another rather than toward me. For example, one girl widely considered by peers and school adults as a bright and cooperative student, expressed exciting ideas but consistently resisted working in small groups where she had to defend her ideas. This student stayed in the program until the middle of the planning period for the final project. When asked why she left, she stated that it was too hard to work with the other students.

Programmatic Power-Sharing. Throughout the program, I was challenged with the question of whether there is a developmentally appropriate critical approach for teaching history and civics wherein the practice is congruent with the theories.[18] What is the right balance between abstract concepts and concrete applications? A teacher with clever props and fun activities can say to middle school students, "This is the way it is/was; isn't that interesting?" and be considered a talented teacher. However, asking middle school students, "What do you think? What would you *do* about it?" creates the stress of confronting wild ideas, fierce impatience, and poorly developed skills.

The theoretical and practical tension between "teaching as community organizing,[19]" and "teaching as discovery,"[20] plagued me. There was the temptation to create early opportunities for a small, winnable action to emphasize the message of education linked to action. I resisted, partly because overt organizing seemed contradictory to the notion of students taking action on their own. Yet, students kept asking, "What is this for?. . . Well then, let's . . ."

Students constantly presented and debated ideas about program direction and content—the words "Can we . . .?", "Why can't we?", "We should do . . ." filled the room most days. The students and I fed off of the excitement and carefully considered all options. The civic action portion of the program sparked more creativity than the historical work, but even there, students learned to question their elders about why they made certain decisions or took certain actions that affect current reality.

Other program areas were not so easily ceded. At the outset, I insisted on healthy snacks and music with "positive" lyrics (hopeful messages with no bigotry or gratuitous cursing). These requirements were value judgments about "what's good for children."[21] Students exercised critical thinking skills by challenging these values, and were invited to bring their own snacks and music if they seriously objected to my offerings. On four occasions, students brought music and I typed up the lyrics to share. Many days students brought their own snacks. On the whole students agreed with these requirements (for example, students often stated that snacks were better than the school hot lunch), but they were not initially arrived at by consensus. This breach of the power-sharing ethic seemed defensible in light of expressed parental approval and my own personal values as a program participant and role model.

Overlapping of Interpersonal and Programmatic Power-Sharing

In most instances, interpersonal and programmatic power-sharing issues overlapped. For example, it was difficult for students to work cooperatively in small groups with unfamiliar students or those with whom there was bad history. Activities were sometimes stalled until students could work through wariness and tension. Another specific example of students' emotional sensitivity were the many comments about the "meanness" of other teachers who were "unwilling" to help with student-initiated projects and clubs.

However, there were several instances when the overlap offered golden "teachable moments": (1) while practicing oral history questions, one student asked me what Washington, D.C. had been like when Dr. King was assassinated. It was a good example of an open-ended question, but more importantly, permitted me to reveal something about myself and to discuss a subject that few adults seemed eager to share with students; (2) while mediating a dispute between two students, I mentioned that similar adult conflicts might be at the root of some of their concerns about school resources; (3) A dispute about snacks became an object lesson in democracy, resource allocation, and shared decision-making, regarding the city budget; and (4) in the community mapping exercise, students walked past their own homes and were able to place themselves in the context of the overall community and to discuss "their" section of the community with authority. In addition, the group stopped by my home to use the bathroom, and gained personal insight to my "place" within the community.[22]

The final student project was the richest example of how interpersonal and programmatic power-sharing issues dovetailed. The objective of the final project was to transform all that had been learned about the history of the city and community, and the vehicles for expressing civic action, into a student response to a community or city problem. The students had three to four weeks to plan and execute their project. It took a while to convince students that they were free to experiment and exercise their creativity as far as it would go.

The first decision concerned the nature of the final project. The possibilities included conducting a large-scale survey of D.C. schools; starting a school garden; building a model of the old and new Takoma School; holding fundraisers for school and city budgets and for THCAP; creating a special event for the annual International Week activities; starting a school newspaper with subscription fees to raise money for THCAP;

organizing a Ward 4 block party for the national Stand for Children mobilization (organized by the Children's Defense Fund); creating 20th anniversary activities for the "new" Takoma School; creating 95th anniversary activities for the school; and conducting voter educational activities for the November municipal elections.

Most of these ideas, with the exception of the anniversary and voter education ideas, originated from students. Stand for Children organizers approached THCAP just as students were beginning to consider a final project and proposed the block party, even offering to assume all of the financial costs of a band/disc jockey, food, publicity, etc.

I asked students to consider what resources were available to them, whom they had met over the course of the semester, and who could help them with the project. The list of resources included: themselves, their families, the nearby high school students, the community newspaper, a public affairs radio programmer, the offices of city council members, the congressional delegate, and teachers and community representatives who had served on the history panel. Students then considered the list of community concerns they generated earlier in the semester, which included environmental/facilities concerns (roaches, holes in walls, condition of bathrooms; and water fountains/water pressure); educational programs (lack of dedicated gym teacher, lack of media teacher, lack of art teacher, no access to the Internet, and better computers with CD-ROM capability); and other issues (quality of school lunches; insufficient games, lack of fun days and club days; and lack of student discipline). Finally, students examined the top three concerns expressed by the Takoma middle students who completed the pre-program questionnaire. They were interpersonal problems, environmental problems around the school and community, and community violence and crime.

After reviewing and discussing each of the options, students voted to plan and hold three fundraisers: a two-week-long, afterschool goodie sale; a car wash in conjunction with the annual Spring Spruce-up; and milk sales in conjunction with the principal's initiative to sell fresh-baked cookies afterschool. Their plan was to raise enough money to correct the environmental and facilities problems within the school.

Initially, I was disappointed and shocked. I pointed out that the financial costs of meeting school and community needs exceeded the proceeds of most bake sales. I reminded students that their and their parents' tax dollars are supposed to pay for school supplies, librarians, photocopy machines, and disinfectant. I suggested that three fundraisers, especially falling in the middle of the citywide testing period, might be overwhelming. I reminded students that the full responsibility for executing the final project would be theirs. Among my expectations was a notion that students would be motivated toward a more "political" activity such as the voter registration activity, or the Stand for Children idea, given their expressions of frustration through the semester on various issues, or at least toward an activity with some longevity such as a school garden or newspaper.

Once I relented, there were struggles about the duration of the goodie sale (the principal intervened and restricted the sale to one week); who should do what work; who should count the money at the end of each day; how to reinvest the daily profits; who should purchase replenishment goods for the sale (some students believed that I should do the bulk of the shopping rather than their parents or themselves); and how to use the final proceeds. The car wash and milk sales teams abandoned their plans at the last minute, provoking a struggle about whether those students should benefit from the year-end fun day that was intended to reward hard work. Apart from mediating these conflicts, I conducted agonizing internal debates concerning desired research outcomes, my role as an adult authority figure, and the impact of the program on my family and personal health. It was also during this period that one of the ugliest instructor-student conflicts occurred concerning money handling and the challenging of authority. This ended with a slashed tire on my car, which created a keen awareness of my status as a role model. In short, power-sharing with middle school students required stamina and mutual trust.

Student Predisposition to Action
Over the course of the semester, countless students asked hopefully whether the program would be offered the next school year. The students who were most likely to *join* the program were those already involved in several extracurricular activities, and to a lesser extent those who expressed some degree of civic/political awareness.[23] Students who *stayed* in the program were those looking for a way to make a difference—either due to dissatisfaction with the status quo or unspent creativity.[24] The difference between the joiners and the stayers was the degree to which students were willing to take initiative to solve problems and to work *inter*dependently.

As one male student stated emphatically, "I don't come here for the snacks [but to make a difference in my community]!" However, an inclination to take action did not necessarily indicate an ability to do so. As young adolescents, the students temporarily forgot the civic purpose of the fundraiser when considering how much fun $250 would purchase at the indoor amusement park. Additionally, some of the more mature students found it difficult to share their ideas and wisdom because they lacked the skills to engage and offer leadership to the more disruptive students.

What limited civic/political awareness students expressed seemed to be gained primarily through their parents and the mass media rather than through regular schoolwork. Despite their active extracurricular schedules, discussions with students indicated that they rarely ventured far beyond the immediate community. When asked during the semester whether the adults in their lives were concerned about the public chaos governing the school and city budgets, students stated that their parents' employment with the local and federal government was a barrier to social protest. Without significant personal experience, students reflected the skepticism of their elders regarding the attentiveness or responsiveness of elected officials, including in-school PTA officers. Nevertheless, students who stayed with the program maintained a belief in their ability to act positively.

One notable inclination was students' avoidance of loud, public, televised work as the only important political work. For example, their pointed rejection of the Stand for Children block party as their final project reflected ego (they stated that Stand was not "theirs"), but more importantly indicated a valuing of more quiet community actions and activities that were closer to home.

This outcome merits an important aside, however. Banks (1973) states that the primary purpose of social action projects should be to provide students with opportunities to develop political efficacy rather than to provide community services, a perspective that is consistent with my own stated biases. In fact, I hoped that THCAP students would be inspired to "loud" action (though, perhaps, on a smaller scale than Stand for Children or the 24-hour street protest by students at the University of the District of Columbia) as a valid tactic toward improving D.C. public schools and public safety.

Yet, I was strongly ambivalent about the Stand for Children proposal on at least three counts. I have an *emotional* preference for "loud, public, televised" political work, having come of age after the radical romanticism of the 1960's. In addition, the liberation of African Americans always has been fueled by justifiable outrage at injustices, and victories have *always* included a combination of protest and behind-the-scenes tactics. However, I have developed an *intellectual* preference for "quiet community action" due to a cynicism that the apparent abundance of protest tactics comes at the expense of well-considered long-term strategies. In addition, there is a widespread belief that "quiet community action" is tame and ineffectual. This is an unfair analysis, I believe, because it denigrates the work of seniors, parents of small children, people with disabilities, the homeless, and any other people who are unable, for whatever reasons, to lead or participate in mass mobilizations. Finally, I invited the Stand for Children organizers to speak to THCAP students in the hopes that students would welcome an "easy out"—they could organize a civic action project that was connected with other students citywide and with a national effort using the financial resources of another organization. Such a decision would also appeal to emotional preferences, a sense of financial efficiency, and my personal weariness near the end of the program. I fought these three competing impulses during the discussion of options and was surprised that only three students voted to hold a Stand for Children block party. This is surely a case where conflicting subconscious cues may have influenced student decisions and outcomes.

Sense of Community
Students developed a sense of community through their observations of other students, through discourse with students, and through collective work and responsibility. For some students, peer support, in the form of special friendships, was essential to their continued involvement in the program.[25] Fourteen of the thirty-one students joined the program at the urging of peers, six of whom came consistently, and four of whom came even after their friend stopped coming. But, for the most active participants, their observations of the attendance and mutual concern of other students were the most important factors for creating a sense of community. When students perceived others as not caring enough about the people or the activities in the program, they withdrew either temporarily or permanently.

As an afterschool program, THCAP competed with cheerleading, sports, music, and "hanging out."[26] Students were free to come and go, even if their parents assumed they were enrolled in THCAP for three days a week. Unpredictable attendance wreaked havoc on small group working teams because it created a lack of consistency and continuity. This became a particular problem with the arrival of spring weather. Students measured the commitment and decision-making authority of one another by the consistency of their attendance.

Other factors emerged as measures of mutual concern. One of the most striking factors for defining community were the snacks, offered at the beginning of each session. Food took on the role of conveyer (students would rush from their final class to get first in line for snacks); comforter (one female student in particular seemed to suffer from clinical hunger); organizing catalyst (several students declared the snacks to be better than school lunches); attention-getter (some of the boys used the food as toy weapons); control mechanism (in the form of snack hoarding); and task organizer (students jockeyed to help prepare snacks). Interestingly, while the students fiercely debated the food at every available opportunity and refused to share food with friends who were not enrolled in the program, there was one notable exception. Not a single student commented on the behavior of the one girl who would leave the group at 4:15 after the snacks were consumed, and who rarely participated in group activities. Asked why, students shrugged and gave vague answers. It is not clear why their sense of community extended to this girl, since her closest friend in the program attended sporadically and would have been unable to defend her friend's behavior if challenged.

The music used at the beginning of each session was another community focal point. As an instructional matter, I preferred to distribute and discuss lyrics prior to playing the music. Students rarely brought in their own selections because they were faced with the challenge of translation from Spanish or with the admitted lack of positive lyrics in their favorite songs. Students teased me about "those old" or "weird" songs, but seemed to appreciate the discussion of the lyrics and usually liked the type and range of music.

The African American students seemed unwilling to learn any Spanish beyond curse words and expressed annoyance when the Latina students held side conversations in Spanish. One Latina was very shy about speaking English although her written fluency was better than some of the African-American students. Over time, she developed more confidence and volunteered to speak publicly on two occasions. Other students were supportive of her efforts, but she was challenged by the other Latina student who expressed a greater need for ethnic solidarity. Eventually, both Latina students left the program for afterschool sports. While I openly lamented the loss of these girls, few of the remaining students shared the loss, expressing indifference or a preference for a homogeneous group.

Students freely discussed their religious affiliations, often referring to biblical passages in discussions of personal behavior, punishment for transgressions, and the call to action and charity. The most active THCAP students were also involved in religious activities such as choirs, home visits, youth groups, etc. as documented by discussions with students and by the pre-program questionnaire. I perceived no evidence of religious bigotry since most students seemed to be Christian, non-affiliated, or indifferent. However, among the most active students, there were many expressions of Christian morality.

Finally, though not insignificantly, the gender composition of the group on a given day determined students' sense of community.[27] The physical energy levels and sexual tension spiked when there were more than three boys present. Both sexes expressed discomfort when the numerical balance tipped in favor of the other sex, with the boys sometimes refusing to join the group on an afternoon when feeling outnumbered. The assumption of leadership in small groups was more fiercely debated in mixed groups: in all-girl groups, seniority and consistent attendance tended to determine leadership; in all-boy groups, leadership was determined by whoever expressed more creativity or initiative on a given day. In general, girls were more likely to stick with a task than the boys, building a track record of accomplishments that fed an overall sense of community.[28] No boys remained in the program at the time of the final project. Some of the observed and stated reasons included: boring subject matter, preference for outdoor activity (including sports and hanging out), a sense that the proposed civic actions were too tame, and a sense that the girls in the program were "taking over." Here again, the remaining students expressed a preference for an all-girl group, even though I expressed a loss of diversity.

Adult Involvement
The greater the adult involvement, the more consistent was student involvement.[29] In some cases, the adult was "remote" from the program, but had nevertheless conveyed to the student an interest in the subject matter, the student's engagement/enjoyment with the program, or a generic interest in productive afterschool activity for the student. In general, the closer the adult was to the program, the more the adult expressed an additional concern for my personal well-being and for program outcomes.

Parental Involvement
Some of the parents did not seem to know where their children were after school, but even these parents shared a primordial concern for their children's safety; they often expressed appreciation when I insisted on signed permission slips or telephone permission to participate in field trips. At the other extreme were two parents who admitted to "forcing" their children to join program. In the middle were those who were aware,

and generally supportive, of program activities. For the most part, these parents also expressed gratitude when I shared concerns about students as a matter of accountability.

Parents were grateful that the program was free of charge. Those who became aware that I assumed most program costs made in-kind donations of money, transportation, and food. Other programmatic support included assistance with preparing testimony for a public hearing, and an expressed commitment by one parent to revise her cynical attitudes toward the school administration (shared openly with her daughter) in light of THCAP'S civic action goals. Parents expressed moral support in several ways. One father made his son write a four-page essay on behavior and responsibility, following a discussion about the student's ambivalent attendance and his "high-spiritedness." As mentioned earlier, some parents expressed concern that I was not strict enough with students. Usually, parents simply thanked me.[30]

In-School Support. Three of the school's teachers expressed interest in the program from the very beginning and encouraged students to participate. Other teachers were eager to share the history of the school and community through oral history interviews and a panel discussion. However, most teachers were oblivious to the program. The most consistent support came from the principal and assistant principal. Some students credit the principal with actively encouraging their participation, although he denied handpicking any participants. In addition, he attended many of the guest lectures, approved all field trips, and intervened in crisis situations upon request. The assistant principal, himself a Ph.D., was supportive of the research aspects of the program.

Community Support. In addition to a $50 contribution from local grocery food store, other community organizations expressed enthusiasm for the program and issued invitations for continued interaction. For example, the community newspaper invited students to submit articles for a fee of six cents per word and offered to promote any community activities generated by students. The public affairs radio programmer invited students to the studio and welcomed ideas for a show.

Rewards

Fair and frequent external rewards, while important to the most active students, were not as important as the internal rewards of feeling smart, feeling proud of accomplishments, and having the ability to entertain one's self.[31]

Again, on a given day, students measured the benefits of program participation by considering the weather, competing afterschool activities (including the fun of doing "nothing"), and the fairness of resource allocation such as the snacks, or the time and attention of the researcher/instructor. In addition, the types of external rewards mattered, ranging from being allowed to speak first or helping prepare snacks, to going on field trips. The most "valuable" field trips were those taking place during the regular school day, generating high participation levels. Some students referred to the program as a "club"—a semantic difference that changed the nature of student involvement. Two of the boys said, independent of one another, "This is the only place where I can cut up," emphasizing the extent to which their lives were programmed with other enrichment activities.

One potential female participant, surveying the multipurpose room, asked me if the program was "just for the smart kids?"—a chilling reminder of how even informal tracking systems become internalized in young students. Despite the strong academic ambitions demonstrated by many participants, such as doing homework during sessions or missing sessions due to volume of homework, participating in an evening Higher Achievement Program, and competing in spelling bees, science fairs, poster contests, there were also students who seemed indifferent to academics, including at least one participant who seemed to have serious literacy problems. Rather, students were rewarded for creativity and leadership, hardly the monopoly of the "smart kids" who were often more conformist.[32]

Interestingly, contrary to the bulk of research on African American achievement motivation, in nearly every instance when students were asked to produce original work—for example, the voter registration drive, the final fundraising project, and the PTA presentation—the students ranked these activities as their favorites.[33]

Instructor Skill
The attributes and skills that would be most useful to an instructor in a program such as THCAP include being well-trained in instructional methods, competency in the subject matter areas, and having a high degree of flexibility, humor, intellect, and perceptivity.[34] As stated earlier, I had no formal training from an accredited teacher education program and the work of the THCAP served as a proxy for a self-reflective student practicum. A high degree of flexibility and a high degree of experiential training with adults and young people at the elementary, high school, and college levels compensated for a low level of formal theoretical training and midrange confidence. A belief in the critical teaching process and my affection and concern for students helped to carry me through.[35]

From the beginning, I tried to keep abreast of changes in students' lives and respond appropriately, such as the accidental street shooting of one student's father, report cards, awards, suspensions, tensions at home and school, romances, and health problems.[36] But, my inexperience showed, especially in the area of classroom management.

Further, it was difficult to manage the distinction between my role as researcher and as a "freestanding" program coordinator. One example was in the desire for male participation to maintain a "balanced" sample, even when the boys clearly had more trouble adhering to the terms of the pledge. Although I expressed far more tolerance for boisterous "male" behavior than did the female students, this bias probably interfered with my judgment. The role confusion was compounded by the fact that my own children occasionally participated in program activities, due to child care difficulties.

It is not certain the extent to which these factors were serious barriers to program effectiveness. In his evaluation, the principal stated that had I been a stronger disciplinarian, I would have had both more control *and* more flexibility. Yet, he also stated that students were "empowered" by the program. It is very likely that more classroom experience would have helped me find a better balance, despite any fundamental contradictions (theoretical and practical) between adult control and middle school student empowerment.

Subject Matter Content
The ostensible subject matter—civic action in the context of a critical examination of history—initially appealed to students with a predisposition to action, and to those with intellectual curiosity about history and civics. Over time, other students expressed interest—either by joining the group or by consistently inquiring—because they saw participants *doing interesting things* "despite" the subject.[37] Students who saw no apparent connection between the program's intent and the issues that concerned them most (meeting basic human needs, ethnic identity, personal freedom, street violence, family conflicts, etc.) said so, and eventually left the program. Each departure disappointed my desire to create and sustain a "relevant" civic action intervention, however each departure was counterbalanced by yet another student inquiry to join the program. An analysis of which students were most attracted to the program (based on interest in the subject matter) and which students stayed (based on subject matter relevance) was beyond the scope of the methodology used here, and bears much more examination.

One student stated, "[The program is] not as boring when we have projects to do," referring largely to my difficulty in making history less abstract. Injected throughout the curriculum and triggered by discussions of current events, the program's history component was more covert. For example, students taught the school's history to one another through the planning and preparation of the PTA presentation on *Takoma Past, Present and Future*. By examining old photos, studying a school and community timeline, interviewing long-term teachers and community activists, writing drafts of their reports, and reading them aloud, students actively discussed school history with very little "instruction" from me. A common question throughout all civics discussions was, "How did we get into this situation?" leading to historical research.[38]

Similarly, students learned about economics indirectly. For example, the endless discussions of fair resource allocation was paralleled with proposed city budget cuts and tax expenditures. The field trip to Capitol Hill on April 15 (Tax Day) coincided with a press conference on tax relief legislation introduced by the D.C. non-voting congressional representative. At the end-of-the-year goodie sale, students and their parents actively discussed how their products (and the pricing of them) competed with those of a nearby gas station/mini-mart. Through the community mapping exercise, students discussed public safety and transportation, health, businesses, education and housing.

The "African American-ness" of the subject was rooted in no particular ideology. In any event, the presence of two Caribbean American and two Latina students broadened historical discussions of race and ethnicity. For example, during a discussion of media images, students discussed the relative absence of Latino images in local media, despite a growing Latino immigrant population, and the overwhelming negative stereotypes in the national media. Unlike jurisdictions where the history of people of color requires major excavation, Washington, D.C. has always been soaking in the bitter juice of race relations and race *cum* class issues. African Americans have always been a very large percentage of the D.C. population and, in recent decades, the majority group; class and political diversity among D.C. Blacks is historically broad. The fact that the current political powers-that-be at the local level are largely African American meant that the analyses of history and civics took a different flavor than might be the case where students and elected officials of color were in the racial minority. One example is the recent tensions between Latinos and African Americans, both those African Americans in relative power, and those at the community level who feel relatively powerless and further threatened by the potential political clout of Latinos. Personal and family experience with U.S. foreign policy, immigration policy, bilingual education, U.S. civil rights and voting rights history, and the relative disenfranchisement of *all* D.C. citizens sharpened the civics discussions among students. To my mind the differing viewpoints enriched these discussions. In the end, however, the academic social studies content seemed to matter less to students than the civic action applications.

Afterschool versus Classroom

The context for this research was an afterschool program and as such, offered a different set of advantages and challenges from those of a regular classroom. In the final section of this article, I address the implications of this kind of work for public school classrooms. However, some of the more generic differences were as follows:

- *Freshness*—As an "outsider," I was oblivious to gossip and students' histories with one another. On the one hand, this fresh eye and ear permitted students a way to interact with one another differently. On the other hand, I was sometimes blindsided by relevant information.
- *Autonomy*—In an afterschool program, the students' personal behavior and decision-making authority, the curriculum, and the nature of field trips are more autonomous than in a regular classroom. Participants are much freer to experiment with text and pedagogy. However, this also has a down side because of limited access to the benefits of bureaucracy.
- *The Benefits of Bureaucracy*—Supplies, faculty interaction, rules, and funds are more available to regular classroom teachers than to afterschool programs.
- *Selectivity*—Students in afterschool programs participate on a purely voluntary basis, rather than because of compulsory schooling laws. Further, the coordinator of an afterschool program is not forced to accept any and all students crossing her threshold in the way that public school teachers must.
- *Commitment*—Students have more difficulty committing to an afterschool activity that parents consider optional.
- *Political activity*—Afterschool programs are freer to engage overtly in political issues than are teachers and students in the regular public school classroom.
- *Scheduling*—In an afterschool program, field trips do not interfere with other school activities and can be of longer duration.

- *Fun*—There is a higher expectation of fun with any afterschool activity. School is "supposed" to feel like work, but a student's free time is supposed to feel more like play.
- *The Presence of Younger Siblings*—this was a function of the limited afterschool options available to parents. The multi-age grouping was not a serious obstacle to program success, but did pose a challenge that classroom teachers do not face.

Theoretical Context

The data suggest that the answer to the research question—Does a critical method of teaching history to middle school students affect their desire and improve their ability to apply historical lessons to contemporary civic challenges?—is a tentative "Yes." Despite the warnings that young adolescents are not cognitively ready or theoretically well-grounded enough,[39] that their political instincts are not sufficiently mature to merit study,[40] that they will stumble upon their culture as a barrier to achievement,[41] and that the community of adults does not sufficiently support young adolescents,[42] the students of the Takoma History and Civic Action Project, the nine most active as well as the other twenty-two participants demonstrated something quite the contrary.

Butts (1993) asserts that public education will not be saved by programs in teacher education whose goal is touted to the public as "critical pedagogy," or "empowering teachers to become transformative intellectuals who are capable of wondering, pondering and critique." He argues that:

> we must not shrink from a goal called "civic virtue" defined by the Founders as a citizen's obligation to promote the public good in a democratic republic . . . we need more than ever not only a good public education; we need a public-good education. We will not achieve either one unless we create a public-good teacher education (33).

This research tends to confirm the complexities of applying theory and the research results of others to classroom practice, particularly using subject matter (social studies) for which the purpose is in constant flux, and for which there are few "correct" answers.[43] Until such time as adults clearly articulate their expectations for a "public-good" education, all pedagogies—traditional and critical alike—may be aimed at a moving policy target yielding widely variable (and perhaps, unsatisfactory) results. Under such circumstances, perhaps neither students nor teachers should be held solely responsible for poor student outcomes.

Nevertheless, the work of several researchers[44] demonstrates that magic can occur in classrooms predominated by low-achieving African American students even within the context of ineffective bureaucracies, and incompatible public policies. Part of this success can be traced to factors such as high expectations, challenging content that requires the development and nurturing of higher order thinking skills, curricular materials that are culturally relevant to students and parents, strong personal engagement between teacher and students, and strong administrative and district support.

However, there is still the question of whether these approaches challenge or enforce notions of social and economic class, capitalism, a vocational approach to learning, and cultural assimilation—in short, some of the conditions and structures that critical pedagogy and liberation theorists argue as the cause for miseducation, disengagement from schooling, and school failure. Further, student outcome measures in these studies still are based largely on standardized, norm-referenced tests, a definition of academic success that is considered narrow even by those who employ the tests.[45] An examination of critical teaching methods, such as was used in this research, still is necessary for a complete understanding of what works in urban middle schools with large numbers of students of color.

In addition, before attempting to answer the research question in its entirety, it is necessary to examine the challenges posed by seven of the component parts of the research question. These components are: *the critical teaching method; the definition of civic action; student motivation and performance; appropriateness; the impact of studying African American and local history; the desire to take civic action; and the application of historical lessons to contemporary civic challenges.*

Critical Teaching Method. This research suggests that it is not simply enough for a teacher to **say**, "In this class we will apply historical lessons to contemporary civic challenges." Rather, the space must exist for students to *act*. To start, one must constantly **ask**: *why is this information important? How does this relate to your life right now?* And then one must ask: ***what can we do about this and when?***[46] In the course of this research, middle school students did not necessarily arrive at these last questions without prompting, but jumped at the opportunity to consider and implement new ideas. For example, the evidence of the voter registration activity showed that middle school students are not yet cynical enough to reject traditional, or even "corny," solutions and are willing to search for new twists.[47] At every turn, students sought something to *do*, even when the evidence of a critical discussion suggested that action was premature.

The teaching method seemed more effective than the subject matter in sustaining student interest, although the exploratory nature of the study did not offer a way to single out the impact of the teaching method on student outcomes, or to contrast it with other teaching methods using the same content. In addition, the instructional method required adaptation for various developmental groupings, since some of the participants were younger students (ages 5–10), most of whom were the siblings of middle school students. On occasion, the younger students were more mature and cooperative than the middle schoolers. However, the program—as designed—was better suited to the cognitive and reasoning abilities of the older students.[48] As a result, the empirical evidence on the critical teaching method used in this research is far from conclusive.

The Definition of Civic Action. For the purpose of theory development and practice, this study defined *civic action* as any public behavior by a group of individuals toward securing or maintaining human rights.

One lesson of this research seemed to be a challenge of the romanticism, held by both veteran and younger activists alike, that is attached to civil disobedience. Student behavior over the course of this program tended to validate this observation. On the one hand, students were tempted to join the loud, public and televised street protests of University of District of Columbia students to fight education budget cuts, and on the other hand, to join quiet, comfortable existing school-based improvement efforts. For the most part, the most active middle school students tended toward a "middle path" that stepped outside of what was comfortable for students, challenging and holding people and institutions accountable, while taking care to "respect their elders." Evidence from liberation movements worldwide indicate that middle school students are certainly capable of civil disobedience, and probably should do so as part of a community recapture of the D.C. public school system. But, within their own sense of personal comfort and within the realm of the "appropriate" role of a critical teacher,[49] the "middle path" seemed to have tremendous value for THCAP students, if for no other reason than that it welcomed people who did not hold or who had not yet formed strict ideological positions.

Student Motivation and Performance. As important as defining civic action for the purpose of theory development, it is essential to discover what civic action means to young adolescents, and the best ways to elicit it. This research suggests that, in many ways, the motivation toward civic action may be akin to the motivation toward academic achievement,[50] in that it is guided by a calculus of effort and benefits and is heavily influenced by parents and peers.

For example, the bargaining approach to schooling is one where adults acknowledge the empirical evidence of continuing employment discrimination—holding for educational attainment—which contradicts the American achievement ideology,[51] yet argue with students about the value of playing to win the formal education "game," even as advocates continue the push for economic and social justice. In the bargain, these researchers validate the self-perceptions of African American youth and their observations of the political economy, but urge more congruence between their educational and occupational aspirations, classroom effort, and those affective behaviors that defeat goal attainment.

Similarly, a civic educator[52] might ask to what extent students trust adults and the civic culture in which they live? How can adults convince students of the value of civic action education if adults are politically apathetic or if students perceive civic action to be ineffective in their communities? Given the external and internal assaults to this age group, is the maintenance of personal safety a more important motivator for civic action at this age[53] than patriotism, for example, or the maintenance of political democracy?

The responses to these questions offer guidance about what motivates middle school students to civic action. This research only hints at these responses. Empirical evidence varied among students in the THCAP research program. The students with good grades were not always the best leaders if they lacked strong interpersonal skills,[54] and the more affluent students were not always more exposed to or aware of civic information if they were also sheltered from the grittier aspects of urban living.[55] Hands-on learning and critical approaches proved unfamiliar and scary to some students. One's success in THCAP, evidenced by active involvement, leadership, and follow-through, did not seem linked to family education, socioeconomic level, or preferred learning style. These questions and observations suggest that the varied challenges to the American achievement ideology evidenced by the curriculum, classroom structure, and range of learning modalities employed in THCAP bear fruit among students who are typically not expected to achieve and whose input into their own learning is rarely sought. In short, the research results suggest that motivation toward civic action, in a twist on academic motivation, may be strong for middle school students that are influenced and frustrated by more traditional expressions of personal power (for example, high grades, conformity with peers, and adult approval), even though they also may express dim faith in the broader civic culture.

But, of course, there are limits to what students can do on their own, and to what one can expect from a semester-long afterschool program.

Despite all of the political fury currently consuming the city; despite all of the information and resources to which students were exposed over the semester; and despite the range of civic action choices generated—it was unreasonable to expect nine students ages 11 to 13 to lead the charge for radical change in the D.C. political and public school systems, as might be urged by some critical pedagogy theorists.[56] Middle school students seem to have different definitions of civic action than adults, based on their assessment of their own abilities to effect change and based on their understanding of what needs to be changed. In addition, their sense of personal power can easily be altered by events such as the accidental street shooting of a peer's parent. As a result, performance expectations of adults may be out of line with what students can and should do.

In fact, the students' insistence on giving the school heavy-duty brooms proved to be a brilliant insight: the head custodian said afterwards that the school had been waiting for eight months for the DC public school system to send the requisitioned brooms and vacuum cleaner. Although the school lacked a librarian until recently, there are now seven new books for Takoma students on the subject of young people and civic action.

Appropriateness. This research does not answer the question of whether there is a *culturally appropriate* approach to critical social studies teaching for middle school students of color that privileges no particular ideology, beyond notions of justice and equality.[57] Certainly, the Takoma students (in their expressed concerns about student respect for me), parents (in comments to me) and school administration (in the principal's evaluation) perceived a cultural incongruity between the teaching methods I used and more familiar, authoritarian teaching methods, even though my methods approached political activity. Ample research supports the notion that there are different attitudes in different cultural groups about which characteristics make for a good teacher,[58] as documented by this effort.

Nor does this research offer more than mere hints into the question of whether there are developmentally appropriate *critical* teaching methods for young adolescents.[59] The history-civics link seems to require a degree of abstract thinking, the ability for which begins to increase at the middle school level, but is not fully formed.[60] Any critical teaching curriculum for this age group should probably contain an equal balance of concrete and abstract information to hold student's attention. More abstract information—such as economics and public policy making—seems to require at least one full school year to master, and perhaps cannot be effectively engaged in a semester-long program such as THCAP.

The impact of studying African American and local history: There is no clear evidence that students applied historical awareness to contemporary civic challenges. While students sometimes referenced historical information and the "significance of historical moments"[61] in conversation, their civic action was not manifestly linked to any particular historical moment or person.

The desire to take civic action: The desire to take civic action may have preceded participation in the program, but became more focused as a result. Research that confirms middle-school girls are highly motivated to be active in social and political issues and are generally far more proactive than the boys[62] was consistent with the high level of participation by THCAP girls. While THCAP students seemed to understand the range of potential civic actions, their desired civic action was localized and within the limits of their perceptions of personal power.[63] Furthermore, despite students' overall seriousness of purpose, the desire to take civic action also needed to be balanced with "down time." As stated in the evaluation by a student who left the program, "you need to have more fun in there." Outdoor activities and play time are still important to middle school students and should be incorporated into any history and civic action curriculum.

The application of historical lessons to contemporary civic challenges: Students took enormous pride in their final project, having controlled the entire operation, wrestled with best way to use proceeds, made an astute assessment of what the school needed, and won peer approval for their hard work. They were challenged to think beyond themselves and their cliques to the larger school and community. Participating students as well as others expressed interest in returning/joining the program should it be repeated. In short, the final nine students perceived themselves as having *made* history, as stated in their informal conversations and reiterated by the principal at an awards ceremony.

Despite these limitations and uncertainties in answering the research question, the research observations suggest that a program such as THCAP can go far toward merging critical teaching theory and practice.

Implications for Practice[64]

In general, a program such as THCAP would benefit from the following: strong planning; a breadth of instructional methods; sensitivity to literacy levels of students; classroom assistance (smaller student-teacher ratio); a strong arts component; an athletic component; bilingual resources; strong theoretical grounding; financial assistance; intensive scheduling; and strong feedback and assessment systems.

In this section I would like to offer insights on the six areas that would seem to be the greatest concern to classroom teachers interested in praxis: adapting an afterschool program for the classroom; subject matter; instructor skill; adult and community support; parental involvement; and power-sharing between teachers and young adolescents.

Adapting for the Classroom. Unless the THCAP curriculum were adapted as a year-long curriculum, the time constraints of classrooms, even those using 90-minute block schedules, would require fewer or more compact curriculum modules, and fewer hands-on activities over the course of a semester. For example, a public classroom teacher might be inclined to forgo the opening (snacks, theme-related music, and discussion of lyrics) for the sake of concentrating on "content." However, the opening served as a way to center students on the task at hand and was an essential part of the content. The size of a typical public classroom also would limit an ability to replicate THCAP; on a given day, there were ten to twelve students in the THCAP classroom, with a maximum of seventeen at any one time. The ability to experiment with text and pedagogy, and to engage in discussions of the efficacy of electoral politics might be difficult for public classroom teachers who are expected to teach in conformance with mandated texts, state standards, standardized test goals, and an uncritical view of American democratic process. In attempting to replicate THCAP, compulsory school laws would ironically force public school teachers to confront the realities of democratic process since all students—representing a spectrum of social, economic, political, gender, and racial/ethnic realities—would be a part of the proceedings. Further, students who did not want to participate would not have the option of leaving the classroom as the afterschool students did, and teachers would be challenged with the task of evaluating perceived student resistance or apathy, postures which are often interpreted as failure. These factors—schedule, class size, student composition, academic goals, and assessment—suggest that a program such as THCAP might better function as an afterschool program, short of a dramatic restructuring of public schools.

Subject Matter. Although THCAP was first conceived as a social studies curriculum encompassing history, economics, and politics, it also drew on music, art, and journalism, and other forms of written expression. In addition, as mentioned above, a stronger arts component and an athletic component might have given the program more appeal to a wider range of students. Such interdisciplinary may be beyond the expertise of a single classroom teacher and require team teaching or a collegiality that is often absent in mainstream public schools. Even in those middle schools where interdisciplinary studies are taken seriously, there are often subject-specific standards that teachers and students are expected to meet that supercede the underlying intention that THCAP students would demonstrate proficiency *primarily* through their civic action project.

As mentioned earlier, middle school students are just beginning to demonstrate an ability to think abstractly as would permit a substantive application of history to civics. But, we teachers might also have a difficult time. We need to discern the *meaning* of historical events and people and, then agree upon the apparent *mandate* of this history, and finally design and execute a civic action response that advances notions of *justice*. This is precisely the critical thinking and action task that a program such as THCAP attempts to do. A classroom teacher might expect to struggle with divergent opinions, emotions, stereotypes and prejudices, differing facility with language, different understandings of morality, and other challenges as s/he and the students reason their way toward definitions of meaning, mandate, and justice. This task might be especially difficult if this teacher also maintains a posture as co-learner and facilitator rather than the knower of complete knowledge.

Instructor Skill. Prior to conducting this research, a mentor reassured me that if students were excited and engaged with the subject matter, my lack of classroom management training would be a minor hindrance to program effectiveness. Common sense and my experience as a parent, I was told, would make up for a lack of formal teacher training. To an extent, the mentor was correct: two-thirds of the students who signed up for the program over the course of the semester maintained moderate to high interest, and half of this group took active leadership in the final civic action project. In the process these students, and in some cases their parents, claimed to have learned more about Washington, D.C. history and civics than ever before. Yet, limited classroom experience should not be taken lightly, and a pre-service or new in-service teacher attempting such a program would benefit from classroom aides and the mentoring of a master teacher. Aides would help supervise the small student work groups and chaperone class trips, while master teachers would help interpret teaching practice and middle school student needs. This is not to say that a program such as THCAP is so labor-intensive that it requires three adults per fifteen middle school students. Perhaps with more classroom experience and one high school student aide, I might have felt more confident and better able to engage the one-third of the students who eventually left the program. However, it is to say that any interdisciplinary work with middle school students that seeks uncertain action outcomes is necessarily more demanding than teaching a single discipline with proscribed outcomes. A teacher attempting the former would need a great deal of support.

Adult and Community Support. Some of the support that a teacher would need would come from other teachers, school administrators, community residents, and local organizations and businesses. For example, students simply could have read some of the existing Takoma history texts. Instead, community residents were willing to meet with students for group oral history interviews, following a reading of the texts. Takoma students could have watched the People for the American Way video showing high schoolers conducting voter registration drives to learn about youth civic action. Instead, the local high school principal and government teacher saw the value of having *middle school* students conduct a voter registration drive with high school seniors. All of the field trips that THCAP students took were participatory; that is, the students were not simply expected to watch what the adults were doing, but they were expected to make presentations, ask questions, take notes, conduct hands-on work, discover how they could participate on an ongoing basis, etc. Such field trips required receptive adult hosts. The interviews with the local elected official (who was not seeking re-election) and the public affairs radio programmer were the result of persistence and not prior connections. In short, a teacher seeking to replicate THCAP needs to be familiar with the community immediately surrounding the school (the students' primary reference point), as well as with the larger civic domain to solicit the assistance of responsive community adults. Without significant engagement with these adults, student understanding of history and civics remains abstract and the program activity becomes pointless.

Parental Involvement. As the first teachers of children, parents help shape the values, opinions, and experiences that students bring to the classroom. By middle school, students are turning as often to their peers to help make sense of the world. Parents are often uncertain how to offer guidance at the same time as permitting their children more independence, and middle schools may not always encourage the same kind of parental involvement as elementary schools. It goes without saying that there is a role for parents to play in the continuing development and education of their children. Yet, the interpersonal and institutional flux of the middle years may create a lack of role clarity. THCAP parents ranged from those who vaguely knew that their children were doing something "constructive" afterschool to those who sought regular contact with me and contributed time, and resources to the program. As mentioned earlier, I cannot say definitively that the involvement of Parent X led to greater interest by Student X and conversely the lack of Parent Y's involvement diminished Student Y's participation. Yet, the parents of middle school students are always "in the room"—through the values that are expressed and in the student's struggle for identity—and I appreciated the direct contact with parents, including the times when they were critical of my teaching style. Welcoming parents into a middle school classroom creates a three-way power dynamic, as opposed to the presumed two-way dynamic of elementary schools where students typically are not expected to have any power.

Power-sharing Between Teachers and Young Adolescents. The whole crux of an effort such as THCAP is to practice negotiating the transfer of curricular and political power from adults to youth, as will occur when one generation dies and another takes over the governance of civic life. To the extent that we value democracy, it requires vigilant exercise.

Yet, even if we claim to believe in democratic practice among adults, it is difficult to cede or share power with children. After all, we are legally and morally entrusted with their care, we are considered shirkers if we allow children to tell us what they want to learn, we create undisciplined, spoiled brats if we fail to impose boundaries and order, and so on. Among some American cultures, there is a very strong ethic of respect for elders that not only supercedes notions of democratic practice, but is considered a pre-condition of academic excellence. In addition, early adolescence is a particularly important period for both youth and the adults charged with transmitting precious cultural information. Witness the rites of passage ceremonies such as bar/bat mitzvah, quincenera, confirmation, that are common occurrences for youth ages 12 to 15. Conversely, middle school students are as likely to withdraw from their peers and from student-teacher interactions as to insist on exuberant participation. What teachers perceive as apathy may in fact be excessive concern about appearing "stupid" or "overly brainy" or "cultural traitors" among their peers. In turn, our efforts to draw students out and mandate their involvement might be considered an anti-democratic wielding of adult power.

So, what does this mean for the teacher who seeks to share power with students? It means that, like the practices of child-rearing and of political democracy, it is the hardest job one will ever love.[65] It is a job that requires the trust and support of parents, peer teachers, the school administration, and the broader community. Such a teacher must be flexible and quick-witted in drawing on interdisciplinary references. This teacher must be able and willing to teach students to reason their way through a web of factual, anecdotal, and emotional information to seek a shared understanding of the subject matter. It means that the teacher must allow students to take chances, get messy, and make mistakes[66] within a non-punitive setting as a way of learning, *prior to* creating a public space for students to commit civic action. And, it means that such a teacher will be very tired at the end of the day.

Notes

1. In this paper, civic action is defined as any public behavior by a group of individuals toward securing or maintaining human rights. It is a spectrum of behavior embracing rebellion (e.g., civil disobedience, revolution), social protest (e.g., marches, demonstrations), public policy (e.g., legislation, law enforcement), and community service (e.g., voluntary charitable or philanthropic action). While civic action may use the tactics of any of these forms of mobilization, its purpose is the full exercising of existing citizenship rights toward overcoming social and economic injustice.

2. The researcher/instructor expected several results from the research, including: the creation of a core group of active students representing the school's gender and ethnic diversity; open and critical dialogue on a range of historical and civic issues and events; student initiative in addressing a school or community concern; a documented change in school and/or community conditions; an increased sense of student empowerment; an increased understanding of appropriate instructional methods for middle school civic action education; and improved teaching skill.

3. The methodology employed in the study was largely qualitative, using the constant comparative analysis method to categorize observations in such a way as to derive a grounded theory in response to the research question.

4. The data presented draw on the relevant research literature, researcher/instructor's field notes and journal, as well as written evaluations by the school principal and student participants in the program, and a pre-program questionnaire.

5. In keeping with research by Wolfgang and Kelsay (1995) and Ross and Bondy (1993)

6. See Morris & Co. (1992); Mackey (1991)

7. See Morris (1992)

8. See Kramer (1990); Jackson-Allen and Christenberry (1994).

9. Consistent with the work of Kramer (1990),

10. See Goleman (1995).

11. This is consistent with the work of Wolfgang and Kelsay (1995) and Goodman (1992). For example, three of the male students indicated that their parents were strict and had high expectations. My observations of parent-child interactions and her conversations with parents confirmed these characterizations. Yet, one of the students, after leading others into mischief, would often implore me not to tell his father, while the other two would deny leadership or involvement altogether. Time and again, one boy was left "holding the bag" while the others maneuvered an

innocent posture. This boy, who is witty, bright, and charismatic, either thought very consciously about his father, or not at all, before breaking class rules.

12 This assertion of adult authority in a democratic classroom is supported by Wolfgang and Kelsay (1995), Ross and Bondy (1993), Meyer (1990), and Guyton (1988).

13 See Wolfgang and Kelsay (1995)

14 See Ladson-Billings (1994); Baloche (1994)

15 See Mack, Jackson, and Lazarus (1995)

16 See Smith and Andrew (1988)

17 This reaction was in contrast to what is assumed to be the preferred learning style of many boys, as suggested by Jackson-Allen and Christenberry, 1994.

18 See Levy (1991); Arnold (1992); Mackey (1991); Gay (1991)

19 As argued by McLaren and Giroux (1986)

20 As counter-pointed by Liston and Zeichner (1987)

21 See Ross and Bondy (1993)

22 A third-generation native Washingtonian African American, I am the mother of two Takoma elementary students, in addition to being an alumna of Takoma School (1969–70).

23 This is consistent with Dunham and Bengtson (1992)

24 As suggested by Clark (1990) and Rettinger (1993)

25 This is consistent with Tanksley (1995), White-Hood (1994), Morris (1992), and Marchant (1991).

26 See Tanksley (1995); Morris (1992)

27 See Morris (1992); White-Hood (1994)

28 See Rettinger (1993)

29 This observation was consistent with work by Walker (1986), Jackson-Allen and Christenberry (1994), Alleman and Brophy (1994), Tanksley (1995), Ford (1994), and Mackey (1991)

30 Although none of the children of "indifferent" parents completed the program, and the students who were most active had the most "involved" parents, there were too many students in the grey area to make a definitive statement about parent involvement. For example, two girls with "involved" parents left the program just as the final project was beginning. One boy of an "indifferent" parent nearly completed the program, leaving the last week. Four of the five students who were asked to leave the program had "involved" parents. There is simply not enough data to assume causality.

31 This is consistent with the motivation research of Midgley, Anderman, & Hicks (1995), Urdan, Midgley, & Wood (1995), Urdan & Maehr (1995), Shade (1994), and Graham (1989)

32 See Smith on Ogbu, page 30

33 This is consistent with the research of Jackson-Allen and Christenberry (1994).

34 For example, see Goodlad (1991) and Dillard (1994)

35 Further, the student evaluation did not specifically ask students to assess instructor skill. There is no question that the task of participating and observing is extremely difficult, especially when the researcher acknowledges a high degree of emotional attachment to the "observed." However, field notes and the written student evaluation tend to support the self-assessment assertions made here.

36 See Ladson-Billings (1994); Foster (1990)

37 See Morris (1992)

38 As suggested by Mumford (1991) and Massialas (1991)

39 See Liston and Zeichner, p. 123

40 See Niemi and Hepburn (1995)

41 See Ogbu (1985); Ford (1994); Fordham (1996)

42 See Arnold (1992)

43 In the context of the D.C. public school system—in particular—there is also a need for an honest and extended discussion of precisely what "public-good" means since the public policy makers who set the economic and political stage for classroom practice include local elected officials, congressional oversight committees, and the U.S. president, in addition to students, parents, teachers, and administrators.

Shaver (1991) asserts that social studies teachers are notoriously skeptical of the functionality of educational research. Further, Darling-Hammond (1993) states that the relationship between research and practice should be to produce knowledge with and for teachers which illuminates the complexities of human learning, for enriching their thinking and practice, and for empowering them to see teaching and learning through many lenses. These insights seem especially useful for preservice teachers eager to apply university-based theories to public school classroom.

44 This research includes the work of Edmonds (1979) Baratz & Stevens (1993), Foster (1993), Hollins (1996), Ladson-Billings (1994), Ford (1992), Haynes & Comer (1993), Slavin (1987), Levine (1994), Braddock & McPartland (1992), Epstein and Dauber (1995), CRESPAR (1996), Project Zero (1996), Clark & Canner (1994), Mizzell (1994) and others.

45 See Mizell (1994)

46 Guyton (1988)

47 See Merelman (1971)

48 This is consistent with insights by Merelman (1971), Van Sledright and Grant (1994), and Niemi and Hepburn (1995).

49 As debated between Liston and Zeichner (1987) and Giroux and McLaren (1986)

50 As is explicated by Ogbu and Simons (1994), King (1994), Dunham and Bengtson (1992), Griggs, et al, (1992), Kramer (1990), Thomas and Larke (1988), and Walker (1986),

51 Described by researchers such as Ford (1990)

52 Such as Clark (1990)

53 As suggested by Hoose (1993), Lewis (1992, 1991), Morris (1992), and Mackey (1991).

54 See Goleman (1994)

55 See Rettinger (1993)

56 See Giroux and McLaren (1986)

57 As proposed by Banks (1991)

58 See research by Mack, Jackson, and Lazarus (1995), Delpit (1988), Dabney and Davis (1982), Ford (1992), Henderson (1988), and Slaughter-Defoe (1991).

59 Liston and Zeichner (122) critique Giroux and McLaren for blurring "the essential distinction between the teacher as educator and the teacher as political activist," maintaining that "critical and emancipatory teaching recognizes that the teacher is first and foremost an educator and only tangentially (if at all) a political activist." Yet, Delpit (1988) argues that an effective teacher of children of color must be something of a political activist.

60 As suggested by Graham (1989) and Merelman (1971, 1986)

61 See Seixas (1994)

62 See Rettinger's research (1993)

63 This is consistent with Guyton (1988)

64 In addition, the research also offers implications for theory development and implications for further research. The theoretical questions concern the social purpose of schooling, particularly in the area of social studies, and through the use of critical and liberation pedagogies, leading to the ultimate question of *what do we want for our children and how will formal schooling help them achieve it?* In the context of this research, an emerging theory of education and schooling would address the power issues between adults and children and the power issues among adults.

The areas of new or continuing research that are suggested by this study include: an increased understanding of the differences between students who are attracted to voluntary civic action education and those who are not; more research into gender differences that impact student motivation, student interests, non-classroom stimuli, and predisposition to civic action; the need to gain a better understanding of African American achievement motivation, especially in school settings in which teachers and students of color predominate; an ongoing need to explore, promote, and enhance the positive qualities, attributes, and cultural frameworks that African American students bring to the classroom; more exploration into which policy postures—rooted in theories of cultural difference, adult remediation, bargaining, and/or emerging theories on achievement motivation—yield the broadest success among African American middle school students; more research into effective methods for teaching history and other social studies to middle school students; the need for reliable quantitative measures of the impact of social studies and civic action education; and more applied research into critical teaching methods in middle school classrooms.

65 At one time the slogan for the United States Peace Corps, I have always thought that it more aptly described any process of raising/teaching children.

66 "Take chances, make mistakes, get messy" is the primary charge of Ms. Frizzle, the fictional science teacher in the *Magic School Bus* public television series, a critical pedagogue if there ever was one.

References

Alleman, Janet and Brophy, Jere. (1994). Taking Advantage of Out-of-School Opportunities for Meaningful Social Studies Learning, in *The Social Studies*, 85, (1), 25–30.

Arnold, John. (November, 1992). A Curriculum to Empower Young Adolescents. A paper at the annual meeting of the National Middle School Association, San Antonio, Texas.

Baloche, Lynda. (January 1994). Breaking Down the Walls: Integrating Creative Questioning and Cooperative Learning into the Social Studies, *The Social Studies*, 85 (1), 25–30

Banks, James. (1991). Social Studies, Ethnic Diversity, and Social Change, in (pp. 129–147): *The Education of African Americans*. Charles V. Willie, and Antoine Garibaldi, and Wornie I. Reed, editors. Prepared under the auspices of the William Monroe Trotter Institute, University of Massachusetts-Boston. New York: Auburn House.

Baratz- Snowden, Joan. (1993). Opportunity to Learn: Implications for Professional Development, in *Journal of Negro Education*, 62, (3), 311–323.

Braddock, Jomills Henry II and McPartland, James M. (1992). Education of Early Adolescents, in *Review of Research in Education*, 19, 135–170.

Clark, Todd. (1990). Participation in Democratic Citizenship Education, in *The Social Studies*, 81, (5), 206–209.

Clark, Terry A. and Canner, Jane (1994). Expecting the Best from Students in Urban Middle Schools, Edna McConnell Clark Foundation Middle Grades Initiative. Princeton, NJ: Educational Resources Group.

Comer, James P. and Haynes, Norris M. (1991). Meeting the Needs of Black Children in Public Schools, in *The Education of African Americans*, edited by Charles V. Willie, Antoine Garibaldi, and Wornie L. Reed. prepared under the auspices of the William Monroe Trotter Institute, University of Massachusetts-Boston. New York: Auburn House.

Dabney and Davis (1982). Referenced in Mack, et al.

Delpit, Lisa. (1988). The Silenced Dialogue: Power and Pedagogy in Educating Other People's Children. in *Harvard Educational Review*, 1, (3).

Dillard, Cynthia. (1994). Beyond Supply and Demand: Critical Pedagogy, Ethnicity, and Empowerment in Recruiting Teachers of Color, *Journal of Teacher Education*, 45 (1), pp. 9–17.

Dunham, Charlotte Chorn and Bengtson, Vern L. (1992). The Long-term Effects of Political Activism on Intergenerational Relations, *Youth and Society*, 24, (1), 31–51.

Edmonds, Ronald. (1979). Effective Schools for the Urban Poor, in *Educational Leadership*, 37, 15–24.

Epstein, Joyce L., and Dauber, Susan L. (1995). Effects on Students of an Interdisciplinary Program Linking Social Studies, Art, and Family Volunteers in the Middle Grades, *Journal of Early Adolescence* 15(1), 114–144.

Ford, Donna Y. (1994). Promoting Achievement Among Gifted Black Students: The Efficacy of New Definitions and Identification Practices, in *Urban Education*, 29, (2), 202–229.

Ford, Donna Y. and Harris, J. John III. (1994). Promoting Achievement among Gifted Black Students: the Efficacy of New Definitions and Identification Practices, in *Urban Education*, 29, (2), 202–229.

———. (1992). The American Achievement Ideology as Perceived by Urban African American Students: Explorations by Gender and Academic Program, in *Urban Education*, 27, (2), 196–211.

———. (1992) Self-perceptions of Underachievement and Support for the Achievement Ideology among Early Adolescent African Americans, in *Journal of Early Adolescence*, 12, (3), 228–252.

Fordham, Signithia. (1996). *Blacked Out: Dilemmas of Race, Identity, and Success at Capital High*, Chicago: University of Chicago Press.

Foster, Michele. (1993). Educating for Competence in Community and Culture: Exploring the Views of Exemplary African American Teachers, in *Urban Education* v 27 n 4, pp. 370–394.

Gay, Geneva. (1991). Culturally Diverse Students and Social Studies, in *Handbook of Research on Social Studies Teaching and Learning*. New York: Macmillan.

Goleman, Daniel. (1995). *Emotional Intelligence*. New York: Bantam Books.

Goodlad, John. (1984). *A Place Called School: Prospects for the Future*. New York: McGraw-Hill.

Goodman, Jesse. (1992). *Elementary Schooling for Critical Democracy*. Albany, NY: State University of New York Press.

Graham, Sandra. (1989). Motivation in Afro-Americans, in *Black Students: Psychosocial Issues and Academic Achievement*, edited by Gordon LaVern Berry and Joy Keiko Asamen. Newbury Park, CA: Sage Publishers.

Griggs, Mildred Barnes, et al. (1992). *Factors That Influence the Academic and Vocational Development of African and Latino Youth*. National Center for Research in Vocational Education (Berkeley, CA). Washington, DC: Office of Vocational and Adult Education.

Guyton, Edith. (1988). Critical Thinking and Political Participation: Development and Assessment of a Causal Model, *Theory and Research in Social Education*, 16, (1), 23–49.

Haynes, Norris M. and Comer, James P. (1993). The Yale School Development Program: Process, Outcomes, and Policy Implications, in *Urban Education* 28(2), 166–199.

Henderson (1988). Referenced in Mack, et al.

Hollins, Etta. (1996a) *Culture in School Learning: Revealing the Deep Meaning*, Mahwah, NJ: Lawrence Erlbaum Associates, 1996.

———, ed. (1996b). *Transforming Curriculum for a Culturally Diverse Society*. Mahwah, NJ: Lawrence Erlbaum Associates.

———, ed. (1994). *Teaching Diverse Populations: Formulating a Knowledge Base*. Albany, NY: SUNY Press.

———, and Spencer, Kathleen. (1990). Restructuring Schools for Cultural Inclusion: Changing the Schooling Process for African American Youngsters, in *Journal of Education*, 172, (2), 89–100.

Hoose, Phillip. (1993). *It's Our World, Too! Stories of Young People Who Are Making a Difference*. Little, Brown & Company.

Jackson-Allen, Jennifer and Christenberry, Nola (November, 1994). Learning Style Preferences of Low- and High-achieving Young African American Males. Annual Meeting of Mid-south Educational Research Association.

Johnson, Sylvia. Introducing CRESPAR, in *Journal of Negro Education*, v 64 n 2, pp. 101–103, 1995.

King, Joyce. (1994). The purpose of Schooling for African American Children: Including Cultural Knowledge, in *Teaching Diverse Populations: Formulating a Knowledge Base*, edited by Hollins. Albany, NY: SUNY Press.

———. (1991). Unfinished Business: Black Student Alienation and Black Teachers' Emancipatory Pedagogy, in M. Foster (ed.) *Readings on Equal Education*, 11, New York: AMS Press.

King, S.H. (1993). The limited presence of African American Teachers, in *Review of Education Research*, 63, (2), 115–149.

Kramer, Linda. (November 1990). Issues of Literacy and School Performance for At-risk and Successful Students in a Multicultural Junior High. National Reading Conference

Ladson-Billings, Gloria. (1994). *The Dreamkeepers*. New York:

———. Toward a Theory of Culturally Relevant Pedagogy, in *American Educational Research Journal*, v 32, n 3, pp. 465–491.

Lewis, Barbara. (1992). *Kids With Courage: True Stories about Young People Making a Difference*. Minneapolis: Free Spirit Press.

———. (1991). *The Kid's Guide to Social Action*. Minneapolis: Free Spirit Press.

Levine, Daniel U. (1994). Instructional Approaches and Interventions that Can Improve the Academic Performance of African American Students, in *Journal of Negro Education*, 63, (1), 46–63.

Levy, Tedd. (1991). Social Studies Instruction: Connecting Students and Their Society, in *Schools in the Middle*, 1, (2), 7–9.

Liston, Daniel P. and Zeichner, Kenneth M. (1987). Critical Pedagogy and Teacher Education, in *Journal of Education*, 169 (3), 117–137.

Mack, Faite R-P, Jackson, Thomas, and Lazarus, Brenda. (February, 1995). Parental Attitudes Regarding the Characteristics of a 'Best' Teacher: Comparison by Gender and Ethnic Group. A paper presented at the annual meeting of the American Association of Colleges of Teacher Education.

Mackey, James. (1991). Adolescents' Social Cognitive and Moral Development and Secondary School Social Studies, in *Handbook of Research on Social Studies Teaching and Learning*. New York: Macmillan.

Marchant, Gregory. (1991). A Profile of Motivation, Self-perception and Achievement in Black Urban Elementary Students, *The Urban Review*, 23. (2).

Massialas, Byron. (1990). Educating Students for Conflict Resolution and Democratic Decision-Making, in *The Social Studies*, 81, (5), 202–205.

McLaren, Peter and Giroux, Henri. (1986). Teacher Education and the Politics of Engagement: The Case for Democratic Schooling, *Harvard Educational Review*, 56(3), 213–238.

Merelman, Richard. (1986). Revitalizing Political Socialization in *Political Psychology*, Margaret J. Herman, editor. San Francisco, CA: Jossey Bass Publishers.

———. (1971). *Political Socialization and Educational Climates: A Study of Two School Districts*, New York: Holt, Rinehart, and Winston.

Meyer, John R. (1990). Democratic Values and Their Development, in *The Social Studies*, 81, (5), 197–203.

Midgley, Carol, Anderman, Eric, and Hicks, Lynley. (1995). Differences Between Elementary and Middle School Teachers and Students: a Goal Theory Approach, *Journal of Early Adolescence*, 15, (1), 90–113.

Mizzell, M. Hayes, et al. (1994). Program on Student Achievement (formerly Program for Disadvantaged Youth): Review and Strategy. New York: Edna McConnell Clark Foundation.

Morris, S.W. and Company. (1992). *What Young Adolescents Want and Need from Out-of-school Programs: a Focus Group Report*. Bethesda, MD: Carnegie Council on Adolescent Development.

Mumford, Richard. (1991). Teaching History Through Analytical and Reflective Thinking Skills, in *The Social Studies*, 82, (5), 191–194.

Niemi, Richard G. and Hepburn, Mary A. (1995). The Rebirth of Political Socialization, *Perspectives on Political Science*, 24, (1), 7–16.

Ogbu, John U. and Simons, Herbert. (1994). *Cultural Models of School Achievement: a Quantitative Test of Ogbu's Theory. Cultural Models of Literacy: a Comparative Study.* Project 12. National center for the study of writing and literacy (Berkeley, CA). Washington, DC: Office of Educational Research and Improvement (OERI)).

Rettinger, Virginia. (1993) The Moral and Political Consciousness of Preadolescents, in *Moral Education Forum*, 18, (4), 2–35.

Ross, Dorene D. and Bondy, Elizabeth. (1993). Classroom Management for Responsible Citizenship: Practical Strategies for Teachers, in *Social Education*, 57, (6), 326–328.

Seixas, Peter. Students' Understanding of Historical Significance, in *Theory and Research in Social Education*, 22, (3), 281–304.

Shade, Barbara J. (1994). Understanding the African American Learner, in *Teaching Diverse Populations: Formulating a Knowledge Base*, edited by Hollins, et al. (pp. 175–189). Albany, NY: SUNY Press.

Shaver, James. (1991). Research and The Teaching of Social Studies, in *The Social Studies*, 81, (6), 239–243.

———, editor. (1991). *Handbook of Research on Social Studies Teaching and Learning.* New York: Macmillan.

Slaughter-Defoe, Dianna T. (1991). "Parental Education Choice: Some African American Dilemmas," in *Journal of Negro Education*, 60 (3), 354–360.

Slavin, Robert E. "Grouping for Instruction in the Elementary School," *Educational Psychologist* (Spring 1987), 109–128.

———, "Cooperative Learning and the Education of Black Students, in Educating Black Children America's Challenge, Howard University School of Education, Bureau of Educational Research, Washington, D.C.: 1987.

Smith, Kitty Lou and Andrew, Loyd D. (April, 1988) An Explanation of the Beliefs, Values, and Attitudes of Black Students in Fairfax County. American Educational Research Association Conference.

Tanksley, Mary Dennard. (1995). *Improving the Attendance Rate for African American Male Students in an Afterschool Reading Program Through Parental Involvement, Positive Male Role Models, and Tutorial Instruction.* Ed.D. practicum, Nova Southeastern University.

Thomas, Gail and Larke, Patricia. (1988). Gender differences among blacks in educational and career orientation, in *Education and Urban Society,* 21, (3), 283-298.

Urdan, Timothy and Maehr, Martin L. (1995). Beyond a two-goal theory of motivation and achievement: a case for social goals, in *Review of Educational Research,* 65, (3), 213-243.

Urdan, Tim, and Midgley, Carol and Wood, Stewart. (1995). Special Issues in Reforming Middle Level Schools, in *Journal of Early Adolescence,* 15, (1), 9-37.

Van Sledright, Bruce A. and Grant, S.G. (1994). Citizenship Education and the Persistent Nature of Classroom Teaching Dilemmas, in *Theory and Research in Social Education,* 22, (3), 305-339.

Walker, Elaine. (April, 1986) The Impact of Schooling on Minority Adolescents' Mobility Aspirations. Annual Meeting of American Educational Research Association, San Francisco, CA.

Whitehood, Marian. (1994). Pride, Heritage, and Self-worth: Keys to African American Male Achievement, in *Schools in the Middle,* 3, (4), 29-30.

Wolfgang, Charles L. and Kelsay, Karla Lynn. Discipline and the Social Studies Classroom, Grades K-12, in *The Social Studies,* July/August 1995, 175-182.

Becoming a Critical Teacher

Raymond A. Horn, Jr.

This is a story about my struggle to become a critical pedagogue in a public high school. Critical pedagogues are rare on the university level, and even rarer on the kindergarten through twelfth grade level of public schools. My story is about being and becoming—a continuous reflection on what I am in relation to what I wish to become. I must immediately disclose the fact that this is a painful process for many reasons that will soon become apparent; but mostly because of the continuous realization of how we are complicit in perpetuating the oppressive structures of our society—or more pointedly how we participate in the truncation of our children's development because of their race, gender, class, ethnicity, or body type. The realization of the deleterious effects of our actions on the development of our children is especially painful since we are part of a caring profession which above all else idealistically promotes the positive development of children.

The telling of my story must be framed in the context of certain assumptions: that there are oppressive structures in our society; that educators consciously and unconsciously perpetuate them; that this oppression has deleterious effects on the development of our children; that these effects can be ameliorated and in some cases negated through a critically contextualized pedagogy; and, that the critical isn't always *critical*.

Essentially, my story is about moving from theory to practice in exposing high school students to a myriad of points of view—including many that have been disenfranchised. The purpose of this broadening is not to promote my point of view, but to promote the students' ability to marshal evidence—to be critical of seemingly simplistic solutions or conclusions. Of course, an integral part of this process is the eliciting of the student's prior assumptions about the issues at hand, and providing a safe space for the interrogation of these assumptions. In these safe spaces students are able to challenge each others assumptions by exploring the consequences of their positions. In addition, the teaching strategies reported in this story aim to disrupt and eliminate oppressive assumptions about race, gender, and class. The story that I shall tell is how theory appears in my practice.

My Background

As a career high school teacher for almost three decades, I have been immersed in educational change which has included the following initiatives: open spaces, open classrooms, individualized instruction, critical thinking, outcome-based education, portfolios, multiple intelligence, cooperative learning, technology, effective teaching strategies, traditional teaching (i.e., lectures, worksheets, objective tests, textbooks as gospel) and many others that have been relegated to the dustbin of education. My roles in these initiatives have included: teacher, department head, curriculum coordinator, student advisor, and educational consultant. My problem is that after all these years I have the sad sense that things never really did change. As my former students' children became my students, my liberal idealism died in the reality of trans-generational illiteracy, pathology, and other negative characteristics of oppression. This conclusion motivated me to seek answers to the question of why educational change invariably fails to better the lives of the major stakeholders in educational systems—students and teachers.

The masters program, which was characterized by transmission of knowledge and quantitative study, provided no answers. However, during my doctoral program I became exposed to qualitative study, critical pedagogy, systems theory, and the postmodern condition. In this context one experience from my public school teaching became a guidepost in my quest to understand change. The only successful change of my career occurred when, in the same year, I became the advisor to the high school newspaper, yearbook, and student government. Within one year these moribund organizations became large, vibrant student-run learning organizations that provided authentic and relevant services for the schools, and provided valuable learning experiences and growth opportunities for the students in these organizations. This one experience with change was different from all others in that the following occurred: students had equitable ownership; a common vision was developed through dialogic conversation; a caring attitude was a significant part of the visions; everyone participated in helping everyone else in acquiring the requisite skills for success; issues of race, gender, ethnicity, and class were part of the dialogic conversation and, as the organization needed to evolve, everyone participated in the accommodation of change. This single intellectual and emotional experience with successful change verified the message found in critical thinking. However, it soon became apparent that there was a distinction between the "at best" benign form of critical thinking, and the "radical political" version.

Critical Pedagogy: My Definition

How critical pedagogy is defined has implications and consequences for teachers and their students. Certain theoretical positions (i.e., current definitions of critical thinking used in the schools; border pedagogy; critical consciousness; critical literacy; and, the political context of critical pedagogy) must be considered or the consequences of what appears to be a critical pedagogy will in actuality promote non-critical thinking and activity. For instance, how critical thinking is currently defined in schools, in most cases, maintains oppressive structures by not eliciting and challenging prior assumptions, and reinforces the disenfranchisement of viewpoints that are not part of the mainstream. The use of narrow and formalistic critical thinking constructs sustain these deleterious consequences. However, to become a border-crosser, to employ critical consciousness through praxis and dialogue, and to be critically literate moves the teacher toward the ideal of being critical in the classroom.

What Is Not Critical Thinking

To expedite this definition, I would argue that there are degrees of critical thinking. The first is certainly not critical, but unfortunately the most pervasive in our schools. This form of critical consists of the critical thinking workshops and gurus who dispense graphic organizers that teach students how to structure data, compare data, synthesize data, and evaluate data. Straight from Bloom's taxonomy come the sequence charts, flow charts, arch diagrams, and "T" charts. The proposition is that when the students use these while watching videos, observing others, or reading a textbook they are thinking critically. Not so!

Another degree of critical thinking, which is analogous to the uncritical action research promoted for teachers as a professional development method, is also problematic. In the classroom the catch phrase "students as researchers" sounds good, but are they critical researchers? The degree of criticality is determined by the focus of the research. Is the research narrowly focused on systematic and scientific technique? Are they constructing their own knowledge or rearranging knowledge constructed by others that is promoted as truth? Are they dealing with issues of power and culture that reveal the oppressive structures and processes of our society? An activity in which students compare Herbert Hoover and Franklin Delano Roosevelt cannot be construed as critical just because it is a comparison, and because it involves research. To be critical implies that the students would have the critical language that would allow the uncovering of the implications of both presidential actions on all members of society—the marginalized as well as the mainstream, and allow the construction of their own beliefs about Hoover and Roosevelt.

Henry Giroux and Critical Thinking
The degree of critical thinking toward which I strive has numerous theoretical roots. Henry Giroux's idea that teachers must be transformative intellectuals proposes that teachers "have the responsibility to question political motives and social inequities with their students in an ongoing effort to create a more democratic and equitable society" (Bennett & LeCompte, 1990). Besides speaking out against economic, political, and social injustice, Giroux proposes that teachers "must work to create the conditions that give students the opportunity to become citizens who have the knowledge and courage to struggle in order to make despair unconvincing and hope practical" (Giroux, 1988, p. 128).

Also, Giroux proposes a border pedagogy that has teachers and students engaging knowledge "as border-crossers," as people moving in and out of borders constructed around coordinates of difference and power" (1992, p. 29). Antecedenal to this type of pedagogy is the understanding that dominant culture uses its power to maintain its position of dominance. This is done through the manipulation of knowledge production in high as well as popular culture. An outcome of this agenda is the creation of borders between those in the mainstream and the "others" who live on the margins. Giroux theorizes that it is the task of teachers to create the pedagogical conditions that allow their students to become border-crossers in order to understand otherness in its own terms (1992). To do this requires the critique of the historically and socially constructed places and borders that we inherit; borders that frame our discourses and social relations. This border pedagogy must create situations in which students are allowed to write, speak, and listen in a language that facilitates the political, social and economic critique of the oppressive structures created by the dominant culture.

Paulo Freire and Critical Thinking

What does a transformative intellectual or border pedagogue do in the classroom to achieve a functional level of criticality? Brazilian educator Paulo Freire provides an answer to this question. Freire sees critical pedagogy as a struggle for freedom—a struggle characterized by conscientization (Freire, 1985), history, praxis, and dialogue (Freire & Macedo, 1996). "Conscientization" (i.e., critical consciousness) is the ability to analyze, problematize (pose questions), and affect the sociopolitical, economic, and cultural realities that shape our lives. Such a level of consciousness requires that people situate themselves in history; the assumption being that we are never independent of the social and historical forces that surround us. That is, we all inherit beliefs, values, and ideologies that need to be critically understood and transformed if necessary" (Freire & Macedo, 1996, p. 199).

Critical consciousness is achieved through praxis and dialogue. Praxis is the relationship between theory and practice in which emancipation from oppression is an outcome of the recursive loop of: theory, action, reflection on action, and new action. Theory and good intentions are not enough. Critical consciousness can only be achieved through praxis and dialogue. Dialogue is a sharing of experience in the context of ideological analysis, and a political project that acts against oppressive practices and institutions (Freire & Macedo, 1996). One powerful political project is critical literacy.

Critical Literacy

Joe L. Kincheloe proposes that all representations (i.e., textbook content, advertising, music, film) have direct political consequences involving power relationships between people (i.e., race, gender, class, age, etc.). Believing this to be the case and wishing to fulfill my moral obligation as a teacher, I must expand my concept of literacy to include these critical concerns. As a critical pedagogue my goal would be to help my students become critically literate in that they would be aware of the explicit and implicit messages in these representations, understand the effects of them on their lives, and act to minimize their effect on themselves and others.

Patrick Shannon proposes that "critical perspectives push the definition of literacy beyond traditional decoding or encoding of words in order to reproduce the meaning of text or society until it becomes a means for understanding one's own history and culture, to recognize connections between one's life and the social structure, to believe that change in one's life, and the lives of others and society are possible as well as desirable" (1995, p. 83). Critical literacy, as proposed by Shannon, provides students with a language of critique that allows students to understand the critical perspective of society's representations, and to act on each to make their "lives better—more fair, more just, more equal, more free" (Shannon, 1995, p. 88). For the students, as well as the teachers, critical literacy must become a pervasive mindset.

As a Pennsylvania social studies teacher my state-mandated curricular outcomes are entitled, "Citizenship." The state of Pennsylvania obviously intends civic education to be the guiding theme in social studies instruction. In keeping with this intent, I agree with Shannon that "critical literacy education is a necessary part of learning to participate actively in civic life" (1995, p. 123). "Perhaps the injustices in our lives continue unabated because too many Americans have constructed identities that accept the impositions of racial, gender, and social class biases, competitiveness, and war as facts of life, without stopping to ask why things are the way they are, who benefits from these conditions, and how we can make them more equitable" (Shannon, 1995, p. 123). Critical literacy implies the ability to deconstruct these identities, question the biases and competition, and take action to promote egalitarian society. Logically, critical literacy will lead to a truly democratic society.

Being Critical in the Classroom: The Ideal
Joe L. Kincheloe has described a critical pedagogue as a person who deals with power and its manifestations; a person who asks *how* we are going to be political, not whether we will be political. This position is different from a more hermeneutical pedagogy that encourages understanding, but avoids politics. The critical pedagogue engages in political action because of the belief that all human activity is politically inscribed. This belief fosters the desire for equity in the curriculum which is achieved by "locating students in history, exploring their personal experience, and analyzing the cultural engagements in which they invest" (J. L. Kincheloe, personal communication, December 10, 1997). These activities create spaces in the classroom where silenced memories are reclaimed, where memory manipulation is brought to light, and where credentialing and sorting is replaced by justice and compassion.

The importance of moving beyond merely watching, understanding, and producing meaning to taking action is further emphasized in Patti Lather's (1993) idea of catalytic validity. Lather proposes that whether a teacher's critical work is successful depends on how well it motivated the students to take political action. Obviously, in an ideal context, the work of a critical pedagogue as described by Kincheloe and Lather will rub against the grain because students and teachers are not supposed to be political because issues of power and representation are not in the traditional venue of students and teachers.

Traditionally, the pedagogy of teachers is more like the banking notion of education (Freire, 1985) where "teachers perceive students as empty containers that need to be filled with pre-established bodies of knowledge. The narrowly defined 'facts' and pieces of information that are transmitted are often disconnected from both teachers' and students' social realities. Students are thus treated as objects that are acted upon, rather than knowledgeable participants in the construction of deep and meaningful learning experiences" (Leistyna, Woodrum, & Sherblom, 1996, p. 333).

The difference between these two pedagogical philosophies is not so much the content, but how the content is interpreted and whether the content *should* be interpreted. A critical pedagogue believes that all meaning is not only socially constructed, but also inherently political. Whether a teacher tells the students what to believe, or allows students to construct their own meaning is a political act. The former sustains whatever culture the teacher is transmitting, and the latter allows divergence from the norm—both are powerful political statements by the teacher. No one would contest E. D. Hirsch, Jr.'s (1988) list of events and people in his presentation of cultural literacy as things that would be valuable for students to know. However, a critical pedagogue would: (1) deny that these are truths/facts; promote critical reflection on the veracity of their established meaning; (2) re-contextualize them to include power relationships; and (3) examine the absent voices, restricted representations, and the silenced memories that inhibit a broader understanding and which are not represented on Hirsch's list.

The implications of these actions are that oppressive structures are challenged by eliciting the prior assumptions of students, and that the teacher no longer reinforces the disenfranchisement of marginalized viewpoints.

Cultural Constraints on Being Critical

For a deeper understanding of anything, context is the key. To more fully understand my experiences with criticality, I will provide relevant personal biographical experiences as well as my definitions. These are all essential in understanding the intent behind the criticality of the activities that will be presented. However, a systemic perspective allows us to understand how this intent is constrained by the culture of the school and that of the larger society. Specific constraints can be indicated as the school culture, the learning materials, the reduction of curriculum into disciplines, power codes, and the lack of critical materials.

The Constraints

The school culture in which I teach is characteristically non-critical. By the time the students arrive they are sufficiently acclimated to the ranking and sorting process (Sarason, 1990) to the point where they know their capabilities, their identity, and their goals. Of course these capabilities, identities, and goals are largely outcomes of their ranking and sorting experiences. This affects my attempts to be critical in many ways. The higher ranking students (and their parents, school administration, and other teachers) work to validate the current rankings, and the ranking processes. Also, when critical activities allow the inequities of the rankings and ranking processes to come to light, the stakeholders (i.e., students, parents, administrators, other teachers) resist the critical insight that arises from these activities and assails them as a waste of time, or as a threat to the prevailing order. Surprisingly, the lower-ranked students join the resistance to critical activities. Therefore, critical activity must be more covert than overt, and infused in the regular curriculum and instruction rather than represented as a radical makeover. More specifically, the critical activities that I crafted are not a complete rejection of traditional school programs and classroom structures but a combining of considerations of difference and its social consequences with the learning of the skills and cultural capital necessary for success within the larger culture (Shannon, 1995).

Besides the deleterious effects of the ranking and sorting function of this type of school culture, the learning materials and the disciplinary structure of the school act to limit critical activity. However, the textbook with the accompanying support materials can be an ally in exploring the effects of power and difference on people past and present. If students are taught to be active critical researchers, then a textbook acts as a resource and a counterpoint to what meanings the student constructs. Also, as a researcher, the student must learn to gather information from diverse sources such as qualitative interviews, traditional library media, audio-visual media, Internet, and critique all information. Instead of accepting the assumptions of the textbook authors, the students can construct their own point of view based upon a critical critique of the information.

A greater detriment to the study of power and difference is the reduction of high school curriculum into separate disciplines. This unnatural construction of what life is like is more difficult to overcome. For instance, in our daily adult lives do we separate math from science, from writing, from speaking? The unnaturalness of the separation of the disciplines can be overcome when every teacher in every discipline promotes the core literacies (writing communication, speaking communication, technological communication, visual communication) as well as integrates math, science, social studies, the fine arts, and language arts in their own discipline. Actively pursuing a holistic or global perspective is in itself a critical activity.

Patrick Shannon (1995) identifies the traditional school skills and content as "power codes" that allow individuals to move ahead in our society. Shannon further points out that knowing these power codes is not enough because "the biases that separate different life-paths continue to operate regardless of an individual's knowledge of 'power codes'" (1995, p. 16). However, as Shannon would agree, learning these power codes is an essential step along with the recognition of the biases that oppress individuals. Therefore, my critical pedagogical strategy is to promote power code literacy along with a critical consciousness.

A final constraint is the availability of critical materials. Materials that present critical viewpoints for high school students are very rare. The kind of critical writing that is available for college students is problematic due to its reading level and the use of graphic language and depictions of situations that many school boards would find unacceptable. This scarcity of support materials puts additional stress on the critical teacher to find time to create these materials, or to develop the skill of creating critical materials. The excellent writing that is available on a college level from the areas of critical theory, cultural studies, and postmodernism needs to be transposed to a level that can be understood by all students. Critical thinkers need to counter the user-friendly barrage of materials from sources such as Disney, American Girls, Barbie culture, and popular media in general that promote the oppressive nature of our dominant culture and objectify our children for purposes of profit. The availability of age-appropriate critical materials would greatly facilitate a teacher's efforts to provide pedagogical opportunities that challenge student assumptions and broaden their consciousness.

My Situation

Realistically, the political context of a school affects a teacher's ability to be critical. My school is a typical hierarchy with a top/down power structure where the power is centralized in the administration. As in most educational hierarchies, teachers have power through that which is given to them by the administration and through the teacher's own efforts in appropriating power. In my school, when the classroom door closes, teachers have significant power over their curriculum and instruction.

My students are generally white, blue-collar with few people of color. Diversity is represented in the few Asian-Americans, and immigrants (mostly Russian). The students are taught in a self-contained classroom by myself (no team teaching) within an 80 minute block schedule in which class size ranges from the mid to upper twenties. The critical activities that will be reported occurred in three ninth grade social studies classes which are somewhat heterogeneously grouped (the composition of my classes affected by the homogeneously grouped math and science classes). The course is an American History course that focuses on domestic policy from 1880 to the present.

The course has a textbook; however, most activities are supported by supplementary materials or student research. The use of numerous types of resources provides a diverse foundation for power code and critical activities. Authenticity through the connection of the past to the present is enhanced through the use of current magazines, newspapers, television media, and the Internet. Within a cultural studies framework the exploration of popular culture across generations guarantees critical study within an authentic, relevant context. In a power code sense, when students function as researchers they learn to access, process, and present information through lasers, computers, and video technology as well as through traditional sources.

The curriculum is traditionally organized in that it begins with post-civil war America and moves to the present. Knowledge about this time period is constructed by the students and myself, not merely transmitted. If I propose myself to be an expert, it is not as a guardian and transmitter of fact, but as an expert in the critical examination and construction of knowledge.

However, to move from the promotion of basic literacy to critical literacy requires the development of critical language. Teaching students to be researchers is not enough to overcome the inequities that pervade our society. Students must have a basic critical vocabulary that allows them to critique not only the information that they uncover, but also the effects of their own behavior in perpetuating oppression. They need to know that knowledge and the use of knowledge is assumptive and inferential. To move from the realm of theory into the reality of practice required me to examine my curriculum for spaces that could be appropriated for critical activity. One ubiquitous space was language. Infusing words that act as powerful codes in our society into my curriculum provided the continuity that critically focused student attention in an authentic and relevant manner.

Learning about Language

To understand an idea is to be able to communicate the idea in a clear and contextually correct manner. Each area of study and each group of people have their own vocabulary that allows them to communicate their unique thoughts and meanings. For students to fully understand the critical perspective of a situation, they need an essential vocabulary that acts as a lens that allows them to discern the hidden criticality of the situation. Fundamental to my goal of infusing criticality in my social studies curriculum was the development of a vocabulary that provides the opportunities for students to express and examine their assumptions. The technical extent of the vocabulary depends upon the age of the students.

Students need to critically examine the following vocabulary because these terms are used by all aspects of society to construct a reality that is compatible with the reality that they wish to promote. Also, these terms are the more formalized codes that mold student assumptions. Incorporating a critical examination of these terms into my curriculum has three important implications. First, it is more difficult for students to uncover their hidden assumptions without confronting this terminology. Second, these terms formalize and legitimize the assumptions that the student has about the world. Finally, the act of dealing with technical distinctions like the political spectrum creates a complexity that forces a reorganization of the student's construction of reality. An example of these implications is the child who claims to be a conservative like her mother and father. Secure in her lack of critique of the word conservative, she confidently parrots her parents' opinions in every situation. She is always secure in her conclusions because she knows that what she says is true because her parents believe that, and their belief is validated by conservatism—of course she is clueless as to what this means. When given the opportunity to explore conservatism in relation to liberalism in different historical time periods, her prior assumptions become problematic and she is forced to accommodate and struggle with this dis-equilibrium.

The following are examples of how I promoted critical inquiry by using certain terms that easily provide opportunities for the students to critically construct and critique knowledge. The repetitive use of this language was guaranteed by thematically structuring the course. The themes were called: the political spectrum; the mainstream, the marginalized, power; and economics. These themes were posed as lenses that could provide a different view of the same situation. Throughout the course a critical activity was initiated by my direction to "put on the power lens, the political spectrum lens, or the economics lens." Students were instructed to compare how different the same assumption appeared when viewed in these different contexts. All ethical considerations were framed in a Kohlbergian context of self-interest, common good, and principled behavior—along with a caring paradigm as explicated by Nel Noddings. Environmental issues were scrutinized in the context of resourcism, preservationism, and ecocentrism (Oelschlaeger, 1991). Additional terms used in an environmental context were cost-benefit analysis, holism, and androcentrism. By using these terms, students were able to coalesce their ideas into a structured assumption, and then have that assumption challenged through interaction with others.

The Political Spectrum
In each time period (i.e., the Gilded Age, the Progressive Era, the Roaring Twenties, the Great Depression, etc.) students examined the political spectrum in the context of reactionary, conservative, liberal, and radical thought. The initial distinction between the Left and the Right involved the different attitudes that people hold about: government involvement in the affairs of people; people's receptiveness toward change; and their orientation toward the past or future as the best of times. The complex nature of these labels became evident as the students surveyed others, examined their own beliefs, and applied these labels to each time period. Quite frequently, students who began the course as self-avowed conservatives soon learned that their assumption about their position on the political spectrum was not valid depending on the historical time period or situation. Some students become upset at the elusiveness of forming simple, concrete labels and formula that tell them what to believe in a given situation.

The Mainstream, the Marginalized and Power
At the beginning of the course students were told that our society consists of people who are part of the mainstream and those who are marginalized. They were also told that power can be used as a lens to determine which people are mainstream or marginalized. Since students were not consciously aware of the concept of power, a collaborative small group activity gave them the opportunity to explore power in our society—how to

recognize power, how people get power, and who has power. This activity presented an opportunity for the students to examine power within their school, especially in relation to each other. Of course, the initial recognition of power dealt with teachers/students, teachers/administrators, coaches/players; but soon the focus shifted to power within the student body. My students were able to discern cliques and peer groups (i.e., Jocks, Rads, Skaters, Nerds, Bandies, Drugies, Preps, Hessians), and examine this structure within the context of who has power, how we know they have power, what kind of power they have, and why they have that power. This activity was clinical and emotional because of its authenticity and relevance to the students. It also provided a way to transfer their personal knowledge and feelings about power to the use of power in American History. The consensus opinion about the Skaters was that they were marginalized. Later, I could ask who the Skaters were during the Progressive Era and how were they different from other marginalized groups.

This activity facilitated the introduction of other terms that related to this theme. Terms like dominant culture, subordinate cultures, race, gender, social class, struggle, oppression, voice, absent voices, silence, spaces, resistance, cultural capital, and representation. These terms now became real entities to the students. Also, the theme of marginalization/mainstream/power was interrelated with the political spectrum theme. Attitudes towards change, government involvement in people's lives, and a past or future orientation took on new meanings.

A questioning sequence that was directly related to their student culture could now be used to create an authentic use of these terms and themes. For instance, one sequence of questions dealt with Skater culture (Skaters are students who identify with the norms exemplified by the skateboarding culture, and through their behavior and dress are distinctive from other student subcultures). Is Skater culture a threat to the dominant culture? How does the dominant culture react to the difference represented by Skater culture? How does this reaction affect you if you are a Skater? If you consider yourself mainstream, how does your behavior reflect dominant cultural values, and consequently how does your behavior marginalize Skaters?

As the students worked with these words in different historical contexts, they frequently had to adjust their assumptions about these terms. Through activities that allowed student interaction, students learned that each person defined voice, resistance, or oppression differently through the diverse ways that historical data can be interpreted. The increasing definitional complexity of these terms caused frustration in most students, but critically broadened the consciousness of all students.

Economics

The theme of economics involved two levels of activity. A power code level dealt with macroeconomic basics such as capitalism, socialism, communism, the business cycle, recession, depression, inflation, stagflation, price stability, full employment, economic growth, fiscal policy, monetary policy, corporations, monopolies, capital, supply, demand, price, scarcity, and cost. However, on a critical level, the questions always involved the previous two themes. What were the human costs? Who benefited, who suffered? Who became marginalized? What was the position of the Right and the Left on the economics of the time period? How did the actions of the Right and the Left affect the mainstream and the marginalized? How was power used in the economic struggle between the mainstream and the marginalized? Student interaction in the form of debates and roundtables become more energized and personal because of the definitional complexity of the language. Students would not only argue about the position of the Right and Left on the economics of the time period, but also on the definition of the Right and the Left.

The economic activities were personalized by having the students locate (hypothetically, or actually if they knew about their ancestors) themselves in each time period. If you were alive at this time, in which group would you belong? Because of your position would you have a liberal or conservative position concerning organized labor, immigration, gender, or race? If you were marginalized how would you feel; how would you act? If you were mainstream how would your actions reflect dominant culture thinking?

A sub-theme emerged in the conflict between the philosophy of Laissez Faire and Liberalism as expressed in the New Deal and later in the Great Society. Students were able to track this philosophical conflict and evolution of both philosophies from the Industrial Period through the Reagan years to current policies. By the end of the course it was clear that one's position concerning economic policy is often dependent upon one's position in society. In these terms students were asked to examine the people of a time period as a market source, a source of labor, and as a component in the determination of corporate profit. Other related ideas such as Social Darwinism during the Industrial Age were analyzed as to its reinforcing effect on certain philosophies and political positions of the time period.

Student production of knowledge through the use of these lenses was not judged to be correct or incorrect. Instead, safe spaces were constructed to allow the students to articulate their positions. In addition, opportunities were presented that allowed students to challenge each other's opinions. Individual opportunities through writing, speaking, and visual communication allowed the students to use this language to critically assess their assumptions.

Using the Language

There was no time where this language had to be memorized and repeated on an objective test. The instructional procedure had the students and myself repetitively using the terminology in an authentic way. Opportunities to use this language were diverse and came in the form of position papers, round tables, critiques of videos and text material, required commentary in an expository or contrast essay or speeches, and projects involving music, visuals, role-playing, or computer-generated products.

Two basic literacy activities were an essay and a speech. The format for both was the STEPS essay format (Interact, 1979) in which the student writes a five paragraph essay that included an introduction, three body paragraphs (mnemonically know as Bing, Bang, Bongo), and a summary or conclusion. This format was also used for the speeches. A rubric was used to determine the grade, and as the course progressed the criteria became more stringent. For example, initially to earn a C grade a student needed the basic parts plus four sentences in each body paragraph, and 250 words. By the end of the course a C grade required an interest catcher and a thesis statement in the introduction, paragraph transitions, topic sentences, a more technical conclusion, and a minimum of 350 words. All essays that were not sufficient were redone until they met the C criteria. Of course, what was just described was power code literacy. To add a critical dimension, each essay always utilized the Bongo paragraph as the place where a critical concern had to be discussed.

One essay required an explanation of Laissez Faire in the Bing paragraph, the Progressive agenda in the Bang paragraph, and the student's position in the Bongo paragraph. A common essay required the presentation of the conservative position in Bing, the liberal position in Bang, and the student's position in Bongo. There were many variations on this theme.

The speeches were of two types—a position paper that will be explained later, and a formal speech organized according to the STEPS format. Whether a speech or an essay, the point was to have the students write and speak as often as possible, and with the inclusion of the critical concerns, the student repetitively had to deal with the critical language in written and in oral form.

In consideration of multiple Intelligences (Gardner, 1993), projects were offered to the students that provided other opportunities to do the same thing except in a different way. Project options included visuals (collages, drawings, timelines, bulletin boards), role playing (skits, debates), music (historical period critiques), and technology (laser disk and computer generated presentations). Once again, each project required power code skills and content as well as critical language and critiquing skills.

An example of how these activities were used as opportunities for critical inquiry would be our examination of immigration in the late 1880s and early 1900s. Stations were established through which the students rotated, and each station dealt with an aspect of immigration. Two stations which required a creative writing and a speech focused on these questions: Who was mainstream and who was marginalized during this time period? How were the marginalized affected by their marginalization? What was the melting pot theory? Were the actions taken by the mainstream to promote the assimilation of the immigrants actually attempts to perpetuate the dominant culture? During this time period what would be the difference between a liberal and a conservative opinion on immigration? Which position is compatible with your position on this issue? What are the consequences of your position?

Hand in hand with the critical use of language is the ability to give voice to one's opinions. The opportunities that I provided for my students to critically explore American History and themselves are akin to giving them voice. Student research and student voice are inseparable. My attempts to provide opportunities for students to voice their assumptions provided lessons about voice for me as well as them.

Lessons About Voice

The overriding goal of a critical pedagogue should be to facilitate the transformation of students into critical researchers. The essence of critical research is to deconstruct the production of knowledge and to use one's voice to make known the intricacies of power, dominance, and oppression. Part of the power of oppression lies in the inability of people to talk about oppression. For students to be critical researchers they need to know how to research (a power code skill); be able to think critically; and be able to, and know how to, give voice to their findings.

Giving students chances to tell their stories and to explicate their meanings are rare in public education; yet it is an essential critical activity. The classroom is an ideal social space that can be used to help students develop a political language, and provide opportunities to give voice to that language. One way to give voice can be to provide opportunities in essays for individual commentary, as explained in the previous section. This type of individual and personal space is a safe beginning for students whose voice and confidence have been severely repressed. Accommodating student voice in individual speeches to a class requires a more trusting environment and a greater degree of confidence. However, the ideal would be to provide a diversity of opportunities that promote free and safe student interaction.

Position Papers

Besides promoting spaces for student voice in writing activities and speeches, I also used the idea of position papers to promote critical student interactions. In the beginning of the course each class period started with two or three position papers. This involved students preparing a position on an issue that would be a minimum of 100 words. They would then read their position to the class. After the speech the class could ask questions about what was said. The topic of the first round of speeches was open to anything involving the school. The second round topic had to be picked from anything that was studied in class up to that point. Generally, a student gave the speech from the front of the room, other students asked clarifying questions or gave opinions, and I would ask what more we can learn about this topic if we applied the lenses of power, political spectrum and economics. Since these ninth grade students were new to the school, the first round topics involved issues such as not being able to carry backpacks to class, getting lost in the hallways, the discipline code, student dress restrictions, semester courses instead of year-long courses, and the 80 minute block schedule. Some positions were unexpected such as when an Asian-American girl gave a quietly passionate speech about prejudice that she experienced in the Middle School, and how she wanted to thank those who treated her like a human being.

Usually the initial opinion and the follow-up questions/comments were agreements or disagreements with the topic. However, the follow-up questions using the critical lenses provided an opportunity for students to broaden their commentary and understanding of the topic. Some of the discussions were quite lively and entirely student interactive. My role was to listen, and when appropriate, ask broader more critical questions.

The second round topics included information from the Industrial Age and the Progressive Era such as urban ethnic and racial segregation; John D. Rockefeller, Andrew Carnegie and their methods; the wealth and opulence of the rich; the poverty of the workers; Social Darwinism; laissez faire; the gospel of wealth; rugged individualism; capitalism and government intervention; progress as uncontrolled growth; early unions; the role of the government in labor relations from 1870 to 1900; use of violence to achieve one's ends; resourcism, preservationism, and egocentrism. In addition, hate crimes were added to the list because of a school-wide initiative addressing this problem in our school. Also, students were allowed to select issues or people not on this suggested list.

The outcome of the second round was that almost all students selected different topics, had definite opinions, argued about these opinions, and felt secure to voice their opinions. A watershed point in the promotion of the class environment as a safe environment, in which to give voice to one's concerns, occurred in the first round. A particularly articulate and successful student took the podium and proceeded to give a clever, witty, and very entertaining homophobic speech. As he proceeded to bash gays to the laughter of his classmates, I struggled with how I would react to this blatant display of prejudice. After the laughter subsided, he asked for questions and an equally articulate girl (who later proved to be a peer leader) responded in a quiet but confident manner with a series of questions and then commentary. Her first questions were: Do you know any gay people? Have any gay people ever hurt you? Very methodically she proceeded with her rhetorical questioning and then ended with her own story about her gay uncle. Her story was a balance of sensitivity and humor that provided an effective counterpoint to the homophobic student's prejudice. Two months later in a roundtable, the same student made another homophobic speech, however this time he was totally ignored by the class. Through this experience I (the teacher—the authority) did not say a word. A deeply prejudiced student felt safe to express his viewpoint, and a classmate was able to voice an opposing opinion while the rest of the class sat in rapt attention.

Round Tables
The position paper strategy was used only for two rounds and then I explained to the students that in learning to give one's voice, one must also learn to listen. Therefore, we would participate in roundtable discussions to practice using one's voice and practice listening to others. Two types of round tables (Benking, 1997) were used for the purposes of

creating safe spaces for students to voice their opinions, thus providing an opportunity to listen to others and teaching discussion strategies and skills.

The structure of the first round table was to have the students sit in a circle configuration. Each student received a time-credit (in the form of a piece of paper; however stones, sticks, etc. can be used) which allowed a person to speak one time. If they wished to speak they would give the time-credit to the teacher and then could speak uninterrupted. Other time-credit options were not using the time-credit (which meant not speaking), or giving the time-credit to another person (giving away your voice). The length of the speech can be predetermined or coordinated with the total available time; however, I established no limits. Consequently, speeches ranged from 15 seconds to 3 minutes. My role was that of facilitator. I started the discussion by asking who wished to speak, and when that person was done I asked if someone else would like to speak. If there was no response then the round table was ended. When a student indicated that she wanted to speak, I would collect the time-credit, or, if a student wished to hear more of what another student said, I would transfer the time-credit. The main rule was that when one talked the rest must listen—whispering, laughing, and questioning were inappropriate behaviors. Also, when your time-credit was gone, you could no longer speak.

Round Table One: The 1930s
The topic of the first round table was the decade of the 1930s in America. The students had just completed a study of this time period, and were told that to practice using their voice and listening to others they had the opportunity to comment on anything about this decade. In both ninth grade classes there were three levels of critique involved in the round table: the student opinions and comments about the 1930s; student behavior during the round table; and a group critique of the student behavior led by me at the conclusion of the round table. In both classes the historical commentary essentially revolved around the course themes and was generally bland except for a few heart-felt opinions about some injustice. This reaction was due to the fact that everyone's focus was on the personality dynamic of this interaction. The class clowns said clown-like comments, the bitter and the negative made bitter and negative comments, and the withdrawn and repressed remained withdrawn. Some students passed their time-credits to the clowns and the bitter to hear more of that type of comment. Others tried to take themselves out of the round table by physically positioning themselves so they would not be

facing the group. Two students interrupted their commentary to voice their anxiety about speaking like this to the group.

In both classes about half way through the round table a student used his time-credit to rebut an earlier comment. This sparked a serious of comments supporting one position or the other, and prompted some students to give their time-credit to these speakers. Also, the student who had made the homophobic comment during the position papers used his time-credit to make another. This time there was no response, and he was visibly upset by the lack of reinforcement.

During the round table I took notes on student behavior and after the round table was concluded, I used these observations to stimulate open discussion about voice and listening. My questioning went something like this: Did you notice that Dave and Jess turned their bodies away from the group and did not participate? What does this mean to you? Keith's comments were not very serious, but three other people gave him their time-credits. Why do you think this happened? What made you decide to speak at the time you did, or why didn't you speak? Would you have liked to speak again? How did you feel when you could not? Did you regret giving up your time-credit/voice? How did it feel to know that people were listening to you? How did it feel to know that people were denying you your voice by disrupting your commentary with laughing or talking out behavior? Discussion about these questions was followed by my comments on the value of speaking first or last, and saving the time-credit for the most opportune moment.

This led to a discussion on the politics of voice in respect to not having voice; not using your voice; people denying your voice by not listening; and the loss to the group when others are not allowed voice or choose not to use their voice. I closed the activity with commentary on the Native American custom of the talking stick and its implications for including all voices in decision making. I also mentioned the Japanese custom of having the young speak first and the old last and the political strategy behind that custom. The students were very excited about this activity and desired to do it again. The activity had consumed the whole 80 minute block, and the students could not believe the class period was over. In both of these classes there were students who were chronic behavior problems, socially-emotionally disturbed, learning disabled, gifted, some medicated with Prozac, some on juvenile probation, and most generally immature. During these 80 minutes all students were on task, tuned in, and behaved appropriately. They were empowered, and therefore interested and responsible.

Round Table Two: Test Results

The second round table was conducted in the same manner, except the topic involved the first and subsequently only traditional objective test given in the course. After three months of activity/performance oriented assessment (rubrics, portfolios), I gave the students a test that involved listing, defining, and short answer questions. Prior to the test they received the questions and the answers in a teacher lecture. The test results were poor, with most students scoring below 60%, and only a handful scoring a 90% or better. After returning the tests, I called for a round table to discuss the test results. The topic was posed as a series of guide questions. They were: What did this test measure? Do your test results accurately describe who you are? Do these test results mean that some students are better than others? Which is a better measure of how well you learned the content and skills—this test or the performance activities that we have been doing? Why did you get the grade that you got? The purpose of this round table once again was to explore the topic and also to learn about the dynamics of voice and listening, and this time to explore the politics of testing (ranking and sorting function, resistance, and power).

The authenticity of the topic and their prior round table experience created a very different round table atmosphere. The comments and actions in both classes were characterized by an unloading of feelings; the opinion that true/false and multiple choice tests were better because they were more skilled in guessing than in memorizing; more and earlier disagreement with other students' positions; not giving away time-credits; seven out of twenty-five in the one class not using their time-credit; and the formation of coalitions to promote one position over another.

At the conclusion of the round table a discussion was held concerning why some choose to speak first or later; why no one gave away their time-credit; why some did not speak; whether the coalition forming was evidence of listening; and why there was no inappropriate behavior. The seven who did not speak either said that they were not interested, or someone else voiced their opinion. In my other class, which is a strange mix between very academically oriented students and poorly skilled and behavior problem students, the comments were similar except for the addition of comments such as "school sucks", "tests suck," and "we shouldn't have tests at all." In this class no one gave away their time-credit except one boy who waited till the very end. When queried about this action, he responded by saying that he wanted to hear what everyone had to say and then he was going to pick the one that he wanted to hear more about. Interestingly, he gave his time-credit to a behaviorally challenged girl whose comments were: I am stupid; I don't know nothing; I'm not smart; I don't want to get rid of the projects and the group work. When given a chance to speak again, she talked about her success with the activity-oriented assessments in relation to her lack of success with the objective tests of her other classes.

After these comments, I explained how traditional testing ranks and sorts students and asked for discussion on this function. This was followed by the idea that some people resist things that they do not like by purposefully failing to perform that task, and does that happen in testing? Finally, I asked them to put on their power lens and discuss testing in terms of power. Once again, the 80 minutes went by unnoticed with the students on task, and with an expression of student consternation over the ending of the class.

Round Table Three: A Different Configuration
The purpose of this round table was to focus on voice and listening, but also to explore the idea of being mainstreamed and marginalized. The structure of this round table was different in that inside the circle were five chairs. Students could volunteer to sit in these chairs and be the speakers. The rest would be listeners. Once again, all would have one time-credit, but the difference was that each of the inner five would make a speech proposing a position or opinion about the topic. At the conclusion of the five speeches those in the outer ring could give their time-credit to the speaker whose position they wanted to hear about or, not give time to anyone. At this time the person who had the most time-credits spoke first, and thereafter each of the speakers were able to speak until their time-credits are depleted. Those in the center had voice; those in the outer ring could only give their voice to others. Heiner Benking (1997) has numerous variations on this technique, one being the selection of the five speakers by the facilitator. In this manner voice can be guaranteed for all factions in a population, and those typically without voice can be guaranteed voice or empowered to be able to bestow their voice on another.

The topic of the third round table was concerned with the assessment of the material that they studied about the 1950s and 1960s in America. The focus question was: Which is the best and fairest way to find out whether you learned the information and skills in the unit on the 1950s and 1960s? I made the proposition that I wanted input on how to assess their learning. In both classes more than five people volunteered to be speakers. I told the class to decide, and in both cases they consensually agreed on five people. In one class, after the initial round of speeches, one person received eight time-credits, another three, and the rest one. Three people did not give their time-credits to anyone. During the phase where each used their time-credits to explicate their position, the rest sat and listened. One girl was very agitated throughout this phase. This was the girl who spoke out against the homophobic speech. After the round table during the debriefing she was the first to speak. She was very upset and quickly blurted out that all five speakers had missed the point and didn't answer the question. She spoke loudly and elegantly about this wasted opportunity by the class to influence the assessment on their learning. I asked her why she did not volunteer to be a speaker and why she did not give her time-credit to another. I also asked how she felt after giving up her voice. Others chimed in with similar comments about knowing that the question went unanswered, but unable to do anything because they no longer had voice. We then talked about whether their opinion was represented, the reasons they selected one speaker over another, and how power was represented in this activity. Finally, I asked who felt marginalized, and many responded. This prompted a discussion about the importance of voice in relation to those who are marginalized and to those who marginalize others. I asked other questions such as: What action would marginalized radicals and reactionaries take in a situation like this? Did the individual who received eight time-credits deserve that kind of power? How did that concentration of time-credits represent power? What would they do over, now that they knew the outcome? How did this round table experience compare to our representative democracy?

The other class reacted in a similar way except one speaker received no time-credits. I asked this person how he felt about this turn of events, and he expressed his frustration and resentment which he directed to the others as well as to the activity. I asked the others to comment on his situation, and the comments ranged from: "He didn't say what we wanted to hear", to "that's how it is in politics—he got voted out." I asked him if this lack of acceptance of his ideas would affect his position, and he responded by pointing out that he believed what he said was right. One student offered that he did not volunteer to be a speaker because "they might not agree with me...and I would feel stupid." Another said that he wanted to speak, but was afraid that no one would give him time-credits. Many regretted not volunteering to speak, and some felt that they gave their time-credit to the wrong person.

Round Table Four: Sexual Harassment in the Classroom
As mentioned, our school year is divided into two semesters in which the students change courses for the second semester. The previous round

tables occurred during the first semester of this school year, and with a new ninth grade class the following occurred.

In another American History class was a seventeen year old boy who had previously failed this course. The rest of the class consisted of thirteen boys and six girls who were fourteen to fifteen years old. The class progressed well; however, after a month, what appeared to be normal "boy-girl" interactions of a less mature level intensified to a level that could be construed as sexual harassment. The behavior consisted of: sexual comments directed at three girls by the older boy and later three ninth grade boys; physical touching of the girls by the boys; and, the boys taking personal items from the girls. All of the boys' behaviors were protested by the girls. One girl became quite angry and upset by this behavior, while the other two had ambivalent reactions to this attention.

One response would have been to initiate the behavior modification sequence as indicated in the school disciplinary code, i.e. a warning, a conference with the student, a parent conference, referral to guidance, teacher-assigned detention, and, referral to the principal which would lead to principal-assigned detention and eventually in-school suspension. In actuality, normal teacher reaction in the school would have been to institute time-outs from the classroom, issue a lot of warnings, talk to the students privately, and lecture the class on proper behavior. An English teacher who specialized in "low" sections taught the older boy for two courses and mentioned that he was actually very intelligent and would respond to non-confrontational reasoning. Throughout the school the older boy was intimidating to other students because of his demeanor and size. By this time the older boy and I had developed a reasonably good working relationship, and therefore, I decided to use a round table to deal with the behavior instead of the conventional procedures.

I introduced the topic of the round table by mentioning that behavior was occurring in the classroom that some people would construe as sexual harassment, and even though the behavior was not intended to hurt others, in actuality it probably did or at least violated their individual rights. I further mentioned that this is a good example of what happens in our larger society, and that we would use this as an opportunity to learn about people's beliefs about this sort of thing. I instructed them to get into a round table circle (I used the configuration described in round table one and two) which they had already experienced. I focused the conversation on the following question: What interpersonal agreements do we need in order to get along in class on an equal and just basis? This was explained as an issue of interpersonal boundaries defined as verbal, physical, and personal possessions. I selected two students and asked the rest to imagine that there was an invisible line between the two, much like an invisible line between two countries. I proposed that each person had the right of control over the space within their line and did not have the right to violate the other's space. Violations of space could be verbal, where one says something hurtful or nasty to another; physical, where one touches another in an unwanted manner; and, personal where one takes the other person's personal possessions without permission. At this point the class agreed that all three violations of space had occurred in our class. I reviewed the rules of the round table and asked if anyone had anything to say.

One of the boys who had been engaging in the harassing behavior started it off by saying that it is the girl's responsibility to know that the guys are merely kidding. The period of silence that followed was broken by another boy giving his time-credit to one who just spoke. He continued by saying that the kind of verbal comments that were being made were OK; however, comments of a racial or perverted nature were inappropriate. Also, he stated that the girls should not bring their possessions to class or should hide them from view. One of the girls who was being harassed followed this by saying that everyone knew this was only kidding, but racist comments would be going too far. Another girl, who was a primary target of this behavior, responded by saying that stealing is wrong and that the guys are going too far in what they are saying. At this point the boys protested her comments with laughter. I reviewed the fact that laughter and derisive comments can deny someone her voice and can be used as a tactic to intimidate another person. I then asked if that was their intent. They replied no, and became quiet. The girl, who was the number one target of the harassing behavior, then spoke. In an angry tone she stated that she had every right to bring her personal possessions to class (hairbrush, books, purse, etc.) and that the sexist comments were out of control. Another boy who was never a part of this problem spoke next and supported the idea that the girls can solve the problem by not bringing their personal items to class.

The older boy who precipitated this problem finally spoke. He started with a sexist comment about girls' need to bring some things to class "if it is that time of the month." This caused an eruption of angry comments from the girls and laughter from the boys. I quieted the room and announced that we needed to temporarily stop the round table to discuss this comment. I asked him if he felt his comment could be understood by others as a sexist and hurtful comment. He replied that he did, and that he should not have said it. The tone of our interchange was calm and clinical. At that point, I asked if anyone had any comments about what was just said, and no one did. So, we resumed the round table. The boy continued by admitting that the sexual slurs were getting out of hand but that nothing seriously physical was happening and that the touching that was going on was acceptable.

At this time the girl who felt that this was merely kidding received another time-credit and reinforced the idea that the girls had no reason to bring a lot of personal items to class, and definitely should not "flash them around." After a speech about how bookbags would solve the problem (students are not allowed to carry these within the school day), the older boy gave a time-credit that was given by him to the girl who was his number one target. She never did use the time-credit.

The boy who earlier mentioned that girls should not bring their possessions to class spoke about how touching other students without permission was wrong because "when we are older we will get in trouble for doing this"; therefore, we must now learn not to do it. The older boy received another time-credit and mentioned that 80 minute classes are boring and that is why he needs to "play" with the others. This was followed by another girl, who was an object of harassment, stating that there should be no physical contact because parents do not want it; and, students must learn that unwanted touching is not all right. At this time silence ensued and no one wished to speak further.

At this time, I formally ended the round table, and asked them to respond to some hypothetical situations that I then posed. First, I proposed a situation. I park my car in a less desirable part of a city and my compact disk player is stolen. Is it my fault because I parked where I did and because I didn't take measures to hide the player? Do I have the right to park safely anywhere and to not have to take extraordinary precautions to protect my personal possessions? The class discussed this and arrived at two conclusions: (1) I would not be very smart in doing that; (2) but it was my right. I then asked if there was any difference between this scenario and what was happening to the girls' personal items. There was no student commentary.

Secondly, I asked if there were people of color in the class (there were none), would it be OK to kid with them about their racial features and cultural preferences. The students were united in their condemnation of this kind of behavior. I then asked what the difference was between racial features and gender differences? Is it OK to say nasty things to a female, but not to an Asian-American or an African-American? At this point there was silence until the older boy asked why I had the power to talk about "stuff like this"? I responded with the fact that sexual harassment is a level two offense (level three bringing the harshest punishment) in our school, and that the consequences were very serious. However, if I merely followed the discipline guidelines, this would become an issue of punishment that would cloud the real issue that needs to be dealt with—sexual harassment. I proceeded to point out that I chose the round table so that we could explore our own feelings and attitudes about this issue and, more importantly, how we can live together for the rest of the semester. He nodded his head in an affirmative gesture and sat back.

At this point, I asked the class to examine the responses of the girls who were the objects of this harassing behavior. I mentioned the practice of blaming the victim, and the victim's facilitation of the undesirable behavior. I asked if any of the comments that we heard in the round table were similar to this, and if we will uncover any of this behavior when we study marginalized people in American History? Unfortunately, as often happens in public education, just as many tried to speak at once, the bell rang, and the class ended.

Eight out of the twenty students spoke, and six others gave their time-credit to students who had already spoken. As the class was leaving, I asked two boys if they didn't say anything because they were intimidated by the older boy's presence. One replied that everything that he would have said was said by others, and the other boy (a physically small student), merely hung his head and walked out.

The reason that I relate this incident is because there were some extraordinary outcomes. I later spoke privately with each of the individuals who were primarily involved in the behavior and everyone said that they understood what they needed to do. The first extraordinary outcome was that this became a non-issue in the class. Occasionally, if a comment was made, a quiet word or a quick glance would suffice as a prompt for the student to stop the behavior. However, my sense is that the students corrected their behavior out of a sense of responsibility to our community instead of out of fear of teacher reprisal. The second extraordinary outcome was the fact that an authentic and relevant issue was handled in such a way that allowed the students to formulate their position, have this position challenged, and make an accommodation that was favorable to all concerned. Actually, a third outcome was the opportunity to relate our experience with sexual harassment to the similar situations of discrimination and oppression that were encountered in our study of American History.

In conclusion, these round tables are unusual activities in that they generate emotions that can be used to energize other ideas, and they act as mediums for the internalization of critical language. Those students who felt marginalized in this activity became emotionally connected to the historical and current marginalized people who they were studying. Also, the real value of round table conversation is that through the round table the teacher is helping students construct knowledge instead of being passive recipients of transmitted knowledge.

Control of Knowledge Production: Students as Critical Researchers

Antithetical to the notion of students being objects of transmitted knowledge is the idea of students being critical researchers. The problem is, not only are students not taught to be researchers, but they seldom experience research in a critical context. In my ninth grade classes, I attempted to resolve this problem by focusing the course on research (as a power code activity) and critical research (as an emancipatory, consciousness raising activity). At the beginning of the course, students developed basic research skills involving finding, accessing, and processing information from traditional library sources as well as technological sources such as laser disks, CD-ROM's, videos, and the Internet. As the course developed, students completed a series of research projects that became progressively complex in research requirements, and that required processing information in a critical context. These activities were proposed to the students as exercises in storytelling. The resultant essay, speech, skit, or visual was construed as a text or narrative which could be read in many ways by different people.

For example, one research exercise involved developing a story that answered the focus question: Which philosophy, laissez faire or the progressive agenda, would have been best for American society from 1880 to 1920? The activity required the students to describe laissez faire and the good and bad points of this philosophy, describe the progressive agenda and its good and bad points, and finally to state their own opinion. To complete this story, students had to access the facts as reported by different groups (business people, workers, minorities, government officials) of the time period (not as reported by the textbook; which was used as only one source) and formulate their own judgment.

Small research activities such as this evolved into larger research projects involving journaling, time planning, a written communication, a speaking communication, collaboration, and self-assessment. At all times the stress was on critiquing other students' narratives and authors of sources that they read, and forming one's own interpretation. A criticism of this approach is that it leads to an enervating relativism, where nothing is right, and everyone's opinion is correct. This is a legitimate concern that is best answered through a discussion of validity, reliability, and trustworthiness of the research method; however, it is not a reason to rely on the textbook as a source of truth.

This point was made to the students by using information on Woodrow Wilson and Helen Keller from *Lies My Teacher Told Me* (Loewen, 1995) to contrast how these people were represented in the textbook. By providing a different viewpoint of these historical people, the students had to reason dialectically within a different point of view. This helped the students realize that a researcher must always critically evaluate information and recognize the inherent bias in all stories. Using a critical research method facilitates the learning of the information and promotes recognition of the different perspectives of the dominant culture and the "Others." Which perspective is correct? The answer must be constructed by the individual student.

Another research technique was the deconstruction of popular culture of each historical time period to learn about the hidden cultural messages. For instance, one of the activities in the study of the 1930s was to view excerpts from popular movies of the time period which included a Marx Brothers comedy, a Busby Berkley musical, Laurel and Hardy, and *The Grapes of Wrath*. While viewing these excerpts, students noted the following information: who was not represented, how women were represented, how people of color were represented, how social classes were represented, how different ethnic groups were represented, who were posed as superior/inferior, and who had power. This information was compared to other sources, thus allowing students to form their own conclusions about power in the 1930s. In this way, popular culture became an important source in the understanding of the representations made by the dominant culture of the time period.

Another review of popular culture involving customs of Christmas was used to reinforce the researcher attitude that there is more to something than meets the eye. The critical language of social class, dominant culture, and appropriation of cultural artifacts for sustaining the dominant culture was used to understand the transformation of Christmas in the United States as detailed by Stephen Nissenbaum (1996). Prior to Christmas vacation, excerpts of Nissenbaum's social and cultural history of

Christmas were used to enhance the relevance of the critical themes of the course.

The development of the students as critical researchers culminated in a final project dealing with the 1980s and 1990s. Instead of memorizing textbook material, students once again constructed a history of this time period that reflected their own research. As before, the same research skills were required; however, in relation to available resources students additionally used magazines of the time period (*Rolling Stone, People, Newsweek*, etc.) and qualitatively interviewed adults. The interviews, along with the diversity of other sources (textbooks, technology, popular media), provided differing historical viewpoints of this time period. The task of the students was to synthesize these viewpoints into their own coherent story of the time period.

In conclusion, did all students become critical researchers? Of course, they did not. However, for the first time, they combined the learning of important power code skills with a critical context in *their* production of knowledge. Whether a student or teacher, one never *becomes* a critical researcher, rather the researcher is always *becoming* critical.

Discipline, Class Time, and Other Sources of Subjugation

As often characterized by teachers, "being in the trenches' requires a major effort to survive the day, much less experiment with one's pedagogy." The pressure from important variables such as classroom discipline and the dictates of the culture in which one teaches often quickly dooms one's best (and critical) intentions. The reception of our critical intent by the students is often, at best, disheartening and enervating. A friend who is a public school superintendent reflects the same opinion, except in relation to the teachers in his school district. He decries the fact that when empowered, teachers tend to even more tightly move to anachronistic pedagogues centered on the textbook, and actively resist changes in their learning environment. When faced with the same conclusion in my dealings with school professionals in a consulting context, and as a participant observer in promoting critical pedagogy with my students, I realized that to understand this resistance required a more extensive deconstruction of the situation and a more detailed systemic view.

My efforts to institute a critical pedagogy in my classes was not well received by the students. A more extensive deconstruction and application of systems thinking (Banathy, 1991) led me to these conclusions about their resistance. First, their own lives are more important than American History. The normal concerns that a child must deal with require significant attention, much less the pathology that results from diverse forms of neglect and abuse. These concerns are paramount to the student; they demand the student's attention. How then do we compete with such emotionally powerful concerns and forces? The answer is to create a relevant, authentic pedagogy in which the authenticity is derived from the links that are established between the student's immediate concerns, and the content and skills that need to be learned. This linkage allows the transference of emotion that is the key force in authenticity.

Students do not like authentic activities because in relation to traditional transmissional pedagogies they are hard; they require work and energy. Part of the student resistance became clear in the round tables when they consistently and openly let me know that multiple choice, true and false assessment was what they wanted because it was easy. Some students were willing to trade a lower grade for the lack of hassle that accompanied this type of assessment. Others clearly did not like the critical analysis of American culture and society because it related directly to their current status in school and in society. Some resented the knowledge that people are objects of manipulation and subjugation by more powerful forces. My conclusion was that resistance in this form validated my ethical intent in moving toward a critical pedagogy. They were not resisting the criticality, they were resisting *the knowledge of their own oppression.*

A second conclusion is that in public schools some students are pathological. Despite medication and parole, they are disruptive. Because of this there is pressure on the teacher to use draconian methods of control that involves curriculum and instruction as well as classroom management techniques. Also, many teachers will admit to the pervasive fear that traditional authoritarian measures of control will no longer work in our litigious society. Students want stability and security as much as teachers and administrators desire the same. Unfortunately, the more effective direction is to build community and utilize the power and caring of all members of the class to create a stable and secure learning environment. I use the word unfortunate because this is the least used measure to sustain a viable, egalitarian learning environment. The situation detailed in Round Table Four is an excellent example of how community building can work in dealing with serious behavior problems—work for not only the teacher's classroom management need, but also for the involved students.

Returning to my friend's comment about the empowerment of teachers and their subsequent resistance, I would argue that this situation is similar to the student resistance in that it is prompted by individual concerns for stability and security—and that it is a product of the educational culture in which they live. We are all aware of the isolation of teachers and the deleterious effects of individualization and balkanization on teachers (Hargreaves, 1994). Contextualizing my friend's comment in a systemic perspective, I wonder if the empowerment dealt with issues of curriculum or instruction, or with issues of control over resource availability, scheduling, arrangement of space, teaming, and interdisciplinary possibilities. Was my friend's empowerment sincere but limited? Did it free people to deal with those powerful, emotional issues that affect their security and stability? I am fortunate in the autonomy that I have over my classes and courses; however, even a seemingly small constraint, such as having to teach to a standardized test, would affect my ability to act critically. The concomitant pressure to "cover the material" would require extraordinary creativity to maintain a critical classroom.

Despite the difficulty in meeting the diverse academic, social, and emotional needs of the students in my classes, things got better. Near the end, a semblance of community was established. In retrospect, I credit this to critical conversation which occurred in diverse ways between students, parents, administrators, guidance counselors, round tables, and impromptu frank class discussions about issues of behavior and failure. These conversations were critical because they all focused on issues of power and control (external as well as internal loci of control). Most conversations involved two or three people except for the round tables and class discussions. These were the catalysts that facilitated community building.

Being and Becoming

To engage in critical activity requires an acceptance of the state of being and becoming—an evolutionary or praxiological state that is essentially a recursive loop of critical reflection. To commit to critical activity is a commitment to the struggle toward egalitarian pedagogical structures and processes. Critical activity, as I experienced, seems to be what Freire described as conscientization or the continuous critically reflective interplay between theory and practice. The act of being critical challenges one's own critical beliefs, forces an exploration of one's identity, which in turn fosters a state of becoming or a reconstruction of one's identity. Being and becoming critical is about finding out who you are and what you represent.

Being critical implies an interaction with the social environment that broadens and enriches one's sense of criticality by providing a greater context that includes the harsh realities of life. The struggle to determine "who I am" in the context provided by interaction with the social environment becomes quite different from the struggle to answer the same question when isolated from the multiple realities of the social environment.

Besides the personal growth that a critical pedagogue encounters, the positionality of teachers in the system provides opportunities to reclaim spaces in the classroom for the promotion of social justice, as well as facilitating the development of criticality in other stakeholders (students, teachers, parents, administrators). Implicit in education is the moral obligation to care about others and oneself. Caring requires the difficult task of recognizing ourselves in the oppression of others and recognizing our complicity in perpetuating oppressive structures. The essence of being and becoming critical is this recognition and the continued commitment to change.

A final thought deals with the imperatives of community building. The incredibly complex problems of our postmodern society can only be resolved through the re-establishment of egalitarian community. To be successful, a sense of community must pervade the entire system. In an educational system, community must be promoted in the classroom subsystem, within the faculty, and between the school and the external local community. In addition, a global perspective must include the sense that we are part of larger communities (i.e., the nation, the world) and therefore must responsibly interact with them. The position of the teacher within the system allows critical teachers to promote community building through the creation of political spaces in all of the sub-systems of which they are a part. Inherent in the creation of these spaces is the need to promote a critical language that will facilitate a critical dialogue. The development of this language can begin in the classroom and grow in use as teachers and students evolve their critical consciousness through their mutual struggle to be and to become critical.

References

Banathy, B. H. (1991). *Systems design of education: A journey to create the future.* Englewood Cliffs, NJ: Educational Technology Publications.

Benking, H.(1997). *Sharing Spaces.* Available http://newciv.org.cob/members/SharingSpaces.htm

Bennett, K P. & LeCompte, M. D. (1990). *The Way Schools Work: A Sociological Analysis of Education.* New York: Longman.

Freire, P. (1985). *The politics of education: Culture, power and liberation.* New York: Bergin & Garvey.

Freire, P. & Macedo, D. P. (1996). *A dialogue: culture, language and race.* In P. Leistyna, A. Woodrum, and S. A. Sherblom (Eds.), *Breaking Free: The transformative power of critical pedagogy.* Cambridge, MA: Harvard Educational Review.

Gardner, H. (1993). *Multiple Intelligences: The Theory in Practice.* New York: Basic Books.

Giroux, H. (1988). *Teachers as Intellectuals: Toward a Critical Pedagogy of Learning.* Boston, MA: Bergin & Garvey.

Giroux, H. (1992). *Bordercrossings.* New York: Routledge.

Hargreaves, A. (1994). *Changing Teachers, Changing Times.* New York: Teachers College Press.

Hirsch Jr., E. D. (1988). *Cultural literacy: What Every American Needs to Know.* New York: Vintage Books.

Interact Company. (1979). *STEPS: An essay writing program on three levels for English and social studies.* Los Angeles, California: Interact.

Lather, P. (1993). *Fertile obsession: Validity after post-structuralism.* Sociological Quarterly, 35.

Leistyna, P., Woodrum, A., & Sherblom, S. A. (eds). (1996). *Breaking free: The transformative power of critical pedagogy.* Cambridge, MA: Harvard Educational Review.

Loewen, J. W. (1995). *Lies my teacher told me.* New York: Simon & Schuster.

Nissenbaum, S. (1996). *The Battle for Christmas.* New York: Alfred A. Knopf.

Oelschlaeger, M. (1991). *The Idea of Wilderness.* Yale University Press: New Haven, CT.

Sarason, S. B. (1990). *The Predictable Failure of Educational Reform.* San Francisco: Jossey-Bass Publishers.

Shannon, P. (1995). *Text, Lies, and Videotape: Stories About Life, Literacy, and Learning.* Portsmouth, NH: Heinemann.

Using a Journal to Develop Reflective and Critical Thinking Skills in Classroom Settings

Valerie J. Janesick

> Beneath the rule of men entirely great,
> The pen is mightier than the sword,
>
> Edward Bulwer-Lytton
> *Richelieu*, 1839, Act II, Sc.2.

Introduction

I write this chapter as a teacher of over twenty years who has found that the best way to teach my students to be critical thinkers is to model those skills which will help them in their quest to be critical thinkers. One such skill I like to teach about and indeed to model, is journal writing. In this chapter, I would like to describe and explain how a classroom practitioner might develop critical thinking skills in by keeping a journal, either as a written journal in a notebook or on the computer in an electronic file. There are many types of journals, of course, which I shall describe in the body of this article. I would like to focus on keeping a classroom journal. A classroom journal is a journal that individual learners, as well as the teacher, construct and create on a daily basis. I have used this approach with adult learners who are student teachers, intern teachers and with doctoral students who wish to improve their classroom practice. My doctoral students who themselves teach, in turn, use this with their students who range in age from elementary to post secondary student ages. I invite the reader to adapt any of these ideas to the level appropriate to their own needs. For this paper, I will focus on the teacher keeping a classroom journal as a tool for deepening critical thinking about classroom practice. I focus on the teacher in this paper in order to begin the journey. The next step of the journey would then be to work on journal writing with learners, the topic for another paper. In the meantime, I begin with a brief overview of the history and importance of journal writing.

A Brief Historical Overview of Journal Writing

Journal writing has a long and reliable history in the Arts and Humanities, as well as various moments in the Sciences. It is not by accident that artists, writers, dancers, musicians, physicians, poets, architects, saints, scientists, therapists, and educators use journal writing in their lives. Virtually in every field, one can find exemplars in those fields all of whom kept detailed and lengthy journals regarding their everyday lives and their life work. In this paper I view journal writing as a powerful heuristic tool and classroom research technique. Keeping a classroom journal may help to illuminate and refine thinking skills at all levels. In addition, keeping a journal may be viewed as an interactive tool of communication between the teacher and the learner.

As we begin this journey of describing and explaining journal writing, it is important to realize the lengthy and significant history of journal writing. While individuals have probably kept journals throughout recorded history for various reasons, some of the first known journals were written in Greek and Roman times. Indeed, St. Augustine and Blaise Pascal kept journals to chronicle moments in their own lives as they tried to find out more about how the mind works. In the 10th century, ladies of the Japanese court wrote precise and candid description of everyday life and the inner workings of one's beliefs and feelings. Often these writers hid their journals under their pillows and so the journals became known as "pillow diaries." These documents went beyond the daily record of life; they were texts that recorded dreams, hopes, visions, fantasies, feelings, and innermost thoughts. Next, the rebirth and awakening of the Renaissance brought with it an era of almost required journal and diary writing. There was an almost understood agreement that one must chronicle the spirit of rebirth and living in personal terms case by case.

The 1660's brought us Samuel Pepys, who for nine years described exactly and in astounding detail the people, politics, sorrows, and joys of life in London. His thick description of the problems of the Church of

England, the monarchy, the Navy in which he served, various wars of the day, the great fire and the plague are brilliant and illuminative records of literature and history. As luck would have it, the first published versions of his diary did not appear till 1825, followed by reissues and new editions well into the late 1890's. It was at this time that the Victorians focused on both letter writing and journals.

Likewise and prior to the Victorian era, a number of spiritual and some religious groups kept spiritual journals. The Quakers, for example, beginning in the 17th century, often and regularly described their spiritual journeys, doubts, questions, and beliefs. John Wesley, founder of Methodism, kept volumes recording his symbolic relationship with his God. Indeed, many Puritans recorded their trust in God, doubt, uncertainty, miseries in their lives, sins, omissions of goodness and so on. The voyage of the *Mayflower* is eloquently and curiously described in journal form. For people who were embarking on new adventures, the journal became an outlet for fears and moments of deep despair on the voyage. The use of the journal from spiritual record to political record flourished as well. Remember, at these points in time, writing was a key and important means of communication. There were no telephones, pagers, computers, televisions, or news media as we know them. For example, during the French Revolution, many writers produced "journals in-time". These were personal accounts of arguments regarding the revolution and which revealed deep and passionate feelings of patriotism, nationalism and disgust for the corrupt monarchy.

Similarly, in this country, during the Westward expansion movement, explorers like Lewis and Clark chronicled their movement West describing relationships with the Native Americans and encounters with existing communities. Likewise, pioneer women not only cooked around the campfires, but took the time to record personal impressions of the Westward movement. Later, these would be chronicled in the play, *QUILTERS*.

This play powerfully documented a history of depression, sorrow, joy, misunderstanding and treachery. There would be no sugar-coating of injustice and bigotry in these diaries. In addition, an eloquent account of the brutality of slavery in this country is chronicled in the Slave Narratives. One cannot turn away from the writings of Olaudah Equiano, Mary Prince, Frederick Douglass, or the Incidents in the life of a slave girl, Harriet Jacobs, by now all classics of this genre. The clarity, suffering, and degradation described in the Slave Narratives inform our understanding of a history of the Black Diaspora. Were it not for these detailed accounts, a critical piece of American history would certainly have been forgotten.

Yet literary and historical figures are not the only journal writers. The field of psychology has long made use of journal writing as a therapeutic aid. The cathartic function of journal writing has been widely recommended by many schools of therapy. Therapists view the journal as an attempt to bring order to one's experience and a sense of coherence to one's life. Behaviorists, Cognitivists and Jungian analysts have used journals in the process of therapy. The journal is seen as a natural outgrowth of the clinical situation in which the client speaks to the self. Most recently, Ira Progoff (1975) has written of an intensive journal. Progoff developed a set of techniques that provide a structure for keeping a journal and a springboard for development. As a therapist himself, he has conducted workshops and trained a network of individuals to do workshops on keeping an intensive journal for unlocking one's creativity and coming to terms with one's self. The intensive journal method is a reflective, indepth process of writing, speaking what is written, and in some cases sharing what is written with others. Feedback is an operative principle for the Progoff method. The individual needs to draw upon inner resources to arrive at the understanding of the whole person, The journal is a tool to reopen the possibilities of learning and living. Progoff advocates:

a Regular entries in the journal in the form of dialogue with one's self,
b Maintain the journal as an intensive psychological workbook in order to record all encounters of one's existence.
c Some type of sharing of this growth through journal writing with others.

The method makes use of a special bound notebook divided into definite categories which include: dreams, stepping stones, dialogues with persons, events, work, and the body. The writer is asked to reflect, free associate, meditate, and imagine that which relates to immediate experience. The latest version of his text (1992) is a definite testimonial to a solid example of techniques for keeping a journal.

Beyond the psychologists, perhaps the two most identifiable writers of journals in our memory are Anne Frank and Anaïs Nin. In fact, *The Diary of Anne Frank* and the many volumes of *The Diary of Anaïs Nin* are published in over 20 languages. Anne Frank's lived experience hiding from the Nazis not only details her feelings of growing up under these conditions, but offer a political and moral interpretation of humanity's failures. On the other side of the coin, Anaïs Nin describes and explains her journey to understand her self, her body, and her mind. Interestingly enough, she also studied Ira Progoff's journal writing method before she died. Although she rejected its structure, she commented on the importance of its purpose and ultimate goal of self-actualization. Even more current, one only has to walk through the display aisles of the major bookstores like Border's or Barnes and Noble and see the many examples of recently published journals. Just yesterday I found the following:

1. Keith Haring Journals
2. The Andy Warhol Journals (this one complete with photos, drawings, and artwork)
3. The Journal of a Viet Nam Veteran
4. The Journal of Someone Dying of AIDS.

The point is that this genre is alive and well, and teachers and learners should not be afraid of trying to keep a journal.

In fact, journal writing is so prevalent now, that one only has to surf the Internet and see thousands of journal resources, examples, and personal histories on line. For example, there is an on-line course on journal writing offered by Via Creativa, a web site entirely devoted to Ira Progoff's Intensive Journal Workshop, chat rooms on journal writing, exemplars of diaries and journal writing, and literally thousands of resources. The reader of this paper will be somewhat overwhelmed by the multitude of sources. As with anything on the Internet, you will have to sift through to see what is best for your learning style. In general, the common thread which unites all these resources on the Internet is the agreement that journal writing is a way of getting in touch with yourself in terms of reflection, catharsis, remembrance, creation, exploration and problem solving, problem posing, and personal growth.

Theoretical Perspectives

While journal writing has its seeds in psychology, sociology, and history, I will rely on understanding the use of the journal from Social Psychology and the Symbolic Interactionists. In addition, what Denzin calls "Interpretive Interactionism" will inform and frame this discussion. Symbolic Interactionists have historically argued that we all give meaning to the symbols we encounter in interacting with one another. Interpretive Interactionists go a step further in that the act of interpretation is also a communication act with one or more interactors.

Basically, the art of journal writing and subsequent interpretations of journal writing produces meaning and understanding which are shaped by genre, the narrative form used, and personal cultural and paradigmatic conventions of the writer who is either the researcher, participant, and or co-researcher. As Progoff (1992) notes, journal writing is ultimately a way of getting feedback from ourselves and in so doing, it enables us to experience in a full and open-ended way, the movement of our lives as a whole and the meaning that follows from reflecting on that movement.

Why Journal Writing?

Students and colleagues have often asked me why should one invest the time in journal writing? To this I can only reply that journal writing allows one to reflect, to dig deeper if you will into the heart of the words, beliefs, and behaviors, we describe in our journals. The clarity of writing down one's thoughts will allow for stepping into one's inner mind and reaching further into interpretations of the behaviors, beliefs, and words we write. For example, a student conducting a mini study in a qualitative methods class wrote in her journal and described some of her inner thoughts:

> I am a bit wary of this research. . . Am I really a researcher because I am taking a class? Can I ever hope to portray what someone else believes or at least says she believes? How will I know if I am being fair? Will I be able to trust this person? Will she trust me? Why should she trust me? Am I being to critical of myself? I am waiting here and she is already 20 minutes late. I hope she gets here soon. . . Here she comes. Now I try to capture this person's thoughts on why she is an administrator. . . .
>
> KS. 97

As we look at this journal entry, one can easily see the learner/researcher in training, asking questions which cause reflection on various issues about the research process. She is beginning to know more about herself and her strengths and weaknesses. To continue with examples of journal writing to illustrate my point on reflection, I would like to continue the bulk of this paper in the form of my own journal about writing this paper.

Monday

I am trying to decide if I should write this paper with a section on describing the various uses of journal writing like keeping a journal of one's dreams, a journal in the form of a dialogue like Ira Progoff suggests. . .

Or, should I write about only keeping a classroom journal? If I do that will I be limiting the options for readers of this paper? Of course, I have had great success with classroom journals with two simple prompts for the teacher to write about. One is: POSITIVE ELEMENTS IN THE CLASSROOM TODAY, and the other is, FRUSTRATING ELEMENTS IN THE CLASSROOM TODAY. I wish I could find the examples I saved from one of my students, who did keep a journal based specifically on these two questions each day. I think I will try to find these. . .

Tuesday
In my quest to find examples, I was most fortunate. Here is an example from J.D., an experienced teacher of some 15 years who teaches middle school in a metropolitan area. What an amazing example of her thoughts on the classroom:

> I love these kids . . . most from broken homes, most thinking I am their parent, advisor, guardian, good cop, teacher, analyst, and coach. I am trying to get them to read more . . . comic books, novels, go to the library, and then get them to write about this. I think I will go for the two page report idea again. It gives me something to reinforce their understanding of what they read and to give them some feedback. I am worried about P. He is always skipping class these days and although I know his brother is home from prison, I wish he would come back to school. I will talk to the principal about this today if I don't forget. I also want to design a new way of evaluating my class without the letter grades we are stuck with. I am reading about the use of portfolios in classroom assessment and I think I will try it this month and get the kids to plan it with me.
>
> J.D. 4-96

If this isn't a good example of what I myself am trying to achieve as a teacher/professor, I don't know what is.

Wednesday
Back to this paper, should I write about the fact that the teacher who decides to keep a journal is a researcher in effect? The teacher is documenting her life history or at least a portion of it. She opens herself up for redirecting her teaching or reshaping it upon reflection of some of her practices and feelings about that practice. Also, the teacher is a kind of historian, documenting life on a daily basis providing a continuous written record. Then, the students who elect to keep a journal, are also in that same situation. Should I mention that not everyone can keep up with the demands of journal writing? The discipline and desire involved nearly outweigh some individuals ability and or time. On the other hand, can this not be for all who are interested in becoming better writers, thinkers, scholars? How does one set time apart for journal writing? I recall the teacher who said she only had twenty minutes after school to write in her

journal and that was it. Then, as she ultimately decided she needed to keep a journal at home as well since once she started to write, she found she was staying at school and writing for at least an hour each day. She got up an hour earlier than anyone in her house and started writing in the early morning hours, a technique advocated by many writers. It seems she had to write about her problems in the class from day to day. I will ask her about this tomorrow and see if she will let me use her examples from her journal.

Thursday
I am so happy H.H. let me see her journal entries. I am going to use only one of her examples regarding a problem in her classroom.

> . . . Once again I have to deal with M. Why is he refusing to write in class and why is he afraid to tell me what is bothering him? He has done this before but we could always talk this out before. . . I am taking a class right now that relates to this directly. . . None of the books or papers is helping me so I am just going ahead and going to try a home visit to talk to his Mom and see if she can help. . . Since I started visiting parents who were unable to come to teacher conferences, I am humbled by what I am learning. . . M's mother is working three jobs to keep the family of three children and herself together. . . I wonder if I would have her courage at this point? She has told me that M. is getting in with the "wrong crowd" and has been involved in questionable activities which is why he is skipping school so often. Even sending someone to check on this has not yielded any positive results. She said she thought this was due to more than "being a teenager" but felt that there were no strong role models for him at home. No relatives live nearby. I brought some of M's work to show her and she felt a bit reassured that at least he was doing something, though she added that "he could do better". I decided I would talk to him tomorrow and ask him to help me organize the class project on voting in the November elections. I felt conflicted upon leaving the house, for I feared that M's Mom needed to talk to someone about her kids and that I wasn't very much of a help at all. I do feel more inspired to be better at letting the kids take over more of the responsibility for class projects. Actually it was M. who taught me this month when he volunteered to lead the book circle discussion.
>
> H.H. 96

When I look at this entry I can see someone still alive and thinking about teaching in a way that makes the basic questions of what and how to teach take on a renewed meaning. Is this a good time to talk about how journal writing can assist one in developing creativity? I am reminded about creativity by Ira Progoff's text, *AT A JOURNAL WORKSHOP: WRITING TO ACCESS THE POWER OF THE UNCONSCIOUS AND EVOKE CREATIVE ABILITY.* I am also reminded that Anaïs Nin didn't like Progoff's method; it was too methodical for her. Yet every time I read that text, I see something new in it. Even reading the publicity blurbs about it, like Joseph Campbell saying "Progoff's Intensive Journal Process is one of the great inventions of our time," makes me rethink my own writing. Tomorrow, I will describe a bit about Progoff's method.

Friday

When did I first hear about Ira Progoff? Now I recall. It was nineteen-eighty-something and I was giving a talk at the University of Alberta in Edmonton on Qualitative Research Methods. In the audience was a former high school teacher of mine who happened to be working on her doctorate and she mentioned it to me in passing. Since that day, I have tried to put into practice as much of what Progoff describes. His intensive Journal Workshop teaches us to be reflective and aware of our unconscious self. He advocates writing a journal as a dialogue with oneself. Can you imagine? I thought I could never be able to do this; then, step by step I started. He began his journal workshops in 1966 and has been refining them ever since. He talks about keeping a daily log. Yes, there is no getting around it—you need to write in this journal every day!!! No resting.! There is only movement forward. He suggests keeping dialogues with key persons in our lives, with our body, with our works, with our roads not taken, with events that were critical in our lives with society, and with our dreams. In other words, we write our journals in dialogue form that prompts us to think in new ways.

Saturday

Progoff got me thinking about all the books on journal writing that have been useful to me and my students. One of my next favorites, after Progoff, is Thomas Mallon's (1995) text, *A BOOK OF ONE'S OWN: PEOPLE AND THEIR DIARIES.* In his overview of diarists and journal writers, he categorizes the writers as follows:

- **Chroniclers**: People who keep their diaries every single day as if recording the news,
- **Travelers**: People who keep a written record during a special time such as a vacation or a trip,
- **Pilgrims**: People who want to discover who they really are,
- **Creators**: People who write to sketch out ideas, and inventions in art or science,
- **Apologists**: People who write to justify something they have done to plead their case before all who read the journal,

- **Confessors**: People who direct ritual unburdenings, conducted with the promise of secrecy or anonymity,
- **Prisoners**: People who must live their lives in prisons or who may be invalids and as a result must live their lives through keeping a journal.

Of course, any writer might be a combination of any of these categories but this might be useful as a tool to understand different approaches to keeping a journal. He gives numerous examples of individuals who fall into these categories to illustrate the importance of keeping a journal. In fact, he became interested in writing his book because he himself has kept a journal for over thirty years. I share that interest with him. I started writing a journal in high school and since then have been faithful to journal writing.

Currently, there are so many wonderful resources on journal writing in popular culture and specifically accessible through the Internet. Recently, in a search on the world wide web, by entering the words "journal writing," I saw over three million entries! In fact, there is a journal-writing course on the web offered by a group called Via Creativa. And there are many web sites on the Progoff method; i.e. , journal writing as a tool for therapy and spiritual growth. I will think about this tonight and write more tomorrow.

Sunday
Last night I couldn't sleep as I thought about all the examples of journal writing in popular culture. First, I recalled Doogie Howser. The television show of a few years ago chronicled a youthful doctor who was a sort of Leonardo DiCaprio type. Younger than his peers in the medical profession, Doogie opened and closed each show writing in his journal which he kept on his laptop. His struggles as a gifted teenager among cynical colleagues and his struggle to know himself were the focus of the journal writing moments in the show. Then, I remembered Bob Packwood's diaries. The Senator actually wrote about his extracurricular sexual activities away from home and family which ultimately was used to force his resignation from the US Senate due to his sexual harassment of young office workers. And of course, who can forget the O.J. Simpson trial? The mass media circus that surrounded this bizarre case was highlighted for me by the fact that the murdered woman's diary was not allowed as evidence *even though it described in great detail circumstances directly related to the case.* All this makes me wonder what would be most helpful to the

reader of this paper. Since the audience is an audience of practitioners in educational settings, I think I need to mention one more resource about journal writing. It is Tristine Rainer's (1978) text, *The New Diary*. Rainer co-taught with Anaïs Nin a course on journal writing to students at a Los Angeles college. She wrote this book, which contains superb examples of journal writing. She, as I, uses the terms *journal* and *diary* interchangeably. She describes seven techniques for journal writing, some very similar to Progoff's technique. Here is her list: portraits, lists, maps of consciousness, guided imagery, altered points of view, unsent letters, and dialogues.

The dialogues come from Gestalt therapies and of course Jungian therapy. In Rainier's text (pp. 104–111), she offers examples of dialogues with the self, the body and works. These examples are fine models for anyone attempting a dialogue. She highlights a Progoff idea, "dialogues with the body," which suggest conversations with the body as a whole. Here is a portion of that example:

ME: Well body, how do you feel?
BODY: Week, shaky, a bit hurt. I feel open and vulnerable. I can't trust my environment yet.
ME: But you'll mend?
BODY: Yes, I'll mend. I don't know how soon. . .
ME: Maybe when you are feeling better, it won't sound so awful.
BODY: Maybe . . . . I'm strong, and I can take it. . .

Obviously, something likes this helps the journal writer relate to the body's messages. In this particular case, the writer was a person who felt disengaged from her body. I recall how many of my students who keep a journal in class resonate with this dialogue technique, though I myself have not tried it yet.

Later on Sunday
I am trying to think about the best way to summarize all the ideas of this paper so far. Especially the reader who is a classroom practitioner may be more interested in the two prompts I wrote of earlier: Positive Elements in the Classroom, and Frustrating Elements in the classroom. I found this example of a Frustrating day from a teacher who just taught music classes all day:

> . . . Oh dear, I am fed up again with everything. And I am particularly fed up with this journal today. Why am I writing about my failures? Are they really failures? Am I not seeing progress with my students because I am so burnt up? Yes that's

right—burnt up not burned out. I love teaching so much and my kids. . . but all the endless bureaucratic Snafus are killing me. I am trying to get my choral group to perform around town at all the schools to raise awareness of violence in our schools and once again, the principal says 'forget it,' because he doesn't want parents to think we have violence in the school. Yesterday , when the two gangs had a fight across the street, he called the police but would not even go outside and lead. Am I only going to work at schools where there is no leadership? Of course I have to keep focusing on the good kids—the breakthroughs like T. who sang her heart out today in her solo and who really wants to go on and study music on a scholarship next year. What's wrong with me that I am getting beaten down by the negative stuff? How can I pull myself to higher ground?
KLL. 1-96

This entry shows the teachers' self-reflection, of course; but now look at this same teacher just four months later.

I looked over my journal from this year and I see a pattern in it. All my complaints and big headaches seem to come from situations where I have no power. Usually, no—make that, ALL the critical incidents I describe in my journal are about the principal, the state regulations, the characters who have some power. But then I see I am playing their game too—I am avoiding confrontations, I am running away from letting myself take control and be Empowered. I have been a wimp. And somehow, I have to deal with my principal. I usually go around him altogether. I also feel like I may need to find a better place to work at this my beloved music.
K.L.L. 5-96

The example goes on at length with this soul searching and although at this point it is not resolved, the writer certainly is thinking through major issues about teaching and learning.

Another Monday

As I try to conclude this piece on journal writing, the major ideas I want to punctuate have to do with journal writing and thought processes. Writing down what we think and feel helps in the journey to improve classroom practice. Some of the examples used in the body of this text may serve to illustrate the individual writer's thinking processes and the willingness to analyze, rethink, and go deeper into a critical stance about one's life and work. Progoff calls this the scope of personal renewal. Others call it reflection. Still others see journal writing, myself included, as a tangible way to evaluate our experience, improve and clarify one's thinking, and finally become a better writer and scholar, if you will. In my own experience of journal writing, and as I see what my students write, I find that we are writing to chronicle our profession. We are talking about examining our own thoughts, beliefs, and behaviors. Many will say that this helps only the writer. Still, if that were the only outcome of writing a journal, I would say that in itself it may help to insure the continuing self-reflection each of us claims as a first step to modeling this for our students. Perhaps this quotation will inspire the reader:

> Oh yes, I've enjoyed reading the past year's diary, and shall keep it up. I'm amused to find how it's grown a person, with almost a face of its own.
>
> Virginia Woolf
> December 28, 1919.

References

Albert, Susan Wittig. (1996) *Writing from Life: Telling your Soul's Story.* New York: Jeremy, P. Tarcher/Putnam Books.

Baldwin, Christina. (1991) *Life's Companion: Journal Writing as a Spiritual Quest.* New York: Bantam Books.

Gates, Henry Louis Jr. (ed.) 1987. *The Classic Slave Narratives.* New York: Mentor/Penguin Books.

Mallon, Thomas. (1995) *A Book of One's Own.* Saint Paul, MN: Hungry Mind Press.

Nin, Anais. *The Diary of Anais Nin*, 1955–1966 (ed.) Gunther Stuhlman. 1976. New York: Harcourt, Brace, Jovanovich.

Pepys, Samuel. *The Diary of Samuel Pepys.* 1970. (ed.) Robert Latham and William Mathews, Berkeley, CA: University of California Press.

Progoff Ira. (1992) *At a Journal Workshop.* Los Angeles: J. P. Tarcher.

Rainer, Tristine. (1978) *The New Diary.* New York: G.P. Putnam's Sons.

Wesley, John. *Journal of the Reverend John Wesley.* 1938. (ed.) Nehemiah Curnock. London: The Epworth Press.

Just Doing It: Towards a Critical Thinking of Visual Culture

Kevin Tavin

> The desire to maintain a specific form of 'critical' thinking rooted in one technology—print—simply does not respect the mutability and diversity of institutions, or of various cultural forms—oral, written, imaged, electronic, in short all that traditionally constitutes popular culture—of transmission of information and value.
> Ava Collins (1994)

Introduction: Uncritical Critical Thinking

Critical thinking is not a new concept to art education. Curriculum reforms centering on "discipline-based" structures of knowledge were understood to help students go beyond merely learning facts or making "stuff," to engage students in critical thinking through evaluating and interpreting artworks (Clark, Day, & Greer, 1987). Yet, the type of critical evaluation, and the critical interpretation that is practiced in most art classrooms today, can be seen as uncritical-critical thinking. Joe Kincheloe (1993) sees students engaged in this type of cognition as removing the ethical and political dimensions of "thinking" unable to confront "why they tend to think as they (do) about themselves, the world around them, and their relationship to that world" (p. 25). In art education, students engage in making art, talking about art, and sometimes even relating art to their lives. Most teachers provide the "art" knowledge for students to bank and limit student inquiry to a vapid form of hermeneutics. Indeed, it is rare to see students questioning the hidden epistemological values that legitimate certain forms of "art" and marginalize others. It is hard to find students reflecting on the dominant cultural fictions and undemocratic systems within the art world. It is even more difficult to find teachers who acknowledge and problematize a student's relationship to hyperreality in any meaningful form of emancipatory pedagogy.

Most students live in hyperreality, with images are pedagogically luminous. However, for countless art educators the brilliance of this postmodern condition is obscured by a dark modernist lens and disciplined squinting. Students negotiate their subjectivities in a postmodern-hyperreal landscape in many, often contradictory ways (Duncum, 1997). Yet, numerous art teachers would prefer to see students as if they were unified beings, living in the nineteenth century. Based upon the same critiques, Matthew Arnold lobbied against mass culture; these teachers try to shelter students from the evil influences around them and contain, in a cold war sense, all forms of unauthorized popular culture from the classroom. Paradoxically, at the same time that many art educators are admonishing students against popular culture, scholars within and across various disciplines have taken up the project of visual culture.

Visual culture, as a pedagogical project, opens the field of visual studies to include vernacular images, mass media, and traditional visual art images. In art educational practice, particularly at the primary level, examples from even the newly acknowledged expanding canon rarely contain images from the popular landscape. On the occasion when these images find their way into the curriculum, they are almost always used as a conduit to enlighten students about the world of fine arts, treated as a frill, or at best occupy a formalistic space (Duncum, 1997).

Art educators must escape from the paradigmatic trap of seeing popular imagery only as a stepladder to the transcendent sphere of high culture in which autonomy, creativity and individuality remain untethered to social and cultural context. Moreover, there is an even greater need to move beyond the positivistic framework that inculcates students into separating art education from the rest of their lives. Art teachers need to problematize images from the whole of students' visual culture. There is also a need for an inclusive view of visual culture in a general education curriculum, particularly at the primary level. Elementary schools are a virtual cornucopia of visual culture, filled with cartoon characters, bulletin boards, posters, and toys. However, elementary curricula almost always ignore the importance of popular images as a means for developing higher order cognition and a more critical understanding of experience, both in and outside the school. Frequently, general elementary educators are responsible for teaching art in their classroom and their opportunities for a critical thinking of visual culture needs to be nurtured.

This article will address the need for art educators to embrace a transformative, critical thinking of visual cultural, from a post-formalist perspective. First, I will provide an overview of visual culture and its proximity to cultural studies. Second, I will discuss art educator's current struggle with visual culture. Third, I will provide a curriculum framework that articulates a transformative critical thinking of visual culture. Fourth, I will provide a scenario in which one pre-service elementary educator, enrolled in a required university art education course, utilized a emancipatory form of critical thinking and provided rich and exciting intertextual connections between various images in visual culture. Finally, I will conclude with a call for a reform of art education from a post formalist perspective and discuss the implication of this shift for elementary educators.

Visual Culture: Honorific Rubric or Performative Hybrid?

There are as many contemporary conceptions of "visual culture" as there are disputes as to its nature, function and legitimacy (Kaufmann, 1996). The notion of visual culture falls within contested spaces and assumes no specific media or boundary while stimulating anxieties through its amorphous and undefined nature. There are, however, some general tenets to which most conceptions of visual culture adhere.

Visual culture usually rejects the notion of a singular discipline and crosses the boundaries of art, architecture, and film, while intersecting with models of anthropology, media studies, philosophy and cultural studies. Visual culture is the study of the social construction of the visual experience and shifts from the history of art to the history of images (Bryson, Holly, & Moxey, 1994). W.J.T. Mitchell (1995) describes visual culture as running throughout:

> critical theory, philosophy, and political discourses of identity formation, sexuality, otherness, fantasy, the unconscious: it focuses on the cultural construction of visual experience in everyday life as well as in the media, representations, and visual arts. (p. 540)

By studying all images from visual culture, the distinction between high and low culture becomes problematic and liberates "art" from the stale canon of masterpieces. One of the key tenets of visual culture, raising arguments both for and against its legitimacy, is its power to slip between and among, collapse and expand, and explode and implode established disciplines and histories. Tom Conley (1996) states:

> One of the pleasures that we gain from the study of the growth of visual culture within the academy, then, is obtained when we discover that it cannot find a

disciplinary place. For that reason its production of analysis, constitutes a space, always in process, in a condition of reinventions that cannot be localized. The attempt to track a pattern . . . betrays the mobility of visual culture insofar as it engages motion, the creation of discourse and space, to the detriment of the delimitation of place, the strategy that defines a discipline. (p. 32)

The anti-disciplinary nature of visual culture is both liberating for some and problematic for others. It proclaims a disorderliness of spaces, breaks down artificial barriers, and undermines confidence in canonized knowledge. Like the postmodern condition, visual culture constitutes a general attempt to transgress the borders sealed by modernism (Jameson, 1983). It proclaims the arbitrariness of all boundaries and solicits resistance from guardians of traditional notions of visual literacy and the purity of the aesthetic. The inter and trans-disciplinary nature of visual culture is due, in part, to the importation of other discursive fields such as cultural and media studies.

Visual culture, like cultural studies, acknowledges popular culture as a significant basis of meaningful and significant inquiry and challenges the authority of the expert whose discourse is sanitized and removed from the dynamics of social power and construction. Henry Giroux (1997) describes three important tenets of cultural studies in the United States. Because these qualities mirror some of the same spheres of visual culture it is important to quote Giroux at length:

First, cultural studies is premised on the belief that the traditional distinctions that separate and frame established academic disciplines cannot account for the great diversity of cultural and social phenomena that has come to characterize an increasingly hybridized, postindustrial world. . . . Second, advocates of cultural studies have argued strongly that the role of media culture—including the power of the mass media, with its massive apparatuses of representation and its mediation of knowledge-is central to understanding how the dynamics of power, privilege, and social desire structure the daily life of a society . . . Third . . . Cultural studies strongly rejects the assumption that teachers are simply transmitters of existing configurations of knowledge. (pp. 235–236)

A critical thinking of visual culture, like cultural studies, would address historical, social, economic and political issues of representation while converging with the inner and outer boundaries of psychoanalysis, semiotics, linguistics, literary theory, phenomenology, anthropology and film studies (Mitchell, 1995). Building on a critical-constructivist pedagogy, students would recognize the need to glean meaning from the myriad of positions they find themselves in and act on their own beliefs. Although a critical thinking of visual culture transgresses multiple disciplines and territories, it is conspicuously absent from the art educational dominion.

Containing Images: Art Education and Visual Culture

Current art educational practices are a hybridization of general educational concepts, modern and postmodern theory, cursory appearances of artistic activity, and the so-called four disciplines of art (art history, art criticism, aesthetics, and art-making). These four disciplines encompass the dominant paradigm known as discipline-based art education (DBAE). This movement, funded heavily by the Getty Foundation, became the focus of curriculum reforms, in part, as a response to the challenge of excellence in education in the early 1980s. The major focus on the four art disciplines promotes a significant distinction between fine art, other disciplines and visual culture (Efland, Freedman & Stuhr, 1996). Although literature supporting DBAE rarely attacks popular artifacts from visual culture overtly, the wholesale promotion of the "greatest works of art" can be viewed as a veiled condemnation of vernacular imagery based on its lack of aesthetic value. At a Getty-sponsored conference in 1987, William Bennett argued that it is important for "disadvantaged children (to) learn about great works and artists that are part of our common culture." Bennett went on to claim that art is among "the best of civilization's products" which can be understood through disciplined inquiry (quoted in Efland, 1990, p. 254). Clark, Day, and Greer (1987) stated, "(i)t is to the arts that we turn when we wish to be assured of aesthetic experience" (p. 140). They believe students who have not engaged in the art appreciation "might be easy prey to manipulation through the use of images in the mass media" (p. 142).

Although advocates for DBAE have campaigned for an inclusive view of visual arts, DBAE practice rarely addresses popular images from visual culture on its own terms. When they do appear, they are usually presented in a cursory manner or critiqued from a formalist perspective. Within most DBAE curriculums, the notion that there is something inherently special about the fine arts remains paramount. Most art educators believe that the high arts are a conduit to creative, humane, honest, and inspiring aspects of ourselves and society (Duncum, 1997). Visual culture, by undermining confidence in canonized, disciplined knowledge, is antithetical to many of these modernist philosophies inherent in DBAE. There is no denying that DBAE has moved drastically from its structural roots and embraced a more open, fluid, interdisciplinary, and pluralistic approach to pedagogy. However, even the most progressive forms of DBAE rarely embrace the emerging field of visual culture. Brent Wilson (1997) states:

> (t)his is precisely what is now happening—the appearance of art related new disciplines that subsume the content of existing art disciplines, add new content, posit new inquiry processes, provide fresh ways of viewing art and culture. The emergence of new art related disciplines may render existing DBAE theories and practice, structures and categories obsolete. (p. 2)

Some art educators who champion the emerging field, and critique models such as DBAE, still find it necessary to secure any discussion of visual culture to canonical works. Kerry Freedman is an art educator who has written several articles which discuss visual culture in art education. In "Critiquing the Media: Art Knowledge Inside and Outside of School" (1997), Freedman begins by arguing that "curriculum is often intended to filter out knowledge not considered legitimate" (p. 46). Through a discussion of Derridan theory, she continues to argue for the inclusion of images from popular culture and mass communication within the curriculum. However, her examples relegate visual culture to the role of a subordinate to the fine arts. Although her theoretical grounding is sound and her intent is stated up front, her methodological and formalist reading of visual culture for the purposes of making art more meaningful reifies the distinction between popular culture and fine art and runs the risk of framing visual culture as a handmaiden to the "real arts."

In her article (1997), Freedman's central focus involves critiquing the film *Batman* through a formalist lens. She references the film's use of Art Deco, Batman's suit with its cold and impenetrable smooth surface "like a metal sculpture," and the joker's costume which displays complementary colors that seem absurd because they clash (p. 49). After Freedman discusses the formal qualities of the costumes and scenery, she moves on to the eclectic art exhibition within the movie which includes work by Rembrandt, Degas, and Renoir. Throughout the remainder of her essay, she discusses other references to fine art within the film. She ends her discussion by stating:

> By incorporating analyses of familiar representations of art, like *Batman,* students develop a keener understanding of the complexities of art. . . . If we want art education to be intellectually challenging as well as enjoyable, we must tackle the difficult job of teaching art knowledge and how art becomes meaningful. (p. 51)

Students do need to be challenged intellectually to make meaningful experiences, but without a stipulation that it has to be tethered to "high art." Being able to analyze *Batman* from a formalist perspective remains in the domain of modernist, critical thinking. This form of critical thinking lures students into the land of formal education with a colorful hyperreal brochure and then provides them with little more than a vapid form of high culture tourism. This does little to raise questions about consciousness construction and identity formation. Paul Smith (1989) sees using popular images in this type of pedagogy as:

> lures and come-ons offered by teachers to students reluctant or unwilling to appreciate the virtues of the canonical curriculum. . . In such cases, the (popular image) is evidently only a teaching aid; its own specificity is rarely addressed, and its interest resides in the light that it can shed on more routine concerns. (p. 33)

This type of instruction is reflective, not reflexive. It reflects the student's experience through a modernist, high art lens. It refuses to step back from "art education" as we know it and allow students to view themselves, their world, and how they come to know it through hyperreality. Through her exploration of fine art within advertising and artistic film styles, Freedman weakens the potential of visual culture to serve as a problematized convex mirror reflecting social and cognitive subjectivities.

Hyperreality in the Hallway:
Visual Culture in the Elementary School

In Freedman's essay, "Interpreting Gender and Visual Culture in Art Classrooms" (1994), she states "(m)iddle and high school students, particularly, can take part in sophisticated levels of critique and reflection on visual culture they see every day, such as television" (p. 169). Hyperreality's flood of signifiers do not seem to be confined to the lives of middle or high school students. Indeed, images from the postmodern landscape penetrate and pervade every aspect of all children's lives in the form of television programs, children's books, advertisements, movies, comics, toys, cereal boxes, video games, fashion merchandise, sport shoes, fast food paraphernalia, and architectural and public spaces. This deluge of imagery and information, which begins at a very young age, falls within what Steinberg and Kincheloe term "Kinderculture," (1997, p. 50) Kinderculture encompasses images from visual culture that bombard students both within and outside of school. These images shape students experiences by capturing their imagination and engaging their desires. These pervasive, immediate, and sometimes ephemeral images construct student's consciousness and their sense of identity, politics and culture.

Within most elementary schools, these images are rarely considered as significant pedagogical sites despite the fact that bulletin boards, hallways, gymnasiums, and individual classrooms are infested with them. It may be that elementary educators believe that popular images from visual culture are mere entertainment or unrefined mass media gimmicks, not worthy of discussion. Henry Giroux (1989) argues:

> educators who refuse to acknowledge popular culture as a significant basis of knowledge often devalue students by refusing to work with the knowledge that students actually have and so eliminate the possibility of developing a pedagogy that links school knowledge to the differing subject relations that help to constitute their everyday lives. (p. 3)

Elementary schools are important sites where general educators and art specialists can develop curricula that challenge narrow or nonexistent readings of visual culture. A curriculum that engages students in expanded critical thinking with images from visual culture can help to re-conceptualize elementary education, childhood, and art. Kincheloe (1993) argues:

> To ignore the social and cognitive impact of hyperreality is to bury our heads in traditionalist sand. It is to embrace a form of educational fundamentalism that seeks safety in the education of a pre-modernist past as the world we once knew collapses around us. (p. 88)

For educators to embrace a critical thinking of visual culture is no easy task. In an educational milieu of modernist fragmentation, concrete cognition and de-politicized pedagogy, many educators would be ill prepared with conceptual tools to provide the means for an insightful analysis of the hyper-complexity of images. Even if educators became skilled at analyzing images, a larger concern involves the negotiation of student voice and action against a backdrop of affective investment. Rethinking the nature of "critical thinking" precludes taking a prescriptive approach to recasting the art education curriculum. However, there are a number of theories one can utilize to refashion art education in a postmodern landscape. What follows is a framework of a critical visual cultural pedagogy and the problems raised by such a project.

From the Outside In: A Framework of Critical Thinking for Visual Culture

The first step in transforming the notion of critical thinking for art education is transforming our understanding of the role popular imagery plays in contemporary society. Jean Baudrillard describes the transition of contemporary society from a production mode to one characterized by the proliferation of signs, simulacra, and images. For Baudrillard, postmodern society is defined by the proliferation and dissemination of images and the entry into a new cultural landscape saturated with images (Kellner, 1991).

When discussing the new cultural landscape, one most consider the technological revolution with new mass communication and information technologies that make up hyperreality. The proliferation of cable television channels generating between fifteen and thirty images per second (MTV not withstanding), the growth of home video, the proliferation of personal computers and the networking of those computers, and the increase of magazine, and book production and accessibility, all profoundly affect the way images are disseminated, exchanged, and circulated. This Cultural Revolution has changed the nature and function of popular images (Collins, 1994).

The proliferation of these images constitutes "visual culture" and as such, need to be understood as a series of complex texts permeated with often contradictory signifying processes. Educators can utilize postmodern theories to extend the notions of reading, writing, and textuality to all images in visual culture. These readings can help educators become aware of the social construction of experiences and the subjectivities of image consumers. This would allow a reading of visual culture to move beyond a simple critique of images to a critique of ideology. Elizabeth Garber points out that visual images are "signifying practices which produce meanings and construct images of the world that affect particular ideological representations of the world" (quoted in Tarlow-Calder, 1993, pp. 146–147). Art teachers could read images as multi-dimensional cultural texts with a wealth of meaning, inscribed from the outside, while seeing themselves and their students as multifaceted beings, socially constructed and over-determined by a range of images, discourses, and codes (Kellner, 1991).

If art educators are going to embrace a critical thinking of visual culture, they will need to transform the critical processes that they have applied to "high art" and adapt it to the hyperreal landscape. jan jagodzinski (1993) states:

> While art educators continue to teach a gaze aesthetic, praising the distinction between looking and seeing, in their classrooms, reminiscent of the time and space of their generation, the baby busters live with glance aesthetic, a continuously changing kaleidoscope of ideas and fashion which are analogous to the 'continuous flow' of television. (p. 90)

The next step would involve understanding the importance of popular cultural texts to our students' lives. Amalia Mesa-Bains (1996) describes the importance of knowing where your students are, as "Experience + Text = Meaning" (p. 32). She believes teachers must be able to draw relationships between students' lived knowledge and that text. In the same vein, Laurie Hicks (1989) argues that the educational process should begin with the student's own phenomenological experience—"the vernacular." She believes educators should "start out with images that originate within the culture and everyday experience of students rather than imposing too quickly academic constraints on what counts as legitimate art" (p. 55).

By taking the social forms and practices of their students seriously, educators can begin to understand the power of popular culture and cultural pedagogy. Henry Giroux (1989) argues:

> the study of popular culture offers the possibility of understanding how a politics of pleasure serves to address students in a way that shapes and sometimes secures the often contradictory relations students have to both schooling and the politics of everyday life (p. 3).

As educators begin to see the pedagogical potency of visual cultural texts, the problem becomes one of student recognition. Students learn to separate popular culture and "real education" at an early age. To most students, one exists in the realm of pleasure the other in realm of "sanctioned knowledge." Many students separate "real texts" defined as novels, poems, and stories, from popular texts, which they see as unproblematic entertainment. Paul Smith discusses the difficulty of articulating the pedagogical power of popular images when he reflects on his own teaching of popular culture. Smith (1989) discusses popular images as Popular Culture Commodity Texts (PCCT) and states:

> Meaning is already understood by students to reside within texts of traditional kind but not always recognized by them as a component of PCCT. Students already think of PCCT's as texts which do not need to be analyzed; rather they often seem self-evident or obvious, texts which, to adopt a distinction of Roland Barthes, signal rather than signify. (p. 34)

The perceived epistemological neutrality of popular signs necessitates the engagement of students in interpreting popular images in multiple and conflicting ways. Popular images need to be problematized and played out in a hermeneutical field of contradictory meanings. Paul Smith sees the conflicting interpretations of one image as "undermining the text's previously silent, unanalyzed passage through (students') lives and marking it as a site of disagreement, not to say struggle" (p. 34).

As students investigate multiple readings of popular images, the role of the teacher could be seen as akin to that of an orchestrator,—facilitating the articulation of students' experience (Smith, 1989). In facilitating discussion, teachers should not appear to be so removed from culture that they can position themselves as a one-way conduit to administer "academic knowledge" to their students. Teachers are too enmeshed in the culture to be free of it (McLaughlin, 1996). The facilitation of student voice should resonate within a discussion of popular culture's discursive formations. Foucault (1972) describes a discursive formation as "present(ing) the principle of articulation between a series of discursive events and other series of events, transformations, mutations, and processes" (quoted in Grossberg, 1992, p. 74). This formation can be seen as an underlying structure of unity, transcending students' individual relation to any particular image. It is within that structure that students can begin to see how certain practices and beliefs have wielded power in ways that seem invisible, natural, or unproblematic. When students read these images as powerful cultural forms, inscribed from the outside, the structuring principles of hegemony can be seen as a pedagogical project. Lawrence Grossberg provides a theoretical elaboration of hegemony as a battle for the popular:

> Hegemony defines the limits within which we can struggle, the field of 'common sense' or 'popular consciousness.' It is the struggle to articulate the position of 'leadership' within the social formation, the attempt by the ruling bloc to win for itself the position of leadership across the entire terrain of cultural and political life. Hegemony involves the mobilization of popular support, by a particular social bloc, for a broad range of its social projects. (quoted in Giroux & Simon, 1989. p. 27)

From this position it is impossible to read images as simply static, one-dimensional entities articulating a discourse of manipulation. Indeed, by engaging students in multiple readings, and exposing the larger discursive formations, the essentialist perspective of top down articulation is disrupted and transformed into a bottom up, or outside in, process of mediation. Stuart Hall (1981) clarifies this issue by stating:

> The meaning of a cultural form and its place or position in the cultural field is not inscribed inside its form. Nor is its position fixed once and forever. . . The meaning of the cultural symbol is given in part by the social filter into which it is incorporated; the practices with which it articulates and is made to resonate.

> What matters are not the intrinsic or historically fixed objects of culture, but the state of play in culture relations (quoted in Giroux & Simon, 1989. p. 9).

By seeing popular images as a site of differentiated politics and multiple ideological positions, inscribed from the outside, students can negotiate the possibility that popular images are neither static manipulative entities nor a terrain of unproblematic entertainment (Giroux & Simon, 1989). When students investigate the images from their cultural landscape as a site of multi-layered and contradictory investments, they see the possibility of recognizing the culturally invisible and can produce their own knowledge. This form of critical thinking allows both students and educators to understand, as John Dewey did, that:

> We rarely recognize the extent in which our conscious estimates what is worthwhile and what is not are due to standards of which we are not conscious at all. But in general it may be said that the things we take for granted without inquiry or reflection are just the things which determine our conscious thinking and decide our conclusions. (quoted in Ross, Cornett, & McCutcheon, 1992, p. 16)

If students begin to recognize the power of cultural pedagogy and reframe their own subjectivities within it, they can be ready to interpret other cultural identities. Thomas McLaughlin (1996), in *Street Smarts and Critical Theory,* describes the process students undertake when they explore new and strange cultural texts. He sees this encounter as helping students

> acknowledge differences and similarities and to recognize the role of their own rules in interpreting the actions of others operating under their own rules. Reciprocally, the encounter with strange texts returns the student to the everyday with sharper theoretical strategies for questioning the premises of his or her own cultural practices. (p. 157)

This form of a critical thinking of visual culture would address historical, social, economic, and political issues of representation while converging with the inner and outer boundaries of psychoanalysis, semiotics, linguistics, literary theory, phenomenology, anthropology and film studies (Mitchell, 1995). Building on a critical constructivist pedagogy, students would recognize the need to glean meaning from the myriad of positions they find themselves in, and act on their own beliefs. In order to provide a transformative aspect to a critical thinking of visual culture, students must assume that social conditions can be improved. They need to understand the underlying values, motivations, ideologies and perspectives that emerge from the process of signification. A critical thinking of visual culture becomes as a tool for social reconstruction as it challenges and offers alternatives to traditional frameworks and processes (Tarlow-Calder, 1993). This type of critical thinking allows both students and teachers to become aware of themselves in new and multifaceted ways. Both teachers and students can create new knowledge and reconstruct themselves for social agency. Joyce King (1994) expresses the need for perspective teachers to gain their own knowledge through experience. She writes:

> prospective teachers need an alternative context in which to think critically about and reconstruct their social knowledge and self-identities. Simply put, they need opportunities to become conscious of oppression . . . it must be discovered in experience. (p. 346)

Floating in the Jean Pool: The Highs and the Lows of Visual Culture

During the fall of 1997, I explored a critical thinking of visual culture while facilitating two sections of a university course entitled, "Visual Arts in the Elementary School." This is a required course in which general elementary and early childhood majors are exposed to the visual arts and its pedagogical applications. This was the third time that I taught this course and, through the impetus of participating in a summer seminar on visual culture, I proceeded to approach the fall semester differently. In previous semesters, the course had three components; an initial unit taught by the instructor, a group project, and an individual presentation in which students would teach part of a lesson for one hour to their peers. In the past, all of the three units were based on progressive discipline-based art education models revolving around one or more works of high art.

I deviated from previous semesters by including essays, lectures, and student projects dealing with the pedagogy of visual culture in the curriculum. I wanted the students to begin to see the power of hyperreality in pedagogical terms. At first, there was quite a bit of resistance. Students articulated that many of the articles "over analyzed" popular culture and others wondered what this had to do with education, more specifically, art education. Most students refused to recognize hyperreality as a political practice and few saw visual culture as a meaningful project to be taken up in their future classrooms. As a result, these students silenced themselves by disregarding the hegemonic power of cultural pedagogy.

My task was clear. I needed to use my students' memories of childhood for the purpose of legitimating the power of cultural pedagogy. I wanted to glean affective investments from the texture of students' mattering maps. Toward the middle of the semester, I assembled the students in a computer lab to discuss their elementary experiences with high art and images from popular culture.

I drew a line down the center of the chalkboard and on one side asked them to list all of the artists that they had learned about in their kindergarten through high school art education. In both sections of the class, no more than twelve artists could be recalled, all of them dead, white, male, and European. They struggled to describe any of the accomplishments of these artists (although half the class remembered Van Gogh cutting off his ear) and had difficulty relating the relevance of these men and their art to their own lives. On the other half of the board I divided and labeled the space into four sections; children's television programs, films for children, toys, and breakfast cereals. I asked the class to list as many images as they could recall from their childhood, accompanied by a brief explanation.

The discourse exposed a celebration of shared private experiences with public forms. As the list promptly expanded, students started singing advertisement jingles and television theme songs while recalling specific episodes and products. They shared dynamic narratives of encounters with toys, recalled the specific imagery on a multitude of cereal boxes, and discussed specific actors on television shows. These memories amplified the echoes of investment that the themes, images, and sounds identified.

I thought of this exercise as a gathering of affective experiences along a horizontal plane, penetrated with inter-subjective associations and shared cultural experiences. It was a direct testimony to the power of corporations to create cultural curriculum through vivid Technicolor and incessant repetition which melds business ideologies, free market values, and childhood pleasure (Steinberg Kinchloe, 1997). When all was settled, we stared at the entire board and I asked my students to identify the dominant site for learning visual culture: inside or outside of school? The class fell silent with a unanimous simper, while everyone gazed at the disparate lists.

As part of a discussion on a critical thinking of visual culture, we examined a project I created which linked hyper-textually, various historical, political, social, and cultural images to an advertisement for Diesel jeans (Fig. 1). The original advertisement was a de-historicized and de-contexualized image of the Yalta summit of 1945 in which women, wearing Diesel clothing (or lack thereof), were digitally placed on the laps of Stalin, Roosevelt, and Churchill. Through *Storyspace,* a hyper-textual computer application, I linked a multitude of images, including, films, television programs, newspaper and magazine articles, and historical photographs to the appropriated image, and re-contextualized it by deconstructing its codes, structures, and shifting contexts. After investi-

Figure 1. *Diesel Web Screenshot,* Tavin (1997)

gating the project as a group, I invited the students to individually experience the text I had created. Each student sat at a computer and engaged my text within a dialogical space. Between the student and text lay a vast pool of diverse themes, issue, and information waiting to be accessed and interrogated with the click of a button. Students engaged the numerous links and nodes to discover windows opening to other windows around them, and to produce their own knowledge.

This project helped generate themes and issues that students wanted to explore further. The stage was set for students to choose their own image to investigate, semiotically and hyper-textually. They were to passionately search in their own familiar landscape for an image, once taken for granted and considered not worthy of investigation. This meant students needed to set themselves in question, to investigate the world.

Resistant Readings and Running Shoes: Critical Thinking in Action

Being at a state institution within the "Big Ten," whose athletic department is sponsored in part by Nike, it is difficult to walk on campus for more than five minutes without seeing the infamous Nike Swoosh. I knew that most students perceived Nike as a popular sports-oriented all-American company whose motto "Just Do it" celebrates rugged individualism. As part of my critical consciousness-raising efforts early in the semester, I handed my students a one-page flier that revealed some of Nike's former and present labor malpractices. One student sporting a Nike sweatshirt reluctantly grabbed the flier and quickly tucked it in his bag. A few months later, when it was time to choose a topic for his hyper-textual investigation, this same student approached me and asked if he could focus his project around a Doonsebury cartoon he saw in which Nike was accused of exploiting workers. He wanted to explore the "truth" behind this and other propaganda.

In the following month and a half, that same student engaged in a process of building a critical generative cognition. That is, a critical thinking that uncovers patterns of relationships and makes new sense of the world (Kincheloe, 1998). By gathering over three hundred visual images relating to Nike's Asian manufacturing network and researching over five hundred articles and essays, he interrogated his own perceptions and began to dis-embed himself from the picture of the world painted by hyperreality. His hunt for meaning led him to contact prominent organizations such as Amnesty International, Global Exchange, National Organization of Women, and Campaign for Labor Rights. Through his contacts previously unrecognized ethical and moral issues became apparent. He started a dialogue with a teacher in New Jersey who had their school play, "Justice: Do It," banned because the principal decided "it was inappropriate for fourth graders to have wrestled with the issue to begin with . . . that it was far too complex for them to have sufficiently understood" (Kerson, 1997, p. 5). On one occasion he had a heated telephone debate with the director of the athletic department at Penn State when he was told that the University fully supports Nike's labor practices. His research culminated in a re-contextualization of visual and written information: a hyper-textual pedagogy in which he carved up, wove and re-wove over eighty-five images within a web of over four hundred connections (Fig. 2).

As part of his overall project, he led the class, who role-played fifth graders, through a search of his imagistic discourse. As he guided the cursor, links opened up texts that disguised and suppressed inequalities, injustices, irrationalities, and contradictions (Goldman& Papson, 1996). First, the Doonsebury images were revealed and contested, each comic strip leading to another. Next, recent advertisements of sports celebrities were juxtaposed with dated television commercials and layered on top of the cartoons (Fig. 3).

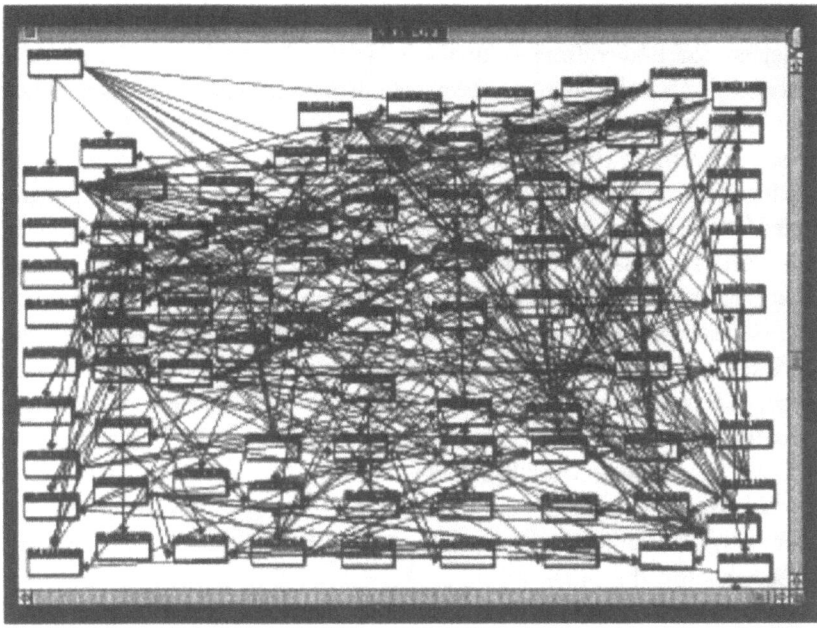

Figure 2. *Nike Web*, Beck (1997)

Figure 3. *Nike Web Screenshot 1*, Beck (1997)

Continuing through the visual labyrinth, Nike advertisements of women playing sports were inter-textually linked to photographs of frail female laborers in South East Asia. Alongside were demonstrators at Niketown and the decapitated sculpture of the winged goddess (Fig 4). Through these and other juxtapositions, the issue of cultural authority was relinquished from Nike to the writer and reader (one in the same) of the new text. Weaving subjugated knowledges with the dominant discourse opened new angles of vision. The intersection of these angles allowed for a new form of analysis that moved beyond a fragmented and isolated perception. Questions were raised as to the nature of the endorsements and the politics of representation. As this de-grafting of code and image continued, the boundaries between global and local, consumption and ideology, and representation and power, and ethics and practice became amorphous, raw, and exposed (Kincheloe, 1993).

This feast of signifiers exposed constituting principles which, on the one hand, accentuate individualism, freedom, democracy, and competition while on the other, erase any complicity with human rights infractions, physical abuse violations, patriarchy, illegal and unethical labor prac-

Figure 4. *Nike Web Screenshot 2*, Beck (1997)

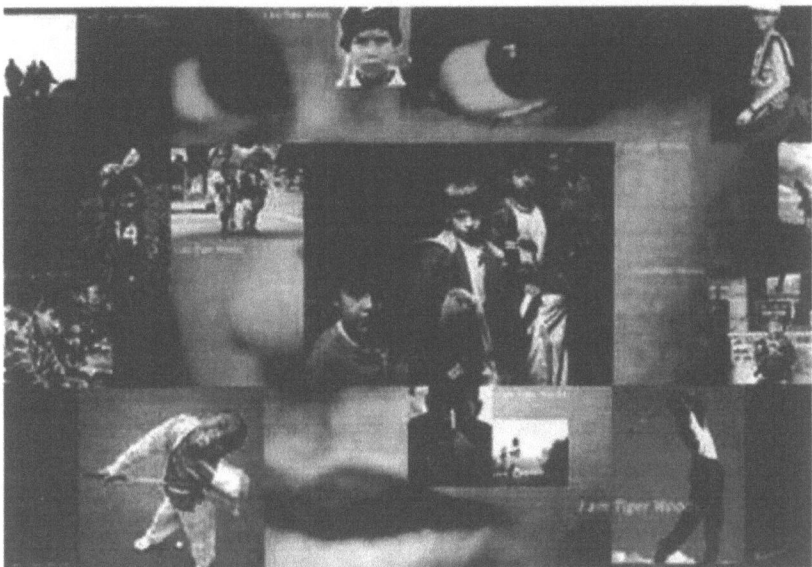

Figure 5. *Nike Advertisement* (1997)

tices, and infiltration and commodification of public schools and universities. As the oscillation between images continued, *Adbusters* parodies of Nike advertisements were used to re-contextualize Nike's responses to criticism. At this point, students were asked to analyze another Nike advertisement with "multicultural children" patched atop Tiger Woods' face (Fig. 5).

After asking other audience members to critique the advertisement, the student presented his own parody of the Tiger Woods image, replacing the "multicultural kids" with subjugated imagery. By placing images of tired female Indonesian factory workers under the caption, "I AM NIKE," he denaturalized Nike's regime of representation and provided new articulations for silenced voices (Fig. 6).

The last part of his project involved inviting the audience members to individually negotiate his hypertext, making their own connections along the way. The student explained that when he gets the opportunity to teach in the elementary school, his fifth graders would further explore globalization, commodification, production, distribution, and circulation of power in multinational corporations. His elementary students would also engage in letter writing campaigns and create their own hyper-textual web from any area of visual culture.

Figure 6. *I Am Nike*—Beck (1997)

Part of the students' production could be to create their own parodies that denaturalize meaning with re-contexualized images. His elementary students could also engage in letter writing campaigns and create their own hyper-textual web from any area of visual culture. Part of the students' production could be to create their parodies that denaturalize meaning with re-contexualized images.

This project allowed everyone in the class, myself included, to investigate ourselves and articulate our goals and identities. By uncovering the dynamics of images which signify de-entities through de-contextualization and de-historicization, this project disrupted, contested, and transformed the suppressed inequalities into an informed inquiry and critique of diverse experiences for mobilizing and sustaining political-civic action.

Conclusion: Hyper-Complexity and Self-Revelation

American culture is rapidly changing and yet art education hasn't quite caught up. The dominant paradigm is organized around conventional discipline based categories which are at odds with the hyper-complex and transgressive nature of post-modernity. Traditional modes of critical thinking have not been successful in understanding the politics of visual culture. Nevertheless, there comes a time when the staleness of disciplined art educational practice yields a self-revelation of its own inadequacy (Mitchell, 1995). That time is now. Art education must disavow the modernist fallacy that sees critical thinking as simply differentiating or distinguishing relevant from irrelevant information. A critical thinking of visual culture needs to go beyond a singular sense of "false consciousness" and acknowledge the multifaceted construction of identity (Jagodzinski, 1993). If art education is going to adapt to the new cultural landscape rather than escape from it, critical thinking must be viewed as a political, social, and cultural practice which addresses all images.

The producers of the visual culture of tomorrow are the students who sit in our class today (Buck-Morss, 1996). These students live in and through mass media. They negotiate their history, ideology, desires, expectations, and multiple and ever changing identities through visual imagery. To ignore this is to deny the dominant site of learning and deny students' voice in shaping their own life. It is a central challenge of a new critical thinking in art education to turn audience members into producers able to combine student intellect and creativity in a project of reflexivity and critique (Sholle & Denski, 1994).

A critical thinking of visual culture offers possibilities for an expanded view of "critical thinking" that is rooted in a performative and transformative pedagogical practice. This new form of critical thinking is needed to help students make sense of the socio-pyschological schizophrenia brought on by proliferation of images in hyperreality (Kincheloe & Hinchey, 1998). Students could begin by articulating their own cultural identity in hyperreality. This interpretation can help students understand the deep structures that form hyperreality and become aware of invisible cultural assumptions. A critical thinking of visual culture would help students contextualize themselves and the images they see within a broader world and help elucidate the way power influences the production of knowledge. David Sholle and Stan Denski (1994) discuss a pedagogy of popular images as allowing "students to speak from their own experience at the same time that it encourages them to identify and unravel the codes of popular culture that may work to construct subject relations that serve to silence and disempower them" (p. 39).

Through making visible the codes that lie beneath the surface of these images and the society that produces those images, students can explore the notion of meaning housed within texts for critical social practice.

They can investigate relationships between images and power, subjectivity and cultural forms, politics and identity, gender and commodity, art and communication, and technology and textuality. They can begin to embrace a new critical thinking of visual culture.

References

Bryson, N., Holly, M., and Moxey, K. (eds). (1994). *Visual Culture: Images and Interpretations.* Hanover, MA: Wesleyan University Press.

Buck-Morss, S. (1996). *Visual Culture Questionnaire*, October, 77(l), 29–30.

Clark, G., Day, M., and Greer, D. (1989). *Discipline-Based Art Education: Becoming Students of Art* in Discipline Based Art Education: Origins, meaning, and development. Board of Trustees of the University of Illinois.

Collins, A. (1994). *Intellectuals, Power, and Quality Television* in Henry Giroux and Peter McLaren (eds) Between borders: Pedagogy and the politics of cultural studies. New York: Routledge.

Conley, T. (1996). *Untitled Response to Visual Culture Questionnaire*, October, 77(l), 31–32.

Duncum, P. (1997). *Art Education for New Times*, Studies in Art Education, 39 (3), 110–118.

Efland, A. (1990). *A History of Art Education: Intellectual and Social Currents* in Teaching the Visual Arts. New York: Teachers College Press.

Efland, A., Freedman, K., & Stuhr, P. (1996). *Postmodern Art Education: An Approach to Curriculum.* Reston, VA: NAEA.

Freedman, K. (1997a). *Critiquing the Media: Art Knowledge Inside and Outside of School*, Art Education, 50 (4), 46–51.

Freedman, K. (1994). *Interpreting Gender and Visual Culture in Art Classrooms*, Studies in Art Education, 35 (3), 157–170.

Giroux, H. & Simon, R. (eds). (1989). *Popular Culture: Schooling and Everyday Life.* New York: Bergin & Garvey.

Giroux, H. & Shannon, P. (eds). (1997). *Education and Cultural Studies: Towards a Performative Practice.* New York: Routledge.

Grossberg, L. (1992). *We Gotta Get Out of This Place.* New York: Routledge.

Hicks, L. (1989). Cultural literacy as social empowerment. *The Journal of Social Theory in Art Education* 9 (40), 45–58.

Jagodzinski, J. (1993). The war of labels: An art educator in search of a sign. *The Journal of Social Theory in Art Education* 13(57), 87–110.

Kaufmann, T. (1996). Untitled response to visual culture questionnaire, October, 77(l), 45–48.

Kellner, D. (1991). Reading Images Critically: Towards a Postmodern Pedagogy, in *Postmodernism, Feminism, and Cultural Politics*. New York: State University of New York Press.

Kerson, R. (1997). *Kids Take Sweatshop Play to Broadway,* National News Reporter.

Kincheloe, J. (1993). *Toward a Critical Politics of Teacher Thinking: Mapping the Postmodern.* Westport, CT: Bergin and Garvey.

Kincheloe, J., Hinchey, P. (eds). (1998). *Postformal Reader: Cognition and Education.* New York: Garland.

King, J. (1994). Dysconscious Racism: Ideology, Identity, and the miseducation of teachers in Stone, L. (ed). *The Education Feminism Reader.* New York: Routledge.

McLaughlin, T. (1996). *Street Smarts and Critical Theory.* Madison:The University of Wisconsin Press.

Mesa-Bains, A. (1996). Teaching students the way they learn in Cahan, S., & Kocur, Z., (eds) *Contemporary Art and Multicultural Education.* 31–38.

Mitchell, W.J.T. (1995). Interdisciplinary and Visual Culture, *Art Bulletin,* 77(4), 540–544.

Ross, E., Cornett, J., and McCutcheon, G. (eds), (1992). *Teacher Personal Theorizing and Research on Curriculum and Teaching.* Albany: State University of New York Press.

Sholle, D., and Denski, S. (1994). *Media Education and the Reproduction of Culture.* Westport, CT: Bergin & Garvey.

Smith, Paul. *The Popular-Cultural-Commodity-Text in Popular Culture: Schooling and Everyday Life.* New York: Bergin & Garvey.

Steinberg, S., & Kincheloe, J. (eds). (1997). *Kinderculture: The Corporate Construction of Childhood.* Boulder: Westview Press.

Tarlow-Calder, P. (1993). *Censored by Omission: Imagery that is Excluded from the Art Education Classroom.* The journal of social theory in art education 13(57), 142-157.

Wilson, B. (1997). *Is Art Education Obsolete?* Partial draft of a keynote address presented at the 1997 International Symposium in Art Education. Taipei, Taiwan, R.O.C.

Critical Thinking in Science—How Do We Recognize it? Do We Foster It?

David B. Pushkin

Consider the following problem I gave my first semester chemistry students last year on their final exam:

50 milliliters of 0.5M Ammonium sulfate are added to an excess solution of Barium chloride. A precipitate results.

1. If you recover 3.25 grams of precipitate, what is your percent yield?
2. How might your result differ if you used 50 milliliters of 0.1M Silver nitrate instead? Please justify your answer quantitatively.

The purpose of sharing this problem is not to show how difficult my chemistry exams can be; nor is it to provide a discourse on analyzing precipitation reactions. I share this problem with you to give you a sense of what students may encounter if critical thinking is an expectation of chemistry teachers. In this problem, students are provided a minimal amount of information, and yet are required to develop a complete picture of a chemical reaction from it. Not only that, but students are posed an alternative scenario—the substitution of one reagent for another—and asked to not only consider the consequences, but justify them in a problem solving manner.

Such a problem reflects no differently the decisions many of these students will make someday in laboratory settings as advanced chemistry students, professional technicians, or even future chemistry teachers. Science itself has grown on the basis of one simple question: *what would happen if?* If one changes the context of a reaction, one observes different results.

Different observations broaden our thinking processes, which in turn, strengthen our decision making and interpretative skills. Our understanding of science becomes more situated and contextual. Our understanding of science becomes broader and deeper. Such a problem provides students an excellent opportunity to develop such thinking and understanding as early as possible during an undergraduate science education.

Well, guess what? Not everyone who teaches chemistry at the college or university level agrees with such expectations of students. Furthermore, such dissenters question the appropriateness of such problems in a first-semester chemistry course for science majors. Why? The reasons are interesting.

1. The second question is ambiguous as to which reagent Silver nitrate will replace. The question is confusing and not well written.
2. The questions are not straightforward enough to dictate to the students what specific answer is desired.
3. A complete balanced chemical equation is not provided. Too much information is missing.
4. The problem attempts to test students on too many concepts.
5. *The students are simply not capable of successfully answering such questions.*

Based on such reasons, perhaps we should respond with some questions:

1. If a given volume of a solution of known concentration is to be substituted, would it not be substituted for a solution of known concentration and of the same volume?
2. Should students not ultimately determine the answers to questions? Is this not what we assess them for regarding their learning?
3. Should students not be able to determine missing information in a problem by the final exam?
4. Is scientific knowledge based on one concept at a time?
5. *When will students be deemed capable? How will anyone know without providing opportunities?*

What can we infer from the criticisms of dissenters? Are they saying critical thinking need not be confusing? Are they saying broad thinking and diverse problem solving skills are not a part of science? Are they saying assessment of learning should reflect fragmented knowledge only? Are they saying students are incapable of thinking? Or, are they saying thinking is really not a part of science?

To take such criticisms literally would force us to wonder if science is taught to empower learners to think, or *dis-empower* them to follow predigested directions and confirm answers. If Sheila Tobias (e.g., Tobias & Tomizuka, 1992) is correct in her assumption that success as a science student is more a function of OQ (obedience quotient) than IQ, then traditional science curricula and pedagogy are primarily designed to stupidify students rather than edify. Is science a process of understanding the world around us and the phenomena we encounter and question, or is it just a bunch of information? What is the purpose of teaching science, or even learning it?

And what does assessment tell us? If traditional assessment intends only to determine how many correct answers students reiterate of bite-sized factoids from short-term memory, then comprehension is merely a construct reflective of trivial competence (e.g., Kincheloe, 1991 & 1993; Pushkin, 1998a). Any sense of scientific understanding is lost in a myriad of algorithmic calisthenics, where students determine decontextualized answers to mathematical exercises that involve little practical relevance at all (e.g., Pushkin, 1998b). If students give correct answers, it is not necessarily due to their understanding of science; it is due to their *cognitive capitulation* to arbiters of knowledge, where thinking is limited to only what arbiters deem worthy of thinking about (e.g., Pushkin, 1998c–d).

Now that the debate as to whether critical thinking should or should not be a cognitive, pedagogical, and curricular goal in college-level science is initiated, the ultimate goals of this chapter are to address the two questions within the title:

- How do we recognize critical thinking?
- Do we foster critical thinking?

How *do* we recognize critical thinking? Perhaps we should first consider the distinctions between higher order thinking and critical thinking. According to Lewis and Smith (1993), higher order thinking involves taking new information and interrelating and/or rearranging it with *a priori* information to develop a new idea or answer to a new problem. However, Fogarty and McTighe (1993) consider critical thinking to involve attributing, comparing/contrasting, analyzing for bias, solving for analogies, and evaluating. Based on these two views, it is clear why higher order and critical thinking are associated with problem solving in science.

The issue, however, is not necessarily whether one form of thinking is superior to the other, but how these views lend themselves to the problem solving emphasized in many first-year chemistry and physics courses.

For example, if one seeks to determine the number of grams of something produced in a chemical reaction, one is merely extending declarative and procedural knowledge—chemical formulas, balancing chemical equations, and converting mass units to mole units, and *vice versa*. Perhaps a physics problem may seek to determine the amount of kinetic energy associated with an object accelerating. As challenging as students or teachers may consider such problems, the level of thinking involved is simply no more than a reflection of confirming objective knowledge, albeit linking it together in multiple steps.

Stoichiometry should be a straightforward concept to teach, and should not generate confusion when it is presented. There is a straightforward approach to solving these problems, and we should see it in the classroom and on tests.

When traditionalists offer such insights regarding the teaching and learning of scientific concepts, particularly the analysis of chemical reactions, critical thinking is neither a cognitive expectation nor pedagogically understood. Traditionalists often preach of the rigor their science curricula offer, yet the only thing rigorous appears to be the repetitive nature of mastering algorithms. When testing is primarily designed to confirm how well first-year students recall, reiterate, and apply facts and rules, higher order thinking is the best expectation one could hope for in such courses.

This is not to say that higher order thinking is detrimental to learning. Higher order thinking skills are important with respect to problem solving, for they do encourage students to use a progression of steps in order to solve a problem. However, based on the examples of determining grams of something produced in a chemical reaction or the kinetic energy of an object accelerating, higher order thinking skills should *not* be mistaken for critical thinking skills. Traditionalists contend these "rigorous" algorithmic exercises do make students think critically; why else assign so many end-of-chapter textbook problems for homework?

Something is clearly missing in terms of what Fogarty and McTighe (1993) contend critical thinking is; the "BIG" picture of science understanding is really not addressed. The problems essentially remain the same, only the "names and faces" change. By traditionalism's decontextualized approach to teaching problem solving, students rarely have opportunities to develop *situated cognition*, a mode of understanding that enables students to solve a variety of diverse problems with flexible mental models.

Where do situational and strategic knowledge come into play? Unfortunately, they do not in the current structure of standard first-year chemistry and physics courses. What are the potential culprits? Faculty? Syllabi? Textbooks? Perhaps, but they are collectively a manifestation of the overall culture of science itself, a culture of conformity and cognitive apprenticeship. We need to ask ourselves if science is a process by which we *come to know*, or a body of canonical information we are *expected to know*. Is science dynamic and evolving, or is it static and standardized? Are we part of nature and a worldview, or are we separate entities, removed from it. Do we create knowledge or do we receive it?

Science, as a positivistic body of canonical knowledge, traditionally views itself in terms of correct or acceptable answers (Pushkin, 1998e). Dawson and Lyndon (1997) refer to this as an essential manifestation of "intelligent behaviour." Segal (1997), noting the words of a scientist, describes science as "purified" and "rational opinion." As science underwent its progression from natural philosophy to discipline of study during the middle of this millennium, the knowledge base became more stable and absolute. The viewpoint of science became more solipsistic and decontextualized from individual thought (Staver, 1998). The wonders of the universe and nature inevitably became what 19th century philosopher Herbert Spencer considered a collection of dead and mostly inert facts (e.g., DeBoer, 1991; Hurd, 1998).

For all our constructs and measures of "learning," one can argue traditionalist discipline-based science offers little valid evidence of it. If traditionalist science is taught from the aforementioned perspective, students fail to demonstrate any significant level of cognition. They fail to use or develop thinking skills, merely reacting behavioristically to academic stimuli. Information is dispensed by a master, passively received by apprentices, reiterated as trivial factoids, and decontextualized to maintain hierarchical power structures (Pushkin, 1998e). Traditionalism sadly quashes efforts for students to develop deep understandings of science, effectively maintaining a hegemonic level of ignorance as well as a distant level of power and authority.

Rather than be learners, students are acculturated as *cognitive capitulators*, blindly surrendering their own thinking processes (Pushkin, 1998d). Rather than empowered, students are rendered *dis-empowered*, traumatically suppressed by their invisible subordination to an ideological manipulation (Bartolome, 1998; McLaren, 1998). Such hegemony discourages students from viewing science beyond a body of information; a vested interest, much less internal locus of control, in learning is lost.

What the hierarchy of arbiters consider effective, efficient, if not at least benign, is far from the nurturing pedagogy that fosters meaningful learning. If all of this is true, how could critical thinking genuinely be an expectation of traditional first-year chemistry and physics courses?

Your aim as our educator was to teach us how to think rather than what to think.
Thank you for this, for unsettling our thoughts, awakening our curiosity, and kindling our minds.
In your classroom, education was always achieved rather than received. For inspiring us to be life-long learners, we are forever indebted to you.

These are the words of appreciation from chemistry students exposed to a constructivist classroom that emphasized critical thinking. Realizing they are part of the process of knowledge acquisition and exchange, students develop more awareness of themselves as thinkers and empowered consumers of knowledge. Unfortunately, these very same students sense something drastically different in traditionalist chemistry classrooms.

I don't just want to understand the what; I want to also understand the how's and why's. Last semester we were expected to do this and any "applied" questions that we would have were more than welcomed to be asked . . . Dr. P. was more than willing to take the time to help us come to the answers we were looking for. This semester, "understanding" is bad and only "troublemakers" attempt to do it. So far, we're only (and I mean only) to memorize equations and plug numbers into them.

The words of Cathy, an aspiring chemistry teacher, sadly indicate how traditionalism is more inclined to keep students in an obedient, passive mode (Pushkin, 1998f). One could argue traditionalism strives to keep students in their apprentice roles within the hierarchy of learning; what Macedo (1994) refers to as *stupidification*. By traditionalists maintaining their status as arbiters of knowledge and gatekeepers to their hierarchy, teaching practices are driven by power structures more than epistemological or cognitive views. Rather than educate to encourage individual growth and independent thinking, traditionalism dictates and demands unquestioned conformity. And yet, epistemological and cognitive views may very well be manifestations of the power structure created by science's culture.

According to Perry (1970), adult learners progress from dualistic thinking to *multiplistic* thinking, a mode reflective of compulsory deference to authority yet not necessarily reflective of internalization. Multiplicity essentially describes an amorphous dichotomy of thought, one for self, and one for authority, depending on the type of authority encountered. Multiplicity is very much analogous to cognitive capitulation; it reflects the surrendering of thought to authority, albeit on a "need-to basis."

Considering the hegemony arbiters use to intellectually beat their apprentices into some form of obedient submission, the cognitive "progression" in traditionalist-dominated science departments is from multiplicity to dualism, quite opposite from Perry's theory. In fact, traditionalism encourages a cognitive *regression*. I contend all apprentices, either science students or teachers, come to the academic setting with a more multiplistic mode of thinking than dualistic. They already possess an inclination to accept knowledge blindly, for the sole purpose of achieving success. Whether or not they internally agree with that knowledge, they appreciate knowledge as a *means to an end*, and accept it as some admission fee to the hierarchy of power.

However, during their cognitive apprenticeship, they "learn" how to narrow their viewpoints rather than broaden them. No longer are there multiple ways to interpret knowledge. For example, the term *diffusion* is viewed quite differently between chemistry, biology, and physics. Yet, as one continues in their discipline-based cognitive apprenticeship, diffusion takes on only one meaning—the "right" meaning, the meaning dictated by the discipline; all other meanings are considered wrong.

If scientific terminology is supposed to be so precise and arbitrary, how does one ever develop an understanding of it? Would this not create a confounding variable for conceptions studies? There should never be debate as to what certain terms mean and to what contexts we apply them. If chemistry's view of diffusion is the only correct view, should the term be completely obliterated from the languages of biology and physics for having an alternative view? If this were appropriate, which disciplines would legitimately be allowed to discuss atoms or molecules? Or cells? Or thermodynamics? Or quantum theory? Not only does science in general have a reputation of intolerance towards those outside science, specific disciplines have equal intolerance towards each other (e.g., Thomas, 1990).

Regarding the second question of my title—*Do we foster critical thinking?*—the answer is clearer than for the first question; not enough! Considering how little traditionalist teachers of discipline-based science recognize and distinguish higher order thinking and critical thinking, it is clear they do not significantly foster or encourage critical thinking by students.

Part of this could be "blamed" on a lack in understanding about these levels of thinking. However, much of it could be "blamed" on epistemological and cognitive views regarding the teaching of science. If the culture of a discipline seeks to eliminate ambiguity, bias, and value from knowledge, there is no point to determining attribution or making evaluations. Knowledge is either acceptable or not; every cause has a definite effect.

This chapter initially introduced us to an example of how critical thinking is addressed in a discipline-based science course. However, this chapter ultimately intended to make us aware of two issues relevant to critical thinking—what represents it, and who believes in it. For lack of experience, or lack of challenging ourselves as teachers, we could all consider ourselves limited in our understanding and application of critical thinking. This is correctable with time, as personal and collective growth will encourage us to probe the minds of students and broaden their understanding and use of science in terms of problem solving.

That is, assuming we truly believe in critical thinking as a cognitive, pedagogical, and curricular goal in our classrooms. If we do *not* stand for intellectual growth and empowerment, critical thinking is simply not a goal. If we do *not* respect multiple meanings for terminology based on context, critical thinking is simply irrelevant. If we do *not* embrace broad and flexible mental models, critical thinking is simply a threat. Critical thinking is more than a learning expectation or mode of problem solving; it is a manifestation of epistemological and cognitive views of knowledge. It always comes back to classroom culture and the culture of disciplines. Critical thinking is a means of understanding nature by a process known as science. Is this, unfortunately, in conflict with the nature of science? This is the question we must ultimately answer.

References

Bartolome, L. (1998, April). The Significance of Teacher Ideology. Presentation at the AERA Annual Meeting in San Diego, CA.

Dawson, C., & Lyndon, H. (1997). Conceptual Mediation: A New Perspective on Conceptual Exchange. *Research in Science Education*, 27, 157–173.

DeBoer, G.E. (1991). *A History of Ideas in Science Education: Implications for Practice*. New York: Teachers College Press.

Hurd, P.D. (1998). Scientific Literacy: New Minds for a Changing World. *Science Education*, 82(3), 407–416.

Fogarty, R., & McTighe, J. (1993). Educating Teachers for Higher Order Thinking: The Three-Story Intellect. *Theory into Practice*, 32(3), 161–169.

Kincheloe, J.L. (1991). *Teachers as Researchers: Qualitative Inquiry as a Path to Empowerment*. London: Falmer Press.

Kincheloe, J.L. (1993). *Toward a Critical Politics of Teacher Thinking: Mapping the Postmodern*. Westport, CT: Bergin & Garvey.

Lewis, A., & Smith, D. (1993). Defining Higher Order Thinking. *Theory into Practice*, 32(3), 131–137.

Macedo, D. (1994). *Literacies of Power: What Americans Are Not Allowed to Know*. Boulder, CO: Westview Press.

McLaren, P. (1998, April). Hope Reinscribed: The Struggle for a Revolutionary Multiculturalism. Presentation at the AERA Annual Meeting in San Diego, CA.

Perry, W.G. (1970). *Forms of Intellectual Development in the College Years, a Scheme*. New York: Holt, Rinehart, and Winston.

Pushkin, D.B. (1998a). Is Learning Just a Matter of Tricks? So Why Are We Educating? *Journal of College Science Teaching*, 28, 92–93.

Pushkin, D.B. (1998b). Introductory Students, Conceptual Understanding, and Algorithmic Success. *Journal of Chemical Education*, 75, 809–810.

Pushkin, D.B. (1998c). Undergraduate Science Education—Improvement, Initiative, and Willingness to Change. *Journal of College Science Teaching*, 28, 8.

Pushkin, D.B. (1998d). How Has Thomas Kuhn Affected My Thinking and Teaching? *Science and Education*, in press.

Pushkin, D.B. (1998e). How do we Know Learning Is Really Learning and Not Cognitive Capitulation? *Science Education*, submitted for publication.

Pushkin, D.B. (1998f). The Epistemologies of Classroom Teachers Through the Eyes of Students. *Journal of Science Teacher Education*, submitted for publication.

Segal, G. (1997). Towards a Pragmatic Science in Schools. *Research in Science Education*, 27, 289–307.

Staver, J. R. (1998). Constructivism: A Sound Theory for Explicating the Practice of Science and Science Teaching. *Journal of Research in Science Teaching*, 35, 501–520.

Thomas, K. (1990). *Gender and Subject in Higher Education*. Buckingham, UK: Open University Press.

Tobias, S., & Tomizuka, C.T. (1992). *Breaking the Science Barrier: How to Explore and Understand the Sciences*. New York: The College Board.

Studies in the Postmodern Theory of Education

General Editors
Joe L. Kincheloe & Shirley R. Steinberg

Counterpoints publishes the most compelling and imaginative books being written in education today. Grounded on the theoretical advances in criticalism, feminism, and postmodernism in the last two decades of the twentieth century, Counterpoints engages the meaning of these innovations in various forms of educational expression. Committed to the proposition that theoretical literature should be accessible to a variety of audiences, the series insists that its authors avoid esoteric and jargonistic languages that transform educational scholarship into an elite discourse for the initiated. Scholarly work matters only to the degree it affects consciousness and practice at multiple sites. Counterpoints' editorial policy is based on these principles and the ability of scholars to break new ground, to open new conversations, to go where educators have never gone before.

For additional information about this series or for the submission of manuscripts, please contact:

> Joe L. Kincheloe & Shirley R. Steinberg
> 637 West Foster Avenue
> State College, PA 16801

To order other books in this series, please contact our Customer Service Department at:

> (800) 770-LANG (within the U.S.)
> (212) 647-7706 (outside the U.S.)
> (212) 647-7707 FAX

or browse online by series at:
> www.peterlang.com

Studies in the Postmodern Theory of Education

General Editors
Joe L. Kincheloe & Shirley R. Steinberg